HANDSWORTH COLLEGE

T07694

17/6/97

£18·99

Children as Witnesses

WITHDRAWN

D1637744

Wiley Series in

The Psychology of Crime, Policing and Law

Series Editors

Graham Davies
University of Leicester, UK

and

Clive R. Hollin
University of Birmingham, UK

Children as Witnesses

Edited by

Helen Dent
West Midlands Regional Health Authority and
University of Birmingham, UK

and

Rhona Flin
Robert Gordon Institute of Technology, Aberdeen, UK

JOHN WILEY & SONS
Chichester · New York · Brisbane · Toronto · Singapore

Copyright © 1992 by John Wiley & Sons Ltd,
Baffins Lane, Chichester,
West Sussex PO19 1UD, England

First published in hardback 1992
First published in paperback January 1996

All rights reserved.

No part of this book may be reproduced by any means,
or transmitted, or translated into a machine language
without the written permission of the publisher.

Other Wiley Editorial Offices

John Wiley & Sons, Inc., 605 Third Avenue,
New York, NY 10158-0012, USA

Jacaranda Wiley Ltd, 33 Park Road, Milton,
Queensland 4064, Australia

John Wiley & Sons (Canada) Ltd, 22 Worcester Road,
Rexdale, Ontario M9W 1L1, Canada

John Wiley & Sons (SEA) Pte Ltd, 37 Jalan Pemimpin #05-04,
Block B, Union Industrial Building, Singapore 2057

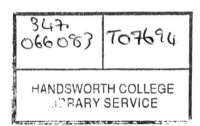

347.
066083

T07694

HANDSWORTH COLLEGE
LIBRARY SERVICE

Library of Congress Cataloging-in-Publication Data

Children as witnesses / edited by Helen Dent and Rhona Flin.
    p.   cm.
    Includes bibliographical references and index.
    ISBN 0-471-93323-6
    1. Children as witnesses.   I. Dent, Helen.   II. Flin, Rhona H.
    K2271.C47   1992
    347'.066083—dc20
    [342.766083]   91–36318
                                                                     CIP

British Library Cataloguing in Publication Data

A catalogue record for this book is
available from the British Library.

ISBN 0-471-93323-6 (ppc)
ISBN 0-471-96178-7 (pbk)

Typeset in 10/12 Century Schoolbook by APS, Salisbury, Wiltshire
Printed and bound in Great Britain by Biddles Ltd, Guildford and King's Lynn

LIBRARY
HANDSWORTH COLLEGE
SOHO ROAD
BIRMINGHAM
B21 9DP

Contents

Contributors

Helen Dent
Editor

School of Psychology, University of Birmingham, Edgbaston, Birmingham B15 2TT, UK.

Rhona Flin
Editor

Business School, Robert Gordon Institute of Technology, Hilton Place, Aberdeen AB9 1FP, UK.

Jan Aldridge

Department of Psychiatry, University of Leeds, 15 Hyde Terrace, Leeds LS2 9LT, UK.

Ethel Amacher

The National Children's Advocacy Center, 106 Lincoln Street, Huntsville, Alabama 35801, USA.

Julian Boon

Department of Psychology, University of Leicester, University Road, Leicester LE1 7RH, UK.

Tascha Boychuck

Center for Child Abuse Prevention, St Joseph's Hospital, Phoenix, Arizona, USA.

Jack Brigham

Department of Psychology, The Florida State University, Tallahassee, Florida 32306-1051, USA.

Ray Bull

Department of Psychology, Portsmouth Polytechnic, King Charles Street, Portsmouth PO1 2ER, UK.

Graham Davies

Department of Psychology, University of Leicester, University Road, Leicester LE1 7RH, UK.

Louise Dezwirek-Sas

London Family Court Clinic, 254 Pall Mall Street, Suite 200, London, Ontario, Canada, N6A 5P6.

Gail Goodman

Department of Psychology, State University of New York, Buffalo, New York State 14260, USA.

Julie Kastanakis   The National Children's Advocacy
                          Center, 106 Lincoln Street, Huntsville,
                          Alabama 35801, USA.

Anne Knox   Department of Psychology, Glasgow
                          Polytechnic, Cowcaddens Road,
                          Glasgow G4 0BA, UK.

Elizabeth Luus   Department of Psychology, Iowa State
                          University, Ames, Iowa 50011, USA.

Stephen Moston   Institute of Social and Applied
                          Psychology, The University,
                          Canterbury, Kent CT2 7LZ, UK.

Kathleen Murray   Department of Social Administration,
                          University of Glasgow, 1 Lilybank
                          Gardens, Glasgow G12 8RZ, UK.

Gordon Nicholson   Sheriffs' Chambers, Sheriff Court
                          House, Lawnmarket, Edinburgh
                          EH1 2NS, UK.

Beth Schwartz-Kenney   Randolph-Macon Woman's College,
                          Lynchburg, Virginia 24503, USA.

Kathryn Sisterman Keeney The National Children's Advocacy
                          Center, 106 Lincoln Street, Huntsville,
                          Alabama 35801, USA.

Stacy Spier   Department of Psychology, The Florida
                          State University, Tallahassee, Florida
                          32306-1051, USA.

John Spencer   Selwyn College, Cambridge CB3 9DQ,
                          UK.

Max Steller   Institut für Forensische Psychiatrie,
                          Freie Universität Berlin, Limonsenstr.
                          27, D-1000 Berlin 45, Germany.

Gary Wells   Department of Psychology, Iowa State
                          University, Ames, Iowa 50011, USA.

Helen Westcott   Public Policy Department, NSPCC,
                          67 Saffron Hill, London EC1N 8RS, UK.

Debra Whitcomb   Education Development Center, Inc.,
                          55 Chapel Street, Newton, MA 02160,
                          USA.

Series Preface

The Wiley series in the Psychology of Crime, Policing and Law will publish concise and integrative reviews in this important emerging area of contemporary research. The purpose of the series is not merely to present research findings in a clear and readable form, but also to bring out their implications for both practice and policy. In this way it is hoped that the series will not only be useful to psychologists but also to all those concerned with crime detection and prevention, policing and the judicial process.

As *Children as Witnesses* illustrates, the last ten years have seen an unprecedented concern, both in the United Kingdom and abroad, for the plight of children in the legal system. The legal system was invented by adults with adult witnesses and suspects in mind. However, increasingly, children are also appearing in court, prompted mainly but not entirely by the growth in cases of alleged child sexual and physical abuse. The frequency with which prosecutions have broken down, due to the inability of the child to "come up to proof" or cope with the rigours of conventional courtroom questioning has led to demands for change.

As a number of contributors emphasise, these requests for reforms in the law and legal procedure have been backed up by extensive psychological research which reveals that children's skills at observation and memory are not as defective as was once thought. Moreover, suggestibility, traditionally considered as a universal trait with which all children were invested, is more tied to particular situations and styles of questioning than it is to the nature of the individual child.

If children's evidence does not require the very specific prohibitions and cautions which have traditionally been attached to it by law, how can children be assisted in giving their evidence in the adult world of the courtroom? A range of techniques are described in *Children as Witnesses* from prior preparation through courtroom visits and explanatory leaflets to the use of videotechnology in the form of live video links and pre-recorded televised interviews. However, all such procedures will be of no avail if juries maintain a skeptical view of the competency and suggestibility of children; a point made by more than one contributor.

Helen Dent and Rhona Flin are well placed to marshal a review of this significant interface between law and psychology. Helen Dent was a pioneer of research on children's competency as witnesses and was among the first to draw attention to the particular difficulties children experienced with conventional procedures such as identification parades. Rhona Flin conducted some of the first research into the feelings and expectations children have as they enter the witness box and on their effectiveness in dealing with the traditional legal techniques of examination and cross examination. Their reputations have ensured that the contributors to this volume are all leaders of their fields with experience of legal systems, not only of Britain but many other parts of the world. All those who wish to discover why psychology has had such a substantial impact on the development of legislation and legal procedure in relation to child witnesses need look no further than this book.

GRAHAM DAVIES
University of Leicester

Preface

In the last decade the topic of children as witnesses has developed from a minority interest studied by a handful of psychologists and lawyers into a subject which now generates international media coverage.

At the time of writing (August, 1991) two major sex abuse cases which will focus on the evidence of children are headline news. On 19 August in North Carolina, USA, the trial of Robert Kelly opened. Kelly was the owner of the now defunct Little Rascals Day Care Center in Edenton and he was charged on 183 counts of sexually abusing 22 children between 1986 and 1989. Six others, including Kelly's wife, Betsy, face trial later.

Much will hinge on the testimony of the children, with an army of experts expected to testify whether children so young can know the truth after so much therapy. (*USA Today*, 19 August 1991, p. 3A.)

The following Monday, 26 August, on the Orkney Islands which lie off the north-east coast of Scotland, a Judicial Inquiry began into an alleged case of ritual sex abuse in which nine children aged from 8 to 15 years, from four families, were removed from their homes in the early morning of 27 February 1991 and taken into care on the mainland of Scotland. The inquiry is not a criminal trial but is intended to examine the handling of the investigation into allegations of ritual sex abuse involving children.

The nine children at the centre of the probe will not give evidence. Instead two independent assessors will interview them and pass on their evidence. (*Scottish Daily Record*, 28 August 1991, p. 9.)

Whatever the outcome of these proceedings, we can be certain that they will produce more questions than answers. Both cases hinge on the reliability and credibility of children's evidence and on the ability of adults to judge that evidence during the investigation of the cases and subsequent legal proceedings. It is hoped that this volume will demonstrate the extent to which both psychologists and lawyers are beginning to search for solutions to some of the problems inherent in any case where children are victims or bystander witnesses.

While this is the first volume on child witnesses to be edited by British psychologists, the contributing authors are from Canada, Germany and the USA, as well as from Scotland and England. The aim of this collection is to present the busy professional reader with the latest and most useful developments in child witness research and practice. Psychological research in this area is of limited value unless it is designed to address real problems arising from the operation of the current legal system. All the authors have a clear, applied focus to their work and the relevant legal context has been provided by specialists who have written easily digestible summaries of the legal status of children's evidence in the countries represented.

All the contributors to this book are either well known and distinguished in their field or are pioneers of exciting and important new developments. We would like to thank them for producing such excellent chapters and for their cooperation in responding to our editorial demands. We also wish to express our gratitude to Michael Coombs and Wendy Hudlass of our publishers, John Wiley & Sons. Michael provided the inspiration for this volume and we suspect that there were moments when he wished that he had not bothered to share this inspiration with us. He and Wendy provided constant support and encouragement and demonstrated a degree of patience beyond the call of duty.

The topics covered in the book start with four chapters on psychological research into variables affecting children's competence as eyewitnesses. All of these chapters contain useful recommendations for the practice of interviewing child witnesses. In the first chapter Dent examines the comparative eyewitness reliability of children with a learning difficulty, normal children, and adults. Goodman and Schwartz-Kenney argue in their chapter that knowing a child's age is not enough and they report the results of a series of experiments which consider the influence of cognitive, social and emotional factors on children's testimony. Moston considers the role of social support (ie the presence of a support person) during interviews and he examines the effect this has on children's recall of witnessed events. This is followed by a chapter on children as witnesses in sexual abuse cases, in which Steller and Boychuck critically examine a technique developed in Germany for assessing the credibility of children's evidence called "Statement Validity Analysis".

The next two chapters both by American psychologists, continue this theme by focusing on the important issue of how child witnesses are perceived by adults, especially those likely to be encountered in the criminal justice system. Luus and Wells present the results of two studies designed to address the question of whether children are perceived to be less credible witnesses than adults when they give testimony in a courtroom-like setting. Brigham and Spier surveyed attorneys, police and child protection workers in order to assess their attitudes to children's testimony and they discuss the opinions and differences of opinion revealed by these groups of professionals.

Recent legal developments are reviewed by legal experts from England (Spencer), Scotland (Nicholson and Murray), and the United States (Whitcomb). In all these jurisdictions the late 1980s and early 1990s have seen significant and sometimes even successful attempts to reform the law relating to children's evidence. These chapters have been written for professionals and researchers who need to understand the legal background without being qualified lawyers themselves.

This is followed by three chapters that examine children actually attending court as witnesses. Flin, Bull, Boon and Knox present results from their observational study of children giving evidence in criminal courts in Scotland. Dezwirek-Sas discusses the first results from a Canadian project which examined the effects of preparing child sexual abuse victims in Ontario for testimony and in the next chapter, Sisterman Keeney, Amacher and Kastanakis describe the procedures they use in Alabama, USA, with groups of child witnesses to prepare them for going to court.

The final chapters, most appropriately, have an eye to the future. Davies and Westcott report on the use and usefulness of videotechnology in the courtroom and Aldridge examines the training needs of professionals who deal with child witnesses.

As someone who has a professional or research interest in child witnesses, we have confidence that you will easily find new and practical information in this book. We wish you good reading.

RHONA FLIN
HELEN DENT

CHAPTER 1

The Effects of Age and Intelligence on Eyewitnessing Ability

Helen Dent

West Midlands Regional Health Authority and University of Birmingham

INTRODUCTION

The child witness has acquired an extremely high profile over the past decade. This has coincided with media exposure to the general public of a far higher prevalence of child sexual abuse than that indicated by official statistics (Bentovim et al, 1988). Though child witnesses who are independent of the crime may be in the majority (Flin et al, in press), nevertheless the child victim of sexual abuse has particularly highlighted the disadvantaged position of the child witness (see Spencer, Chapter 7, this volume).

Additional to the disadvantage occasioned by rules of evidence are the negative beliefs and attitudes of some professionals and jurors towards the ability of the child witness (see Brigham & Spier, Chapter 6, this volume; Luus & Wells, Chapter 5, this volume). One potential cause of such views may have been the rather unfavourable picture of the child witness portrayed by research in the early part of this century (see Goodman, 1984, for a review). Recent research has started to create a more positive but more complex image. The aim of this chapter is to contribute to current knowledge about the effects of age and also of intelligence on eyewitness performance.

Children as Witnesses. Edited by H. Dent and R. Flin
© 1992 John Wiley & Sons Ltd.

PSYCHOLOGICAL RESEARCH

Psychological research on the comparative reliability of child and adult witnesses has not so far provided clear results, partly due to the small number of studies and to their widely varying methodologies, which rather limits the conclusions that can be drawn from this work. Research at the beginning of this century produced dramatic demonstrations of children's suggestibility in the laboratory and the courtroom. This work helped to contribute to the conception of the child as a dangerously suggestible witness, who, by implication, would be less reliable than an adult witness. These early studies did not produce comparable data from adult subjects and it was not until the work of Loftus and colleagues (Loftus, 1975) that data emerged to show just how unreliable and suggestible adults could be.

Over the past 12 years, there has been a substantial increase in experimental studies investigating the abilities of children as witnesses (eg Ceci et al, 1987; Davies et al, 1989; Goodman & Schwartz-Kenney, Chapter 2, this volume). Of particular relevance to this chapter are those that have directly compared the reliability of children's and adults' recall of a witnessed event. Some studies have used live events (eg Goodman & Schwartz-Kenney, Chapter 2, this volume; Goodman & Reed, 1986; King & Yuille, 1987; Marin et al, 1979; Poole & White, in press), some have used film or video (eg Dent & Stephenson, 1979; Cohen & Harnick, 1980; List, 1986), and at least one a series of slides (Parker et al, 1986). It is rare, partly due to ethical concerns, for live events to contain specific criminal elements and the studies mentioned in this chapter did not do so. Crimes of various kinds are more commonly shown when the event is prerecorded and this was the case in the studies cited above which used some form of prerecorded event. The length of the various incidents, the delay prior to recall, the number of recall sessions, the medium in which recall was elicited (written vs oral) and the interview techniques have all varied between the studies, as have the ages of the subjects and, not surprisingly, the results. However, some common findings have emerged from these studies.

First, with the exception of free recall from the older adults (mean age 68 yr) in List's (1986) study, adults performed as well as or better than children. Secondly, with the same exception, older subjects produced more complete recall than younger ones in free recall conditions. When questions were asked, one study (Marin et al, 1979) found all age groups (6–7 yr, 9–10 yr, 13–14 yr and adults) to be equally reliable for both objective (non-leading) and suggestive (leading) questions. Overall, however, a more complex pattern of results has emerged. For example, when answering objective questions, children aged 6 and 12 years have been found to be as reliable as adults (Marin et al, 1979; Cohen & Harnick, 1980), whereas children aged 9 and 10 years have been found to be less reliable (Cohen & Harnick, 1980; List, 1986). When suggestive questions were used, some researchers have found children aged 6 and 12 years to be as reliable as adults (Marin et al, 1979; Cohen & Harnick, 1980), whereas others have found children aged 6 and 9 years to be less so (Goodman & Reed, 1986; Cohen & Harnick, 1980).

One important conclusion to be drawn from these studies is that children as young as six years *can* be as reliable as adults when answering both objective and suggestive questions, but we now need to know more about the circumstances in which each age group can perform optimally and whether under these circumstances there is an age trend of superiority.

CHILDREN WITH LEARNING DIFFICULTIES

It is increasingly recognized that the group of children who have been termed "mentally retarded", "mildly mentally handicapped" or children with "learning difficulties" are an important group to study. They are at particular risk of sexual abuse (Bentovim et al, 1988), they are more likely to live in inner cities (Ramey et al, 1984) where there is a greater chance of witnessing crime, they have been shown to have particular memory problems (Brown, 1974), to respond optimally to a different interview technique from children of normal intelligence (Dent, 1986), to be less complete, less accurate and more suggestible than children of normal intelligence (Pear & Wyatt, 1914), and to be resistant to suggestion for items for which there is a strong memory trace (Gudjonsson & Gunn, 1982). For these reasons it is particularly important to include these children in studies of eyewitnessing.

THE PRESENT STUDY

The study being reported here is an experimental investigation of the comparative reliability of children with a learning difficulty (LD), other children and adults. In applied research it is clearly important to be able to demonstrate the applicability and substantiveness of the findings. Therefore, in order to enhance the conclusions that can be drawn from the findings, two important principles have been incorporated into the design. The first is that of realism or, as it has also been termed, ecological validity. This has been accomplished as far as possible by using an unexpected live event as the to be remembered material. The second principle is that of replication, which has been accomplished by employing the same experimental design and method as previous work by the author carried out with mentally handicapped children (Dent, 1986) and with other children (Dent & Stephenson, 1979).

The study was designed to investigate the following questions:

1. Is there a difference in the ability of children with a learning difficulty (LD) and other children to report details of a previously witnessed scene?
2. Is there a difference in recall ability between these two groups and a group of adults?
3. Do each of the groups respond optimally to different interviewing techniques?

The Design of the Study

The design and procedure of the study involved an unexpected incident which was staged in the classrooms of three subject groups: children (LD), other children and adults. One week after the incident each subject was seen by a trained interviewer who used one of three standard interview techniques. The interviews were recorded on audio-cassette tape, later transcribed and scored for accuracy, and the resulting data subjected to statistical analysis.

The Incident

The incident was designed to be comprehensible to every child and to be plausible to adults. It lasted for four minutes.

Two actors, a woman and a man, posing as Dr Whewell and her assistant Mr Kelly, entered the classroom. Dr Whewell informed the teacher that she had come to investigate teachers' reactions to noise levels in the classroom, and she asked permission to take the teacher's pulse. During the incident, Mr Kelly walked round the classroom carrying a cassette recorder and microphone, which enabled an audio recording of each incident to be taken. Dr Whewell then took various items out of her briefcase, including some toys, biscuits and medical equipment, as she searched for a stopwatch. The toys and biscuits were deliberately included as items likely to be of particular interest to the children. Finally, she took the teacher's pulse, then left with Mr Kelly, but returned briefly to retrieve a book which she had "forgotten".

The students in each class were unaware that the incident was staged and that they would later be questioned about it. In one school of open plan design, a child was overheard saying, "That woman's gone and forgotten her book *again!*". Each classroom teacher was rehearsed in order to achieve as much consistency as possible between situations.

The Subjects

1. One hundred and two (50 girls, 52 boys) children aged 9 and 10 years of "normal" ability were recruited from an "inner" city and suburban school. The majority of the children were Caucasian; a small proportion were Asian and Afro-Caribbean.
2. Seventy-eight (25 girls, 53 boys) children (LD) aged 8–12 years (mean age = 10) were recruited from special schools and from remedial classes in the same schools as group 1. They were defined by their teachers as children with a "learning difficulty" and were of approximately the same racial proportions as group 1.
3. Sixty-five (48 women, 17 men) adults aged 16–41 years (mean age = 21) of "normal" ability were recruited from various further education colleges and youth training schemes. No university students were included and many of the adults had attended the same schools as the children in group 1.

The Interviewers

A small group of adult male and female interviewers were trained by the experimenter. Each one interviewed several children individually using one of three techniques. The techniques were chosen in this instance because they were used in the author's previous studies (Dent & Stephenson, 1979; Dent, 1986), and originally because they had been observed to be the strategies most commonly used in police interviewing.

Interviewing techniques

The three interviewing techniques employed in this study were:

1. Free recall. This interview involved minimal prompting of the subject and consisted of standardized instructions plus a few permitted prompts.

2. General questions. This interview consisted of standardized instructions, followed by 14 open-ended, non-leading questions, for example "What did the man do while he was in your classroom?"
3. Specific questions. The same instructions as for General questions were followed by 72 detailed questions involving maximal, but non-leading, cues, for example "Did the man give anything to your teacher?". All questions were checked by a lawyer, who confirmed that they would not normally be considered to be "leading". Each interview technique was carefully designed so that subjects did not receive any more information during questioning than was given in Free recall. The interviews were recorded on audio-cassette tape and later transcribed for analysis.

Data Scoring

The transcripts of the interviews were scored for the numbers of correct and incorrect points of information included in each subject's account. A checklist containing 180 points of information about the sequence of events, the appearance of the actors and their equipment was used for this purpose.

The total number of correct points in each report was taken to be a measure of *completeness*. *Accuracy* of each report was calculated by taking the percentage of correct points to correct plus incorrect points found in each report.

Completeness and accuracy scores were taken for the total recall in each case and for several subdivisions of total recall. The main subdivision was for action versus description, since previous research has shown children to experience difficulty with description, particularly of people (Dent, 1982; Davies et al, 1989). Descriptive recall was further subdivided into descriptions of the female actor, the male actor, the toys and biscuits in the female actor's bag and other objects in the female actor's bag.

Finally, the script of the incident and the checklist were given to a high-ranking member of the West Yorkshire police force who constructed a list of the points of information concerning the appearance of the two actors that, in his opinion, would be most useful in a police investigation. Completeness and accuracy scores were taken for these measures.

Analyses of variance and Newman–Keuls *post hoc* analyses were performed on the completeness and accuracy scores for each measure. Details of these analyses will not be included here but are in the final report of this project (Dent, 1987; see also Dent, in preparation, for a fuller discussion of these results).

RESULTS

Accuracy of Recall

Without exception, all three groups of subjects, children (LD), other children and adults, gave equally accurate reports in response to Free recall and General questions. When Specific questions were asked, the accuracy of the children's reports decreased to a level significantly lower than that of the adults' reports, except when they were describing the objects in the female actor's bag. For this information, all three groups gave equally accurate responses to specific questions.

"Police" Accuracy Scores

Recall for the appearance of the female and male actors was also scored using a short checklist of those items identified by a police officer as being of particular value in an investigation.

The scores showed the same pattern as before, with subject groups being equally accurate in response to Free recall or General questions and the adult group being most accurate when answering Specific questions.

Completeness of Recall

The completeness of the reports given by the children (LD), other children and adult subject groups followed a more complex pattern than found with the accuracy of those reports. For most measures, the adult groups gave more complete reports than both child groups in response to Free recall and General questions. When Specific questions were asked, the children (LD) gave the least complete, with children and adults providing equally complete reports.

However, when describing the objects in the bag, the subject groups were equally complete in the Free recall and General questions conditions. Similarly, when giving the "police" description of the female actor, the subject groups were equally complete in all three interview conditions. When giving the "police" description of the male actor, the subject groups were equally complete in response to General questions.

Male–Female Comparisons

A consistent trend throughout all measures, interview conditions and subject groups was that of female superiority in both completeness and accuracy of reports. This trend was not, however, found to be statistically significant.

Summary of Results

Close consideration of the figures involved for all measures revealed that General questions most consistently elicited the best blend of completeness and accuracy for all three subject groups. However, Free recall consistently produced the most accurate reports, therefore a recommended interviewing strategy would be to use this technique first, followed by the open-ended style of General questions.

Specific questions produced a large increase in completeness but at the expense of accuracy, particularly with the two child groups. The adults' reports were not so adversely affected by the increased prompting involved in Specific questions. Nevertheless, whenever this technique is used it is important to be aware of the probability of a lower level of accuracy in the information obtained.

DISCUSSION

Comparative Reliability

The most important result to emerge from this study is that children aged 8–12 years, of a wide range of abilities, can be just as reliable witnesses as adults. This does, however, depend upon the manner in which they are interviewed. The results from the study clearly show that whereas both children (LD) and other children were as reliable as adults when giving Free recall or answering General questions, they were less reliable when answering Specific questions. A major strength of this project is that it has replicated earlier findings that children give very accurate recall of various types of witnessed events when this is elicited by Free recall or General questions (Dent & Stephenson, 1979; Dent, 1986).

This finding has strong implications for the manner in which children are interviewed at all stages of an investigation. If child witnesses are allowed to relate their report with minimal prompting, either as free recall or in response to general, open-ended questions, then the results of the present research suggest that they would not be significantly less accurate than adult witnesses.

Delay prior to recall is another important factor which can affect reliability. In this study, the subjects were interviewed just one week after the incident. An earlier study with the same age group of children

(Dent & Stephenson, 1979) has shown that memory deteriorates sharply over a period of two weeks and then more gradually up to two months after witnessing the event. Reduced accuracy has also been found in the recall of children aged 5–9 years after a five-month delay (Flin et al, in press). Such deterioration affects both the completeness and the accuracy of what is remembered. Though the present research project did not directly address this issue, the previous research findings (Dent & Stephenson, 1979; Flin et al, in press) would suggest that evidence from witnesses should be obtained as early as possible. A videorecording of the interview could fulfil the dual purpose of being a record of the witness's earliest, most vivid and complete memory and showing how the recall was elicited (see Davies & Westcott, Chapter 13, this volume). This would enable recall elicited by methods which have been shown to preserve accuracy to be distinguished from other recall. Such practice could be especially useful with child witnesses, since their accuracy of recall has been found to be particularly adversely affected when detailed and probing questions are used.

Completeness

With regard to the total amount of recall given by each subject, this study has replicated a general finding (see Davies, 1991) that completeness increases with age and with the level of prompting used. This creates a major dilemma for the interviewing of child witnesses, since increased prompting (from free recall to specific questions) has been found in this and in previous studies (Dent & Stephenson, 1979; Dent, 1986) to be accompanied by a sharp decline in accuracy. Recent research is opening up some creative solutions to this problem. Wilkinson (1988) has managed to produce a significant increase in the completeness of the reports of preschool children, without an accompanying detriment in accuracy, using a context reinstatement technique. Moston (Chapter 3, this volume) has achieved a similar result using peer social support.

Recall for Items of Particular Interest to Children

The design of the incident in the present study deliberately included items likely to be of particular interest to children such as toys and biscuits, in order to see whether these would be any better recalled than other details by the two child groups. This was indeed the case, in that all subject groups were equally accurate in their recall of the toys and biscuits in all interview conditions. Specific questions did not have the usual adverse affect on the accuracy of the children's recall for toys and biscuits. This finding tends to indicate that the children's recall of these objects was particularly clear since previous research (Gudjonsson & Gunn, 1982) has shown that susceptibility to suggestion is lower for more clearly remembered details.

However, with regard to completeness, adults gave more correct information than the two child groups in the Free recall and General questions conditions, but in the Specific questions condition, children (LD) and adults gave significantly more correct information than the children. This finding reinforces the notion of vivid memories being resistant to suggestion and, further, indicates that the children (LD) paid particular attention to the toys and biscuits.

These results certainly support previous findings (Goodman et al, 1987; Gudjonsson & Gunn, 1982) that witnesses of all ages and abilities will give particularly reliable reports about those objects or events in which they are most interested.

Forensically Relevant Recall

A relatively unusual manipulation of the data was to identify which descriptive items would be likely to be of particular use in a police investigation. The aim was to see how the three subject groups' recall would compare for these items. As with the other measures, the three groups were equally accurate when Free recall or General questions were used, but adults were significantly more accurate than the children when answering Specific questions.

This pattern of results strengthens the conclusion that children's testimony can be as accurate as adults', since this applies not just to general recall of an incident, but also to those aspects which may be of particular interest in a police investigation. Moreover, some of the children's accounts were as complete as the adults' for the "police" descriptions.

Optimal Interviewing Techniques

This study was also designed to shed light on which interviewing technique would prove optimal with each of the experimental subject groups, children, children (LD) and adults. The results indicated quite clearly that, though increased completeness could be obtained by use of Specific questions, this was at the expense of accuracy, particularly for the two child groups.

The fundamental problem of how to elicit total and accurate recall from a child witness has generated many practical and research attempts to find good solutions. In cases of suspected sexual abuse, the task of eliciting recall is made much harder when a child is reluctant to divulge information. Various interviewing strategies have been developed by clinicians to encourage children to talk (see Vizard, 1991 for a review). However, these are not always compatible with rules of evidence, since when children cannot otherwise be encouraged to talk, most make use of overtly leading questions. This is not necessarily an unreasonable clinical strategy, given that children, and indeed adults, are often embarrassed to talk about sexual matters Children may be aware of real, or may imagine dreadful consequences of telling; and recent research findings have shown how very reluctant children can be to reveal information they have been asked to keep secret (Pipe & Goodman, 1991). Nevertheless, there is still concern that, when used outside the courtroom, leading questions will produce fabrication alongside reluctantly provided recall.

A recent and promising research development is focusing on methods of adapting Geiselman and colleagues' (1985) cognitive interview for use with children (Geiselman et al, 1990). The cognitive interview has been found to elicit more complete and accurate recall from adults than "standard" police interviews (Geiselman et al, 1985), but it has not yet been shown to be as effective with children as with adults. A research programme at Southampton University is currently investigating further ways of modifying the cognitive interview for use with young children (Memon & Bull, in press). Other directions that appear promising at the moment are the use of statement validity analysis (Steller and Boychuk, Chapter 4, this volume); improved training for police officers and other interviewers (Aldridge, Chapter 14, this volume); giving thorough and detailed preparation to children before their court appearance (Dezwirek-Sas, Chapter 11, this volume; Sisterman Keeney et al, Chapter 12, this volume); and adapting the courtroom proceedings to the child's needs (Nicholson & Murray, Chapter 8, this volume; Davies & Westcott, Chapter 13, this volume).

SUMMARY

The research reported in this chapter has given support to the view that the recall of child witnesses can be as accurate as that of adult witnesses. When accuracy is the prime consideration, an interviewer should make use of free recall or general questions, at least in the first instance. However, children may be reluctant or unable to disclose certain information without more detailed prompting. More research is needed on how to reduce errors of omission in children's recall without increasing errors of commission. Some interesting developments in this direction have been briefly mentioned.

ACKNOWLEDGEMENTS

This research was supported by Grant Number 48716 from the Home Office Research and Planning Unit and was conducted while the author was employed by the University of Leeds. The views expressed in this chapter are those of the author and do not necessarily represent the position or policy of the funding body.

REFERENCES

Bentovim, A., Elton, A., Hildebrand, J., Tranter, M. & Vizard, E. (1988). *Child Sexual Abuse within the Family*. London: Wright.
Brown, A. (1974). Strategic behaviour in retardate memory. In N. R. Ellis (Ed.). *International Review of Research in Mental Retardation*, Vol. 7. New York: Academic Press.
Ceci, S. J., Toglia, M. P. & Ross, D. F. (Eds) (1987). *Children's Eyewitness Memory*. New York: Springer-Verlag.
Cohen, R. L. & Harnick, M. A. (1980). The susceptibility of child witnesses to suggestion. *Law and Human Behavior*, 4, 201–210.
Davies, G. (1991). 'Research on children's testimony: implications for interviewing practice. In C. R. Hollin & K. Howells (Eds). *Clinical Approaches to Sex Offenders and Their Victims*. Chichester: Wiley.
Davies, G., Tarrant, A. & Flin, R. (1989). Close encounters of the witness kind: children's memory for a simulated health inspection. *British Journal of Psychology*, 80, 415–429.
Dent, H. R. (1982). The effects of interviewing strategies on the results of interviews with child witnesses. In A. Trankell (Ed.). *Reconstructing the Past. The Role of Psychologists in Criminal Trials*. Stockholm: Norstedts.
Dent, H. R. (1986). An experimental study of the effectiveness of different techniques of questioning mentally handicapped child witnesses. *British Journal of Clinical Psychology*, 25, 13–17.
Dent, H. R. (1987). Interviewing child witnesses, an experimental study of the comparative reliability of child and adult witnesses. Final Report of research supported by the Home Office Research and Planning Unit, Grant No. 48716.
Dent, H. R. (in preparation). Cognitive development and eyewitnessing ability.
Dent, H. R. & Stephenson, G. M. (1979). An experimental study of the effectiveness of different techniques of questioning child witnesses. *British Journal of Social and Clinical Psychology*, 18, 41–51.
Flin, R., Boon, J., Knox, A, & Bull, R. (in press). The effect of a five month delay on children's and adults' eyewitness memory. *British Journal of Psychology*.
Geiselman, R. E., Fisher, R. P., Mackinnon, D. P. & Holland, H. L. (1985). Eyewitness memory enhancement in the police interview: cognitive retrieval mnemonics versus hypnosis. *Journal of Applied Psychology*, 70, 401–412.
Geiselman, R. E., Saywitz, K. J. & Bornstein, G. K. (1990). Cognitive interviewing techniques for child witnesses and witnesses of crime. Report to the State Justice Institute (grant no. SJI-BB-11J-D-016).

Goodman, G. S. (1984). Children's testimony in historical perspective. *Journal of Social Issues*, **40**, 9–31.

Goodman, G. S., Aman, C. & Hirschman, J. (1987). Child sexual and physical abuse: children's testimony. In S. J. Ceci, M. P. Toglia & D. F. Ross (Eds). *Children's Eyewitness Memory*. New York: Springer-Verlag.

Goodman, G. S. & Reed, R. S. (1986). Age differences in eyewitness testimony. *Law and Human Behavior*, **10**, 317–332.

Gudjonsson, G. L. & Gunn, J. (1982). The competence and reliability of a witness in a criminal court: a case report. *British Journal of Psychiatry*, **141**, 624–627.

King, M. A. & Yuille, J. C. (1987). Suggestibility and the child witness. In S. J. Ceci, M. P. Toglia & D. F. Ross (Eds). *Children's Eyewitness Memory*. New York: Springer-Verlag.

List, J. (1986). Age and schematic differences in the reliability of eyewitness testimony. *Developmental Psychology*, **22**, 50–57.

Loftus, E. F. (1975). Leading questions and the eyewitness report. *Cognitive Psychology*, **7**, 560–572.

Marin, B. V., Holmes, D. L., Guth, M. & Kovac, A. (1979). The potential of children as eyewitnesses. *Law and Human Behavior*, **3**, 295–305.

Memon, A. & Bull, R. (in press). The cognitive interview: how and why it may improve the memory of an eye witness. In J. F. Romero Rodriguez & D. P. Farrington (Eds). *Psychology, Crime and Law: British and Spanish Research*.

Parker, J. F., Haverfield, E. & Baker-Thomas, S. (1986). Eyewitness testimony of children. *Journal of Applied Social Psychology*, **16**, 287–302.

Pear, T. H. & Wyatt, S. (1914). The testimony of normal and mentally defective children. *British Journal of Psychology*, **6**, 388–419.

Pipe, M. E. & Goodman, G. S. (1991). Elements of secrecy: implications for children's testimony. *Behavioral Sciences and the law*, **9**, 33–41.

Poole, D. A. & White, L. T. (in press). Effects of question repetition on the eyewitness testimony of children and adults. *Developmental Psychology*.

Ramey, C., Campbell, F. & Finkelstein, N. (1984). Course and structure of intellectual development in children with high risk for developmental retardation. In P. Brooks, R. Sperber & C. McCauley (Eds). *Learning and Cognition in the Mentally Retarded*. New York: Laurence Erlbaum.

Vizard, E. (1991). Interviewing children suspected of being sexually abused: a review of theory and practice. In C. R. Hollin & K. Howells (Eds). *Clinical Approaches to Sex Offenders and Their Victims*. Chichester: Wiley.

Wilkinson, J. (1988). Context effects in children's event memory. In M. Gruneberg, P. Morris & R. Sykes (Eds) *Practical Aspects of Memory: Current Research and Issues*. Chichester: Wiley.

CHAPTER 2

Why Knowing a Child's Age is Not Enough: Influences of Cognitive, Social, and Emotional Factors on Children's Testimony

Gail S. Goodman

State University of New York at Buffalo

and

Beth M. Schwartz-Kenney

Randolph-Macon Woman's College, Lynchburg

In the summer of 1990, the US Supreme Court ruled on a sexual abuse case involving two young sisters, 5 and 2.5 years of age (*Idaho vs Wright*, 1990). The 5-year-old had disclosed sexual abuse to a family friend and later to a doctor. The doctor then interviewed the 2.5-year-old after performing a medical examination on her. During the doctor's testimony at trial, from which we quote below, he was permitted to recount the child's answers to four leading questions. These four questions became the focus of the appeal to the Idaho Supreme Court

Children as Witnesses. Edited by H. Dent and R. Flin
© 1992 John Wiley & Sons Ltd.

and then to the US Supreme Court. (A refers to the doctor's answers and Q to the attorney's questions.)

A. "Do you play with daddy? Does daddy play with you? Does daddy touch you with his pee-pee? Do you touch his pee-pee?" And again we then established what was meant by pee-pee, it was a generic term for genital area.

Q. Before you get into that, what was, as best you can recollect, what was her response to the question "Do you play with daddy?"

A. Yes, we play—I remember her making a comment—about yes we play a lot and expanding on that and talking about spending time with daddy.

Q. And "Does daddy play with you?" Was there any response?

A. She responded to that as well, that they played together in a variety of circumstances and, you know, seemed very unaffected by the question.

Q. And then what did you say and her response?

A. When I asked her "Does daddy touch you with his pee-pee?" she did admit to that. When I asked, "Do you touch his pee-pee?" she did not have any response.

The doctor testified that the child then volunteered that her daddy " ... does this with me, but he does it a lot more with my sister than with me" (*Idaho vs Wright*, 1989). A psychologist who testified for the defense argued that the questions were leading and would therefore be likely to result in a false report, and the Idaho Supreme Court agreed, overturning the conviction. The US Supreme Court affirmed the State court decision to overturn the conviction, although for a complex mixture of reasons.

How likely are children to provide false information when asked questions of a leading or even a misleading nature, that is, how suggestible are children? Does elicitation of question-induced errors change with age? Are there conditions under which age differences appear and other conditions under which age differences disappear? Or, is knowing a child's age enough?

In this chapter we will describe several studies conducted in, or in association with, our laboratory that examined contextual factors that affect children's testimony, especially their responses to leading and misleading questions. The studies highlight a general theme: that although age differences exist in children's abilities to remember events, a variety of contextual factors (eg social/emotional influences, the children's understanding of the purpose of being interviewed) may interact with memory to determine the quality and quantity of children's eyewitness reports. These contextual factors can play an important role in determining not only children's accuracy but also their willingness to report an event.

Thus, in each study, we were particularly interested in exploring the joint effects of context and memory. We were also particularly interested in linking our work to issues that frequently arise in actual child sexual abuse cases.

WHY FOCUS ON CHILD SEXUAL ABUSE

Although our research is designed to investigate the accuracy of children's testimony generally, we have made special efforts to orient our work toward issues raised by child abuse cases, especially cases of alleged child sexual abuse—and for good reasons. Although children testify as victim or bystander witnesses about a variety of other crimes, no other crime in the US criminal court system seems to involve children as witnesses to the same extent that child sexual abuse does. For example, a recent survey of prosecutors in Florida revealed that child sexual abuse cases constitute half of the child witness cases they handle (Leippe et al, 1989, in press).

However, it is well known that a far greater number of children experience or witness crime, and give reports about it to authorities, than ever testify in court (Goodman et al, 1988). Prevalence studies indicate a shockingly high frequency of child sexual abuse and in recent years there has been a substantial increase in the number of sexual abuse reports to social service and police agencies (American Association, 1988).

As a result, more and more children are being interviewed about this kind of crime well before a court case ever develops. When they are interviewed, use of leading questions—which, legally speaking, may simply mean that the questions are direct and specific—is very likely to raise the issue of children's suggestibility. Therefore, we have been interested in simulating the kinds of leading questions that might be used in a precourt interview.

Finally, we have aimed our research at children's testimony concerning child sexual abuse because, in recent years, cases of such abuse have been particularly controversial, especially when the prosecution relies heavily on children's testimony and the defense leans heavily on claims of children's suggestibility. We have been especially interested in testing the claim that nonabused children are highly suggestible when asked leading questions. It is important to understand that our work has not been oriented toward examining the testimony of actual sexual abuse victims but rather toward testing nonabused children's proclivity to make statements, either spontaneously or as a result of leading or misleading questioning, that might result in false accusations of sexual abuse.

As will be seen below, our studies indicate that age differences do occur at times in children's response to leading and misleading questions, including questions that might be of considerable consequence if asked in a child sexual abuse investigation.

However, contextual factors can eliminate, exaggerate, or even reverse these age differences. Current developmental theory provides a framework for making sense of this variability in children's performance.

AGE DIFFERENCES IN CHILDREN'S EYEWITNESS TESTIMONY

When the performance of very young children is compared to that of older children and adults, it is common to find age differences in both the completeness and the accuracy of reports. We cannot expect very young children to have the memory ability or cognitive sophistication of adults, although even 3-year-olds can sometimes provide a surprising amount of accurate information about meaningful life events (Goodman & Aman, 1990; Jones & Krugman, 1986). Nevertheless, age differences in suggestibility are not always found in studies of children's testimony (eg Marin et al, 1979), a result that some professionals find perplexing.

Actually, many current theories of cognitive development (eg Chi, 1986; Fischer, 1980; Vygotsky, 1934/1978) lead us to expect that age differences will not necessarily appear on eyewitness tasks. According to these views, children's cognition is not strictly bound by developmental stages, nor is it strictly age-bound, as legal thinking might suggest. Instead, children's abilities are typically uneven, with children having more sophisticated skills when events are familiar, tasks are simplified, surroundings are supportive, and the social/emotional climate is favorable. Although limits on children's optimal performance exist, so that the most sophisticated performance of a 3-year-old in an optimal situation rarely if ever matches or exceeds the most sophisticated performance of a 10-year-old, a broad range of abilities can be found at any one age (Fischer, 1980). Thus, a young child tested under supportive conditions may perform as well as an older child tested under less supportive conditions (Price & Goodman, 1990). This leads us to expect many age-by-task-by-context interactions when we study eyewitness tasks (Melton & Thompson, 1987).

Like other abilities that change with age, suggestibility is not a stable feature of childhood. We conceive of suggestibility as a characteristic that varies as a function of a variety of factors, including memory strength, feelings of power or powerlessness, the extent of social pressure, and comprehension of what is being asked and why it is being asked. Because suggestibility is not viewed as a stable trait, our conception does not preclude the possibility that suggestibility varies in accordance with the circumstances of an interview. It also does not preclude the possibility that effective training procedures can be developed to bolster resistance to suggestion (Warren-Leubecker et al, 1991).

Until recently, most researchers with an interest in children's testimony have not intentionally sought to investigate age-by-task-by-context interactions. Instead, children's testimony for neutral or stressful events has been studied, and age differences in free recall, answers to questions, and photo identification accuracy have been noted. These studies are important, but in the actual contexts in which children testify, matters are often much more complex than the studies suggest. A variety of social and emotional factors impinge on child witnesses, and these can determine whether or not age differences in children's ability to report events arise. This principle is illustrated in one of our studies that examined the effects of repeated interviewing and "reinforcement" on the accuracy of children's testimony about a stressful event.

EXPERIMENT 1: THE EFFECTS OF REPEATED INTERVIEWS AND "REINFORCEMENT"

In sexual assault cases, children are often interviewed repeatedly. What are the effects of multiple interviews on the accuracy of children's reports? Some fear that multiple interviews are likely to lead to inaccuracies, especially if the interviewer asks leading or misleading questions and reinforces the child's response with comments such as "You are doing really well"; "You have a good memory" (Underwager & Wakefield, 1990).

However, most research to date indicates positive or null effects of repeated interviewing on children's testimony (Brainerd & Ornstein, 1991; Dent & Stephenson, 1979; Tucker et al, 1990). In our own work, we were particularly interested in children's reponses to repeated misleading questions, especially misleading questions related to abuse allegations (Goodman et al, 1991a).

We also wanted to test the notion that "reinforcement" would lead to increased error of commission in response to our repeated questions.

When interviewing young children, clinicians and researchers typically find that it is important to build and maintain rapport, help the children feel comfortable, lower their anxiety and keep them interested in answering questions. However, as mentioned earlier, forensic interviewers have been criticized for using such techniques because positive statements (eg "You have a good memory"), tangible rewards (eg cookies and juice), and an especially warm atmosphere are thought by some to heighten young children's suggestibility. We tested this notion by having half of the children in our study interviewed in an especially warm manner (eg given frequent compliments, many smiles, and cookies and juice) and the other half interviewed in a more neutral, cool manner (eg given no compliments, few smiles, and no cookies and juice).

To capture some of the elements of a victimization experience, the children in our study were questioned, either once or repeatedly, about a stressful event—receiving an inoculation at a medical clinic. The inoculations were part of the children's normal health care and were not imposed by us. A number of other studies of children's memory for stressful events have been conducted (Goodman et al, 1991b; Mertin, 1989; Peters, 1991; Tucker et al, 1990) and relevant clinical research has also expanded markedly (eg Jones & Krugman, 1986), but none of these studies has examined children's responses to repeated, misleading questions, and none has examined effects of a social/emotional factor such as "reinforcement" on children's memory for a stressful event.

In our study, 72 3–4-year-olds and 5–7-year-olds were recruited from families who came to a medical clinic for the children's routine inoculations. The families were generally from the lower socioeconomic strata, and a variety of racial and ethnic groups were represented. We videotaped the children while they received their inoculations and interviewed them later about the experience. Approximately half of the children in each age group were interviewed only once after a four-week delay (single interview condition). The other half were interviewed twice, once after a two-week delay and then again after a four-week delay (repeated interview condition). By comparing the two groups' performances at the four-week interview, we could determine the effects of repeated interviewing.

The interview itself consisted of a free-recall question followed by a set of specific questions (eg "Was your mom or dad in the room with you?" "Did the nurse listen to your heart?") and misleading questions (eg "What time did the clock on the desk say it was?". when, in fact, there was no clock in the room, and "She didn't wear a white coat, right?", when, in fact, the nurse wore a white coat). Many of our specific questions would be considered leading in a court of law. A subset of the questions which we will discuss separately from the rest, were designed to be similar to those that might be of special importance in a child abuse investigation (eg "Didn't she touch your bottom?" "The nurse told all the other kids to keep a secret. Didn't she tell you to keep a secret?"). We refer to these as "abuse" questions.

Our results were consistent with former research in indicating that repeated interviewing did not reduce the children's accuracy of report and, if anything, actually improved it. Specifically, children interviewed twice were less suggestible in response to the misleading questions and the abuse questions at the time of their second interview than at the time of their first interview. Compared to a single, delayed interview, repeated interviewing made the children more, not less, resistant to false suggestions. This finding is of particular importance because of the belief, held by many in our legal system, that repeated interviewing of children increases the likelihood of obtaining a false accusation due to increased suggestibility.

Our results were also consistent with previous research in uncovering age differences in children's testimony. Older children made fewer incorrect statements in free recall and were better able to answer the specific and misleading questions correctly. Interestingly, significant age differences in the proportion of correct answers to the specific questions were not accompanied by significant increases with age in the proportion of commission errors made. In other words, older and younger children did not significantly differ in the proportion of commission errors made to the specific questions, many of which would be considered leading in a court of law.

As will be explained next, this was not necessarily the case with respect to the children's responses to the misleading and abuse questions. Whether or not the children were interviewed with reinforcement influenced the appearance of age differences in response to these questions.

Significant effects of reinforcement were sporadic but when they existed reinforcement was almost always found to strengthen the accuracy of children's reports, especially those of younger children. Specifically, in response to the abuse and misleading questions, age differences in commission errors—present in the no-reinforcement condition—disappeared in the reinforcement condition. In the no-reinforcement condition, the younger children made more commission errors to such questions as "Didn't she touch your bottom?" and "She didn't have any clothes on, did she?" than did younger children in the reinforcement condition or older children regardless of reinforcement condition.

These findings indicate that although age differences in children's testimony can be demonstrated across the age range studied, the appearance of differences is often contingent on more than just age. Social influences, such as "reinforcement"—which presumably made the interviewer less intimidating—can have an important effect in optimizing children's performance (see also Moston, 1987).

EXPERIMENT 2: CHILDREN'S REPORTS OF GENITAL TOUCH

The inoculation study just described indicates positive effects of social influence on children's accuracy, but social influences can also serve to dampen rather than enhance a child's willingness to report an event. A study conducted by Saywitz et al (1991) illustrates this point.

Children who suffer sexual abuse may fail to report it for many reasons; for example, they may be embarrassed about what happened, they may not remember the event or may not have interpreted it as abuse, or they may have been instructed not to tell. For such children, an open-ended, free-recall question many fail to elicit a report. Some professionals feel that specific questioning directed at the abuse may at times be required. Other professionals object to the use of specific questioning with children, fearing that it is leading and will elicit false reports of sexual abuse in nonabused children. Some of these professionals contend that only very general open-ended questions should be employed (eg "What happened yesterday at your preschool?" or "Did anything ever happen to you to make you feel uncomfortable?") or that children's free play will reveal sexual abuse without the need for any questioning (see Idaho vs Wright, 1989). The Saywitz et al study permitted us to weigh the relative advantages and disadvantages of asking children specific (leading) questions.

The study concerned children's reports of genital contact. Some have argued that the situations we studied previously were too unlike situations about which children might testify in sexual abuse cases, situations in which nonsexual touching of the genitals might be misinterpreted as sexual contact. Of course, it is difficult to design a study in which children's genitals are touched, but it was again possible to take advantage of an already existing medical procedure.

More and more doctors in America are including genital examinations of children in their regular medical exams. For female children, these examinations involve visual inspection and touch of the vaginal and anal areas. Saywitz et al took advantage of this fact by testing female children's memory for a medical examination that included a genital component.

The 72 5- and 7-year-old girls in the study were scheduled for a regular doctor's examination at a medical center and received identical examinations, with one exception. Half of the children received the genital examination and half did not. The latter half received an examination for scoliosis.

After either one week or one month, the children were interviewed individually about the experience. In the first part of the interview, the children were asked to recall what happened last time they went to the doctor's office. Each was then given a set of anatomically detailed dolls and asked to demonstrate what happened. Finally, the children were asked a set of specific and misleading questions about the experience. The final questions were the most important. For these questions, the interviewer held up an anatomically detailed female doll and asked the child "Did the doctor touch you here?", pointing to the doll's vaginal area. If the child said "Yes", she was asked to provide greater detail (eg how it felt and how the doctor did it). The interviewer then turned the doll over and asked "Did the doctor touch you here?", pointing to the doll's anal area. Again, if the child answered in the affirmative, the interviewer asked for more detail.

The power of this design lies in its ability to test for false reports of genital contact while also revealing failures to report actual genital contact. If children who did not receive a genital examination reported that the doctor touched their genitals, a false report of genital contact would be obtained. If the children who in fact had a genital examination failed to mention the genital touch, a failure to report genital contact could be noted. Moreover, because children's reports were solicited through free recall, demonstration with anatomically detailed dolls, and leading questioning, the likelihood of their revealing genital touch or falsely reporting it could be examined for each type of questioning.

Saywitz et al found that children in the genital condition were unlikely to report the genital part of the examination in free recall, even when using the anatomically detailed dolls (see Table 2.1). It was only when asked specific, leading questions that the majority of the children finally revealed that genital touch had actually occurred. The same pattern appeared for vaginal and anal touch. These findings argue against the notion that it is unnecessary to ask children specific questions about genital touch.

For the children who did not have the genital examination, none falsely reported genital touch in free recall or when using anatomically detailed dolls. However, when asked the specific, leading questions three of the children gave false affirmations for one of the genital questions. Two of the children falsely affirmed anal touch and one child

Table 2.1. Number of children reporting vaginal and anal touching as a function of examination condition in experiment 2: accurate reports and errors

	Free recall	Demonstration	Question
Reports of vaginal touching			
Examination			
Genital (N = 36)			
Accurate report	8	6	31
Omission error	28	30	5
Scoliosis (N = 36)			
Accurate report	36	36	34*
Commission error	0	0	1
Reports of anal touching			
Examination			
Genital (N = 36)			
Accurate report	4	4	25
Omission error	32	32	10*
Scoliosis (N = 36)			
Accurate report	36	36	34
Commission error	0	0	2

*One parent did not want this question asked.

falsely affirmed vaginal touch. Two of the children could provide no detail when asked how the doctor did it and how it felt, but a third child (a 7-year-old) said the doctor used a stick.

These findings indicate that the likelihood of obtaining a false report of genital contact by asking a leading question must be weighed against the likelihood of children not revealing genital contact unless they are directly questioned about it. At least for the type of genital contact we investigated, which was nonpainful and took place in the context of accepted medical practice, most children did not reveal genital contact unless specifically asked, and most did not falsely report genital contact when asked about it in a leading way.

There are several possible reasons why the children failed to report the genital contact unless directly asked about it. It is possible that the genital part of the examination was not remembered well. However, there is also reason to believe that the genital contact was embarrassing, at least for the older children. Evidence for this interpretation can be found in the pattern of data for the children's reponses to the free-recall question, the doll demonstration, and the combined specific and misleading questions. One would expect age differences in the children's testimony . As can be seen in Table 2.2, predicted age differences did appear for children in the scoliosis condition. Compared to 5-year-

Table 2.2. Number of propositions accurately reported in free recall and demonstration task and proportion of questions answered correctly in experiment 2 as a function of age and examination condition

| | Condition | | | |
| | Scoliosis | | Genital | |
	5 years	7 years	5 years	7years
Free recall	19.69	35.94	23.94	20.58
Demonstration	43.56	68.36	49.08	46.02
Questions	0.72	0.79	0.73	0.81

olds, 7-year-olds in that condition recalled more accurate information, demonstrated a greater amount of accurate information with the dolls, and answered more of the questions correctly. However, this was not true for children in the genital condition. In that condition, 7-year-olds provided no more correct information than 5-year-olds in free recall and also demonstrated no more correct information than 5-year-olds with the dolls. It is unlikely that they did so because 7-year-olds in the genital condition had a less complete memory for the doctor's examination; these children produced the highest mean performance when questioned directly about the experience. Rather, it appears that 7-year-olds in the genital condition were less willing to reveal all of what they could recall.

This study provides evidence concerning the relative advantages and disadvantages of asking children leading questions about genital touch. The data suggest that leading questions may at times be important in obtaining accurate information about genital touch from children. At the same time, there is some danger of obtaining a false report. The study also suggests that social factors such as embarrassment can eliminate age differences in children's reports. Because of older children's more sophisticated social understanding, they may realize that talking about genital touch can be embarrassing. If so, this social factor may have led in our study to the elimination of the age differences one would expect for free recall and doll demonstration, age differences that were apparent for the children in the scoliosis condition.

EXPERIMENT 3: KEEPING SECRETS

So far, the studies discussed lend support to the notion that social/emotional factors can have important effects on children's reports. As revealed in experiment 1, social/emotional factors can at times eliminate age differences by raising younger children's performance so it is equivalent to that of older children, perhaps by reducing intimidation. As revealed in experiment 2, social/emotional factors can eliminate age differences by decreasing older children's performance, perhaps due to older children's more sophisticated understanding of what is and what is not a socially acceptable topic of conversation. In the third experiment, to be discussed next, we have found that social factors can, at times, actually result in the reversal of age differences, so that younger children's reports are *more* complete and accurate than older children's reports.

This experiment dealt with the reports of children who were instructed by a loved one to keep a secret (Bottoms et al, 1990). As mentioned above, child victims of sexual abuse may be admonished not to tell anyone about the sexual activity. Research to date suggests that 5–6-year-olds can easily be intimidated into silence by strangers who instruct the children not to tell (see Pipe & Goodman, 1991). How much more powerful, one can imagine, would be the force of a secret when it represents a pact between a loved one and a child.

We were also concerned with the influence of age on children's tendency to keep events secret. Parents have told us informally that their young children do not understand the concept of a secret and cannot withhold their impulses to tell. Piaget (1926) thought that children would first be able to keep secrets around the age of seven years. Although current research clearly indicates that Piaget's estimate was wrong, he may have been correct in assuming that a certain level of cognitive development must be attained before children fully understand the concept of a secret. This does not necessarily mean, however, that young children will not keep some events secret. Whether or not they do probably depends on motivation. Threats, for example, may provide a compelling motive even for young children (Bussey, 1990).

To explore the effects of secrecy instructions on children's reports, 48 3–4-year-olds and 5–6-year-olds were tested. Each child and his or her mother came to the laboratory. The child first played with a research assistant while the mother was instructed for her role in the study. Once the mother's instruction was completed, she and her child were asked to wait in a playroom that included a large bookcase filled with attractive toys.

Children in the "secret" condition were told that the research assistant had forgotten some papers in another building. Before leaving, she asked the mother and child to wait, telling them they could play with any of the toys *except* the ones on the bookcase, which were supposedly needed for the other children. Once she left, the mother, as instructed, gradually engaged the child in play with the forbidden toys. For example, the child and the mother blew bubbles, played with a costume, and turned on an audio-cassette of the Chipmunks singing. Also, when the mother went to touch a Barbie doll on the shelf, its head popped off and the mother hid it behind the other toys while the child watched. We term these events the "critical activities".

After playing with the toys, the mother told the child not to tell for fear that she (the mother) would get into trouble. As a reward for keeping the secret, the mother promised to buy the child a toy like his or her favorite toy on the shelf. Children in the no-secret condition experienced the same events, with three exceptions. First, the research assistant never instructed the child and mother not to play with certain toys. Thus, playing with the toys on the bookcase (engaging in the critical activities) was not forbidden. Secondly, the mother did not tell the child to keep the activities secret. Thirdly, although the mother promised to buy the child a favorite toy, she did not imply that the gift was contingent on keeping any activities secret.

Each child was immediately interviewed so that she or he could be debriefed before leaving for home. During the interview the child was asked a free-recall question concerning what had happened with the mother in the waiting room, followed by a set of more direct questions about what had occurred. For half of the children, the questions were quite leading (eg "You saw the Barbie doll, didn't you?") whereas for the other half they were less so (eg "Did you see the Barbie doll?"). Our purpose in varying the form of questioning was to explore whether leading questions are necessary to elicit children's secrets.

In the no-secret condition, the typical age superiority appeared in free recall. Older children recalled significantly more correct information about the critical activities than did younger children (an average of 9.17 units for 5–6-year-olds and 2.33 units for 3–4-year-olds). However, in the secret condition, the age advantage disappeared. Regarding the critical activities, older children recalled somewhat less than younger children (an average of 3.09 units for 5–6-year-olds and 5.00 units for 3–4-year-olds). Instructions to keep the activities secret were effective in dampening the older children's but not the younger children's free recall. A similar pattern occurred when the children's answers to the direct questions were considered, but the findings are even more dramatic. In the "secret" condition the mean proportions of correct answers to questions about critical activities were 0.80 for the 3–4-year-olds and 0.59 for the 5–6-year-olds. In the control condition the means were 0.78 for the 3–4-year-olds and 0.92 for the 5–6-year-olds. In this case, the older children in the secret condition correctly answered many fewer of the questions than did the younger children, reversing the direction of the usual age difference. When asked questions such as "You blew bubbles with your mom when you were in the waiting room?", older children in the secret condition often said "No", "I don't think so", or "I don't remember".

This study indicates that social influences can have a powerful effect on children's testimony. Although older children may at times be more capable than younger children of reporting an event, social influences can eliminate and sometimes even reverse the typical age advantage. Older children's advanced cognitive skills and knowledge of the world often support more complete and accurate memories but they also permit them to appreciate the social significance of their statements, in this case the possibility that their mothers might get into trouble and that they might not get a valued toy.

Interestingly, the children's willingness to report the secret activities was not affected by the form of question asked. Regardless of the use of more or less leading questions, older children tended to withhold information about secret activities. In contrast, Clarke-Stewart et al (1989) found that strongly leading questions were successful in eliciting information that children had been told to keep a secret. As Pipe and Goodman (1991) point out, the leading questioning in the Bottoms et al experiment was not as forceful as in the Clarke-Stewart et al study and perhaps was insufficient to pry the secret from the children. Also, the children in our study were told by a loved one to keep the secret, whereas children in the Clarke-Stewart et al study were told by a stranger. It is still an open question whether more strongly leading questions would have pried from the older children a secret that threatened to get their mothers into trouble.

EXPERIMENT 4: EFFECTS OF AUTHORITY AND INVESTIGATIVE CONTEXT

In our study on secret keeping, children thought their mothers had done something wrong, but they were not led to believe that their mothers had done something harmful to the children themselves. A prominent feature of child abuse investigations is that someone is accused of doing something "bad" to children. This contextual factor, which is of potentially weighty influence, concerns the investigative context in which children are interviewed. How do children respond when they are interviewed by a police officer who states that something bad may have happened and that an actual investigation is in progress?

In the study to be described next we examined whether children's susceptibility to leading and misleading abuse questions is increased when they believe that an investigation is taking place and they are interviewed by someone who appears to be a police officer (Tobey & Goodman, in press). The main question we asked was whether, when the "forensic realism" of the study is increased, children become more suggestible in response to questions of high relevance to abuse.

Twenty-six 4-year-olds came individually to the laboratory on the pretext that their parent, not the child, was needed to answer questions in a study. The child was told that he or she would be baby-sat while the parent completed a questionnaire in another area of the building. The child was left alone in a room with a "baby-sitter" who engaged the child in a series of activities. The activities included the child putting on a doctor's costume, having her or his picture taken, and playing Simon Says. After approximately 11 days, the child returned to the laboratory, again under the impression that he or she was simply accompanying the parent.

When the child and parent arrived for the second session, the child played briefly while the research assistant talked to the parent in another room. When they emerged, each child in the "police" condition was told that a police officer was there and needed to talk to the child. The child and parent were then taken to a room where a uniformed police officer was waiting. After building rapport with the child, the police officer explained that he was concerned that the baby-sitter might have done something bad last time the child was there and it was important to find out from the child exactly what happened. The parent had been instructed to express concern and ask if other children were involved, to which the officer replied that he couldn't say because the investigation was still in progress. Before leaving the room, the officer explained that his "partner" would talk to the child.

The partner, a female research assistant who was dressed similarly to the police officer, entered and built rapport with the child. The parent then left the room, and the questioning began. The partner proceeded to interview the child about what had happened when the child played with the baby-sitter. The interview included a set of abuse questions (eg "Did the man take any of his clothes off?" "He took your clothes off, didn't he?"). The child was debriefed immediately after the questioning.

Children in the control condition were treated the same way, except that they and their parents did not meet with the police officer and were not told that something bad might have happened. The children were interviewed by the same research assistant who played the role of the police officer's partner. (Interviewers were blind as to whether the children were in the police or control condition.)

Thus children in the police condition were led to believe that the baby-sitter might have done something "bad" and that a police investigation was going on, whereas the other children were not interviewed under these pretenses. We found that both groups of children were highly resistant to the abuse suggestions. The single commission error was made by a child in the police condition who said "Yes" when asked if the baby-sitter kissed him. However, the free-recall and spontaneous statements of two children in the police condition were adversely affected. For example, in response to the free-recall question, one child said "I think he was putting the hospital cap on, but he might try to do something bad, really bad, yes siree". Also, in response to the question "Was the man mean?", this child was the only one who answered "Yes". These findings are consistent with those of Clarke-Stewart et al (1989), who found that children's answers to specific questions often remained accurate in the face of a misleading interview even though their *interpretation* of the event could be manipulated. However, most of the 4-year-olds in our study changed neither their answers to the abuse questions nor, as far as we could tell, their interpretations of the event. Thus, a contextual factor affected the free recall of a few but not most young children; it did not significantly affect the children's responses to the leading and misleading abuse questions. The children we tested—only four years of age—remained highly resistant to the abuse suggestions.

CONCLUSION

In summary, many factors influence a child's ability and willingness to report an event accurately. Although children's cognitive abilities increase with development, age alone should not be considered the sole determinant of a child's capacity to provide reliable eyewitness testimony. As the studies we described earlier in this chapter illustrate, children's abilities can be affected, positively or negatively, by the social/emotional and contextual factors inherent in a situation.

In our experience, some young children are easily intimidated when interviewed by a stranger, and intimidation can heighten suggestibility. This impression is supported by our findings on the effects of reinforcement. If intimidation can be lifted, young children's ability to resist false suggestions can be improved, although susceptibility to suggestion may not be eliminated completely. Nevertheless, even young children interviewed in the context of a police investigation can resist a number of false suggestions relevant to charges of abuse.

Older children's more sophisticated cognitive abilities enable them not only to be more confident of their memories but also to recall details about an event and to answer questions about it with greater accuracy. But these same abilities also permit older children to realize the social implications of their statements, which may lead to the withholding of information out of, for example, embarrassment or feelings of protection for a loved one. Thus, although older children may be capable of recounting an event, they may not be willing to do so. Knowing a child's age in itself is not enough.

ACKNOWLEDGEMENTS

Preparation of this chapter was supported by grants to Gail S. Goodman from the National Center on Child Abuse and Neglect, United States Department of Health and Human Services. We thank the National Center for their support.

REFERENCES

American Association for Protecting Children (1988). *Highlights of Official Child Neglect and Abuse Reporting 1986*. Denver, CO: American Human Association.

Bottoms, B. L., Goodman, G. S., Schwartz-Kenney, B. M., Sachsenmaier, T. & Thomas, S. (1990). Keeping secrets: implications for children's testimony. Paper presented at the American Psychology and Law Society Meeting, Williamsburg, VA, March 1990.

Brainerd, C. & Ornstein, P. (1991). Children's memory for witnessed events: the developmental backdrop. In J. Doris (Ed.). *The Suggestibility of Children's Recollections*. Washington: American Psychological Association.

Bussey, K. (1990). Adult influence on children's eyewitness testimony. Paper presented at the American Psychology and Law Society Meeting, Williamsburg, VA, March 1990.

Chi, M. T. H. (1986). *Trends in Memory Research*. New York: Kreger.

Clarke-Stewart, A., Thompson, W. & Lepore, S. (1989). Manipulating children's interpretations though interrogation. Paper presented at the Society for Research in Child Development Meeting, Kansas City, MO, April 1989.

Dent, H. R. & Stephenson, G. M. (1979). An experimental study of the effectiveness of different techniques of questioning child witnesses. *British Journal of Social and Clinical Psychology*, **18**, 41–51.

Fischer, K. W. (1980). A theory of cognitive development: the control and construction of hierarchies of skills. *Psychological Review*, **87**, 477–531.

Goodman, G. S. & Aman, C. (1990). Children's use of anatomically detailed dolls to recount an event. *Child Development*, **61**, 1859–1871.

Goodman, G. S., Bottoms, B. L., Schwartz-Kenney, B. M. & Rudy, L. (1991a). Children's testimony for a stressful event: improving children's reports. *Journal of Narrative and Life History*, **1**, 69–99.

Goodman, G. S., Hirschman, J., Hepps, D. & Rudy, L. (1991b). Children's memory for stressful events. *Merrill-Parlmer Quarterly*, **37**, 109–158.

Goodman, G. S., Jones, D. P. H., Pyle, E. et al (1988). The child in court: a preliminary report on the emotional effects of criminal court testimony on child sexual assault victims. In G. Davies & J. Drinkwater (Eds). *Do the Courts Abuse Children?* Leicester: British Psychological Society.

Idaho v Wright, 289 S. Ct (1989).

Jones, D. P. H. & Krugman, R. (1986). Can a three-year-old child bear witness to her sexual assault and attempted murder? *Child Abuse and Neglect*, **10**, 253–258.

Leippe, M. R., Brigham, J. C., Cousins, C. & Romanczyk, A. (1989). The opinions and practices of criminal attorneys regarding child eyewitnesses: a survey. In S. J. Ceci, M. P. Toglia & D. F. Ross (Eds). *Perspectives on the Child Witness*. New York: Springer-Verlag.

Leippe, M. R., Romanczyk, A. & Manion, A. P. (1991). Eyewitness memory for a touching experience: accuracy differences between child and adult witnesses. *Journal of Applied Psychology*, **76**, 367–379.

Marin, B., Holmes, D., Guth, M. & Kovac, P. (1979). The potential of children as witnesses. *Law and Human Behaviour*, **3**, 295–306.

Melton, G. B. & Thompson, R (1987). Getting out of a rut: detours to less traveled paths in child-witness research. In S. J. Ceci, M. P. Toglia & D. F. Ross (Eds). *Children's Eyewitness Memory*. New York: Springer-Verlag, pp. 209–229.

Mertin, P. (1989). The memory of young children for eyewitness events. *Australian Journal of Social Issues*, **24**, 23–32.

Moston, S. (1987). The suggestibility of children in interview studies. *First Language*, **7**, 67–78.

Peters, D. P. (1991). The influence of stress and arousal on the child witness. In J. Doris (Ed.). *The Suggestibility of Children's Recollections*. Washington: American Psychological Association.

Piaget, J. (1926). *The Language and Thought of the Child*. London: Kegan Paul, Trench, Truber.

Pipe, M. E. & Goodman, G. S. (1991). Elements of secrecy: implications for children's testimony. *Behavioral Sciences and the Law*, **9**, 33–41.

Price, D. W. W. & Goodman, G. S. (1990). Visiting the wizard: children's memory for a recurring event. *Child Development*, **61**, 664–680.

Saywitz, K., Goodman, G., Nicholas, E. & Moan, S. (1991). Children's memories of a physical examination involving genital touch: Implications for reports of child sexual abuse. *Journal of Consulting and Clinical Psychology*, **59**, 682–691.

Tobey, A. E. & Goodman, G. S. (in press). Children's eyewitness memory: Effects of participation and forensic context. *Child Abuse and Neglect*.

Tucker, A., Mertin, P. & Luszcz, M. (1990). The effect of a repeated interview on young children's eyewitness memory. *Australian and New Zealand Journal of Criminology*, **23**, 117–124.

Underwager, R. & Wakefield, H. (1990). *The Real World of Child Interrogations*. Springfield, IL: Charles C. Thomas.

Vygotsky, L. S. (1934/1978). *Mind in Society: The Development of Higher Psychological Processes*. Cambridge: Harvard University Press.

Warren-Leubecker, A., Hulse-Trotter, K. & Tubbs, E. (1991). Inducing resistance to suggestibility in children. *Law and Human Behaviour*, **15**, 273–286.

CHAPTER 3

Social Support and Children's Eyewitness Testimony

Stephen Moston

Kent University, Canterbury

INTRODUCTION

One of the most debated topics within the literature on children's eyewitness testimony concerns the effects of stress on recall performance (eg Bales, 1986; Doris, 1991; Peters, 1987). Research has primarily focused on stress at the time that an incident occurs, rather than the stress experienced while recalling events. The introduction of videotechnology in the courtroom stems from a realization that the stress involved in giving an account of an event exerts a particularly debilitating effect on children (Davies & Westcott, Chapter 13, this volume). Here then, low levels of recall are attributed to the social environment present at the time of the interview rather than implying an inherent weakness in memory. This chapter considers one method of manipulating the social environment at the time information is recalled, namely, through the provision of social support.

It is easy to underestimate the extent to which children can be anxious in eyewitness interviews, even if the event under discussion was not in itself stressful. In experimental studies of children as witnesses some authors report (usually in footnotes) that several children were so upset that they could not take part (Marin et al, 1979),

Children as Witnesses. Edited by H. Dent and R. Flin
© 1992 John Wiley & Sons Ltd.

or would only participate if accompanied by a parent (Goodman & Reed, 1986). Why then should interviews be so stressful for children? When they are interviewed either as witnesses or in experimental tasks, children are usually isolated from other people to as large an extent as possible. Thus the child is deprived of his or her traditional support networks at a time of stress, namely, questioning by the police or social services. This typically occurs because of fears that their evidence might be contaminated through contact with others, or that the presence of others might either distract or inhibit the child (see Moston & Engelberg, in press) Initially, these strategies seem eminently reasonable. In cases of sexual abuse there is a very real possibility that a child will retract an allegation after discussion with other people (eg a non-offending parent). Although the isolation of children is necessary in some cases, the policy has been generally pervasive, even when the people supporting the child could have no possible motive for encouraging his or her silence or non-cooperation.

The arguments concerning the negative effects of others often represent somewhat simplistic assumptions about the effects of social support on task performance. While it is true that children's recall may on occasions become distorted or inhibited because of the presence of others, it would be wrong to suggest that social support is inherently problematic. The effects of the provision of social support, both positive and negative, will vary depending on the needs of the interactants and the type of interaction between them.

The apparently negative attitude towards the provision of social support can most probably be put down to a general lack of faith in the ability of children as witnesses. There is the fear that children are so suggestible that their evidence will be corrupted if either they discuss an incident with anyone or the interview involves prompting. Consequently, by isolating the child, any later accusations of suggestion can be reduced. For example, in the final report on the Bexley project (Metropolitan Police and Bexley Social Services, 1987) on the inter-agency cooperation between social services and police departments, it was suggested that interviewers should "reduce as far as possible the number of people in the room, but this must be balanced with the needs of each child and the wishes of the parent" (p. 49).

In the official evaluation of the Bexley project, Charnley (1987) showed the number of cases in which third parties (support persons) were actually present during interviews. Charnley was only able to carry out an evaluation of 33 cases, slightly less than half of the total number included in the project. Of these, 25 interviews (about 75%) were carried out with a "third party" present. Consequently, it is clear that the recommendation in the Bexley report to avoid the presence of third parties was not strictly implemented. From these figures it is apparent that children do "need" someone with them during interviews. Typically this person was the child's mother, although in some cases other people were present. In such cases the support person is present in order to provide emotional support, rather than to facilitate the communication process. Thus, in the USA it has been advocated that adults can be present to act almost as interpreters in that they can translate the child's personal language into more conventional terms (Murray, 1988).

There is an apparent contradiction in the literature regarding whether or not parental presence either increases or reduces children's anxiety in stressful situations. In a study of children's long-term behavioural adjustment following time spent in a hospital, Vernon et al (1967) found that maternal presence had a calming effect on children's (aged 2–6) distress during anaesthesia induction but made little difference during a non-stressful procedure such as admission to the hospital. However, Gross et al (1983) found that parental presence in the doctor's treatment room during an injection led to more intense and longer lasting crying in children than when the parent was not present. This was interpreted as a form of protest, since the children probably believed that the parent would give comforting responses at the signal of distress.

The reasons why parental presence can increase the child's distress were more carefully analysed by Melamed and Siegel (1984), who looked at the different reactions of parents during medical procedures on children in hospital. After categorizing parental behaviours, they found that children with mothers who talked to them assuringly and calmly were less stressed than those whose mothers showed signs of agitation and distress. It was concluded that a form of emotional contagion from the parent to the child was taking place, through non-verbal as well as verbal means.

One reason why parents may be distressed when supposedly helping their children is that when providing support many people feel threatened by those who are suffering, possibly as a result of anticipating increased demands upon them (Wortman & Lehman, 1985). As a consequence they rely on automatic or scripted support behaviours such as assuring someone that "It's natural to be upset" or saying "I know how you feel", both of which can imply that the distressed person's suffering is of little consequence. Wortman and Lehman suggest that the person closest to the person in need of help may have the least tolerance for that person's distress. They may resent that person's "excessive" suffering and lose patience with them. Therefore, in analysing sources of support it may be necessary to look beyond family members and friends to other sources of help, such as those who have previously experienced a similar problem. These similar others may respond to discussions of feelings with interest rather than anxiety or fear.

The presence of others may also have an inhibitory effect on task performance. Harari and McDavid (1969) looked at the effects of asking children to tell, or "fink", on another child who has committed some transgression. In summary, this study found that children would not "tell on" another misbehaving child if they were interviewed in the presence of a peer (or the offending child), even though they would readily admit to knowledge of the mischievous incident. The Harari and McDavid study has implications for studies of social support in the context of eyewitness research. For example, in a case of sexual abuse where a child is asked to talk about a relative (eg the father), the presence of a relative or family friend may well prove inhibiting. Here, when the child believes that the parent, or other source of support, does not want him or her to talk, then he or she is more likely to say nothing. In such cases, social support clearly is harmful. However, we may reason that when those providing support have no reason for encouraging the child's silence, or rather that the child does not perceive them as having any reason, then their presence may in fact be beneficial. The recommendations in the Bexley report fail to make this distinction between suitable and unsuitable sources of social support.

In other situations, the existence of social support may have a facilitative effect on task performance. For example, Lindner et al (1986) looked at the interaction between environmental characteristics and personal perceptions of support, as calculated by the Social Support Questionnaire (SSQ). Social support was defined as an experimenter's offer of assistance (if it was needed) to adult students (classed as high or low in social support resources) who were about to work on a story completion task. The experimenter told the subjects that she would be available to help them throughout their work, for example to answer any questions that might come up. Although no subject requested help, those subjects who had low scores on the SSQ performed significantly better than a comparable group who did not receive these instructions. Their performance was within the same range as that of high SSQ subjects. The administered support did not raise the performance of the high SSQ subjects, in comparison with that of an untreated control group.

The same pattern of results emerged in a similar study by Sarason and Sarason (1986). This study incorporated a new feature, namely, one where after the task the subjects completed a questionnaire on their thoughts during the task. This was related to a measure of the number of available others to whom individuals believe they can turn to in time of need (SSQN). The low SSQN subjects in the control group with no support reported higher levels of cognitive interference than the other groups, particularly the low SSQN subjects receiving support. Higher cognitive interference may result from higher levels of perceived stress. Subjects may feel under greater stress and thus worry more or attempt to distract themselves with off-task thoughts. Sarason and Sarason (1986) suggest that with an increase in self-confidence, low SSQN subjects may be able to focus their attention more completely on the task at hand rather than on self-preoccupying thoughts, such as worry over their ability to accomplish the task.

Social support may have either a beneficial or detrimental effect on task performance. In the case of child witnesses, it is clear that children giving statements or evidence do prefer to be questioned in the presence of supportive others (Goodman et al, 1988), although on occasions the presence of a support person may well be counterproductive. With regard to the effects of social support on children's recall memory, there is little evidence to sway opinion in either direction. The present chapter attempts to rectify this omission.

A series of three studies is described. Each investigates the effects of social support, as provided by peers, on children's free-recall descriptions of witnessed events. Peer support was chosen because children do derive support from peers (Nelson-LeGall & Gumerman, 1984; Sandler et al, 1985) and they are less likely than adults to attempt to control the recall interview or reinterpret statements (Kruger & Tomasello, 1986). That is, when assisting children in completing tasks, adults often feel obliged to make a direct contribution, even when they can offer little in the way of practical assistance. Study 1 assesses the effects of peer presence on children's recall of a witnessed event. The peer providing support knew nothing about the event. Support in study 2 is provided by peers who have discussed the event with a witness. Study 3 assesses the individual and combined effects of peer presence and discussion on children's recall.

STUDY 1: THE EFFECTS OF PEER SOCIAL SUPPORT ON CHILDREN'S RECALL OF A WITNESSED EVENT

The subjects in this study were 20 seven-year-old and 20 10-year-old children who had witnessed a live staged event which took place in their classroom at school. In addition to the witnesses, 20 other children (10 for each age group) also took part. These additional children did not witness the staged event, having been taken out of the room on the pretext of seeing their head teacher.

In the live event a man entered the children's classrooms on the pretext of looking for someone. The children witnessed the event in groups of about 20. The man spoke briefly to the teacher in the classroom before explaining to the class that he was looking for a (fictitious) boy. He wrote the boy's name on the blackboard and then left. The event lasted less than two minutes. About 10 minutes later the children were taken from the room and individually asked to describe the man, what he had said and done. The interviewers were not present during the staged events in any of the studies. Half of the children in each age group were interviewed alone (control), while the other half were questioned in the presence of one of the children who had not been present during the staged event. This non-witness was not instructed to take any direct part in the proceedings, although free to do so if he or she wished. The study was simply concerned with the effects of the presence of a second child on the free recall of a child witness. A simple form of social support, namely the mere presence of another child, was thus examined. The children were interviewed by a single adult interviewer in a room familiar to them from within their school.

As expected, the older children recalled significantly more (mean recall of nine correct items) than the younger children (mean recall of five correct items), but the presence of another child during the interview had no effect on the amount of information recalled, or its quality. The potentially inhibitory effect of a peer (eg Harari & McDavid, 1969) did not emerge, although this was not surprising given that in this case the non-witnesses were unlikely to disapprove of their colleagues' cooperation in the task. Accuracy was consistently high across age and experimental groups, with 90% of all statements being correct. In summary, the first study found that the presence of another child had no effect whatsoever on the witnesses' quantity or quality of recall.

STUDY 2: THE EFFECTS OF PEER INTERACTION BETWEEN WITNESSES AND NON-WITNESSES ON CHILDREN'S RECALL OF A WITNESSED EVENT

In the second study, the non-witnesses were to take a more important part in the proceedings. Instead of being mere observers, they would have the capacity to make a direct contribution, should they want to or should the witnesses request it. The subjects were once again aged seven and 10 years. There were 18 witnesses and nine non-witnesses in each age group, comprising a total of 54 children. An attempt to extend the age range of subjects to include younger children (aged four years) was entirely unsuccessful. The children would not discuss the witnessed event together and the presence of another child proved to be too much of a distraction for the witnesses. This part of the study was, therefore, abandoned.

Before the recall interview (centring on a staged event similar to that in the first study), the witness and non-witness were asked to discuss the event (informed peer support condition). The witness was told that he or she was going to be questioned about the event just seen. He or she was to tell the non-witness what he or she had seen as they would be asked to describe the event together. The children were allowed as long as they wished to talk together, although discussions rarely exceeded five minutes. While the children discussed the event, the interviewer left the room.

The children were then interviewed together. Now, as well as providing social support, the non-witness could also be of practical assistance by offering prompts. Although it was the witness who was asked to describe the witnessed event, the non-witness was asked to help his or her classmate to tell as much as he or she could remember and to make sure that no mistakes were made. As in the first study, the performance of the children in these recall pairings was compared to a control group of witnesses who did not discuss the event with anyone and who completed the recall task in isolation (child alone condition). The contributions of the non-witnesses during recall, that is, both correct and incorrect descriptions of the event, were included in the data analysis provided the statements were not contradicted or rejected by the witness.

The mean numbers of correct statements in free recall given by each age and experimental group are as follows: age 7, child alone, 5.3; child with informed peer, 12.8; age 10, child alone, 11.8; child with informed peer, 16.0.

The results were examined using a two-way analysis of variance, with the independent variables of age (7 vs 10 years of age) and experimental group (control vs experimental support condition). There was a significant effect of age ($F = 13.32$; $df = 1,32$; $p < 0.001$) and experimental group ($F = 19.40$; $df = 1,32$; $p < 0.001$) on the mean numbers of correct statements. There was no interaction effect.

The effects of the social support manipulation were particularly striking for the younger subjects interviewed with a peer, who recalled more than twice as much correct information as the control group. There were no differences in the accuracy rates of the groups. The experimental manipulation thus had an entirely positive effect on the free-recall memory of the children.

Very little of the correct information recalled by the experimental groups originated with the non-witnesses. Their contribution accounted for only a small fraction of the improved recall of the experimental group (an average of less than one additional item per child). In fact, the non-witnesses tended to say very little during the interviews, only asking a handful of questions and offering very few prompts. The spoken contributions of the non-witnesses (eg mean length of utterances, number of conversational turns and number of words spoken) all failed to correlate with the number of correct (or incorrect) statements in free recall.

These results were initially taken as evidence that the recall improvement stemmed from the very presence of informed peers, rather than as a result of their oral contribution during the interview. That is, as in the studies by Lindner et al (1986) and Sarason and Sarason (1986), the presence of a potential source of credible help, even though it was not called upon, enhanced task performance. There was, however, one drawback in reaching this conclusion. The second study also incorporated the variable of discussion prior to the interview. This confounding variable could possibly have accounted for the improvements in recall instead of the notion of informed social support. Several studies with adults (eg Sarason, 1981; Winstead & Derlega, 1985) have shown how discussion prior to task performance can influence behaviour. For example, Costanza et al (1988), in a task in which adults had to guide a tarantula through a maze, showed how prior discussion (provided it was centred either on the task at hand or on a totally unrelated matter, but not discussion of feelings) could lead to lower scores of anxiety and depression as well as having behavioural effects (namely how close subjects got to the tarantula). Consequently, a third study looking at the independent and combined effects of discussion and social support was carried out.

STUDY 3: THE EFFECTS OF DISCUSSION AND SOCIAL SUPPORT ON CHILDREN'S RECALL OF A WITNESSED EVENT

A total of 98 children (56 witnesses, 42 non-witnesses), half from each of two age groups (seven and 10 years), took part in the study. The event which the children were to be questioned about involved an adult confederate of the experimenter entering a room in which there were four children. The man spoke to each child, asked their names, told them that later on some people would be coming to talk to them and that he was going to show them how to use a tape-recorder. He did this by asking them to say their names into a microphone and then replaying the tape. The event involved the children moving about the room and talking with the man. It lasted nearly five minutes.

This study examined the independent and combined effects of peer presence and discussion on children's free-recall memory. Four types of interview were conducted for each group of four children. These were as follows. (1) Child alone, no discussion (control, as in the first two studies). (2) Child with peer support, but with no prior discussion (replicating study 1). (3) Child alone, after discussion. (4) Child with peer support, after discussion (replicating study 2). Three of the interviews (types 2, 3, and 4) required the participation of a non-witness.

For the after discussion interviews, the witness and non-witness were asked to discuss the event prior to the recall interview. As in study 2, the witnesses were told that they were going to be questioned about the event they had just seen. They were to tell the non-witnesses what they had seen as they would be asked to describe the event together. In the child alone after discussion group, the instructions were slightly modified and the witness and non-witness were separated just prior to the recall interview. For all of the interviews requiring two people, same-sex pairs were used.

The mean numbers of correct statements in free recall given by each experimental group (collapsed for age) are as follows: child alone, no discussion, 6.0; child with peer support, but no prior discussion, 5.4; child alone, after discussion, 7.4; child with peer support, after discussion, 10.4. These results show that the combination of both peer presence and discussion (informed peer support) resulted in improved recall. The mere presence of a peer, as in the first study, had no real effect on recall, although average recall in the peer present condition was slightly lowered. Discussion without peer presence appears to have had some benefits, although these are clearly not of the magnitude of discussion combined with peer presence.

The children's correct statements were analysed using a three-way analysis of variance, with age (seven and 10 years), peer presence (peer absent and peer present) and discussion (absence and presence of discussion) as between-subjects factors. Unlike the previous two experiments, there was no effect of age on recall ($F = 1.769$; $df = 1,48$; $p > 0.05$). There was a significant effect of discussion on recall ($F = 13.99$; $df = 1,48$; $p < 0.001$), but not peer presence ($F = 1.769$; $df = 1,48$; $p > 0.05$). There was a significant interaction effect between discussion and peer presence ($F = 4.670$; $df = 1,48$; $p < 0.05$).

As in the second study, the non-witnesses contributed very little information, either correct or incorrect. Overall, the non-witnesses said very little during the interviews; the majority of their responses seemed to be supportive statements that agreed with the description of the event, such as "yeah", or simple repetitions of statements (witness: "He had glasses"; non-witness: "Glasses"). There were a few examples of non-witnesses prompting recall by asking questions ("Did he have a beard?"), or simply reminding the witnesses of things they had said earlier ("You left out the colour of his hair"). However, such prompts were quite unusual and rarely helped to increase the recall performance of the witnesses.

As with the previous studies, the children made very few errors in their free-recall statements and those that were made centred on physical descriptions of the man. The most common errors were concerned with colour, such as the colour of the actor's trousers (five times) and the colour of his shoes (four times). The low numbers of errors were reasonably evenly distributed among the different groups (all comparisons non-significant, $p > 0.05$). The correct statements as a percentage of the total number of statements showed that the children were generally giving accurate accounts of the event. About 89% of all statements were correct. Variation by age and experimental group was negligible.

DISCUSSION

The third study confirmed that the interaction between discussion and peer presence during an interview leads to an increased level of recall relative to those interviewed alone (control), those with an uninformed peer present, or those alone but after discussion. Discussion alone appears to have some effects, but these are not of the magnitude of discussion plus peer presence. Consequently, for peer interaction between a witness and a non-witness to be an effective aid to recall, the person with whom the witness interacts must stay with him or her throughout the recall process. The presence of a peer without any degree of prior interaction between the participants has no effect on recall.

It may be that the presence of an informed peer makes the interview less intimidating by virtue of the fact that the child knows that someone else already knows his or her account and may be called upon to endorse this if necessary. Whether or not the second child actually does back him or her up does not appear to matter It is the very existence of this option that seems to be of importance. As Sarason and

Sarason (1986) suggested for adults, perhaps the increase in self-confidence following the provision of effective social support allows children to focus more on the task at hand. It is not simply a rehearsal effect. General observations of the children during the studies bear out this conclusion. Those interviewed in the presence of an informed peer approached the task with a degree of enthusiasm and confidence not apparent in other groups. Children interviewed alone often show a real reluctance to talk during interviews and seem only too pleased when their "ordeal" is over. In contrast, those interviewed with informed peer support were more likely to spontaneously continue discussions with the interviewers, even after the interview was formally ended.

The form of discussion employed here (problem centred) is only one of several forms of preparation that could have occurred. It may be that discussing feelings (eg fears) prior to an interview, even if the aim is to alleviate fear, may increase levels of stress (see Costanza et al, 1988). Alternatively, one could try discussing how to perform the task to the best of one's ability, or even topics that distract the child's attention from the stressor.

Generally, the present studies show a method of enhancing children's free-recall memory without distorting the accuracy of their accounts. The social environment at the time that information is recalled, as manipulated here, does have a strong bearing on the quantity (but not the quality) of information that is recalled.

The idea of children interacting as an aid to effective recall is likely to be counter to some people's preconceptions. Children as witnesses are typically viewed in a very negative light, and with regard to the general idea of peer interaction, in any form, one might say that the only thing more unreliable than one child witness is two child witnesses. Collaboration between children is seemingly viewed as an undesirable state. Defence lawyers would probably attack two witnesses more aggressively than a single witness, since they can play on the court's general fears concerning children's alleged excessive suggestibility. For example, in a trial involving a single child the defence lawyer may be hard pressed to explain the source of the child's supposed fantasies. However, when there are two children it is somewhat easier to presuppose some childish mischief-making gone wrong.

Although this study cannot directly address such questions, it does at least show that the idea of interaction itself is not inherently unreliable. Simply by talking together children do not allow their accounts to become wild fantasies. Neither in discussion with a non-witness nor through subsequent prompting was recall undermined. This is almost certainly due to the fact that children rather than adults were used as supporters. In discussion with a peer, as opposed to an adult, there is little reinterpretation of statements (Kruger & Tomasello, 1986) and so the integrity of the account does not change after discussion.

Suggestibility of the kind feared by those opposed to collaboration stems from two basic sources. These include conflicts of knowledge, or "expert" knowledge-based authority, the basic principle here being "I know more about it than you do". Alternatively, it may stem from cases where the non-witness has greater social power than the witness, as in the case of an older child or adult (see Moston, 1990 for a recent review). The advantage of discussion with a non-witness peer is that these problems do not arise. The peer is not an expert and does not have superior social status. Any erroneous suggestions are thus low in credibility and are easily identified and dismissed.

It may be that if two witnesses were to discuss an event then this might alter their joint account, but this problem would not be unique to children, as studies with groups of adults, including police officers, have shown (eg Stephenson et al, 1983). Discussion among two child witnesses prior to their joint interview may cause one child to adjust his or her account into line with that of the other. However, when the second person has no knowledge of the event (a non-witness), then there is no reason to suppose that he or she will influence the witness, unless there is some motive for doing so.

It is difficult to directly apply the present findings to interviews with children who have witnessed serious crimes. More research involving the use of adults as support persons is clearly necessary. There is some urgency to this research as the concept of social support for child witnesses is now becoming a salient issue. For example, the recent practice direction for Scottish judges (1990) advises the permitting of a relative or other supporting person to sit alongside the child while he or she is giving evidence, but it also states that several factors should be taken into consideration before implementing this procedure (see Nicholson & Murray, Chapter 8, this volume).

The results discussed in this chapter suggest that social support can have considerable beneficial effects on children's free recall of information. However, only one elementary form of support has been examined. It may be that other forms of support have a more detrimental effect. The conditions in which support can be advantageous or otherwise need to be clearly defined. If they are not, then rules governing the use of support persons may exclude potentially reliable sources of support while including unreliable sources. The situation may come to mirror that for juvenile suspects having committed criminal offences. Under the Police and Criminal Evidence Act (Home

Office, 1984) all juvenile suspects must be interviewed in the presence of an "appropriate adult". In practice, this often means one of the juvenile's parents. Unfortunately, many parents are clearly inappropriate in that they may apply coercive pressure to the child (typically to make them confess). With regard to child witnesses, it is equally possible that many obvious sources of support are possibly unacceptable. It is often the case that the person who has the most interest in helping someone is, regrettably, the least suited to do so (Wortman & Lehman, 1985). There may be a strong case for court-appointed guardians and not necessarily parents or other involved parties to act as support persons for child witnesses.

ACKNOWLEDGEMENTS

The author was funded during this research by an Economic and Social Research Council Competition Award.

REFERENCES

Bales, J. (1986). Courts try to lift the burden on abused children. *The American Psychological Association Monitor*, **17**, 20–21.

Charnley, H. (1987). *Child Sexual Abuse: Joint Investigative Report. The Metropolitan Police and London Borough of Bexley, Social Services Department. Evaluation Report*. London: HMSO.

Costanza, R. S., Derlega, V. J. & Winstead, B. (1988). Positive and negative forms of social support: effects of conversational topics on coping with stress among same sex friends. *Journal of Experimental Child Psychology*, **24**, 182–193.

Doris, J. (1991) (Ed.). *The Suggestibility of Children's Recollections*. Washington: American Psychological Association.

Goodman, G. S., Jones, D. P. H., Pyle, E. A., Prado-Estrada, L., Port, L. K., England, P., Mason, R. & Rudy, L. (1988). The emotional effects of criminal court testimony on child sexual assault victims: a preliminary report. In G. M. Davies & J. Drinkwater (Eds). *The Child Witness: Do the Courts Abuse Children?* Leicester: British Psychological Society.

Goodman, G. S. & Reed, R. S. (1986). Age differences in eyewitness testimony. *Law and Human Behavior*, **10**, 317–332.

Gross, A. M., Stern, R. M., Levin, R. B., Dale, J. & Wojnilower, D. A. (1983). The effect of mother–child separation on the behavior of children experiencing a diagnostic medical procedure. *Journal of Consulting and Clinical Psychology*, **51**, 783–785.

Harari, H. & McDavid, J. W. (1969). Situational influence on moral justice: a study on "finking". *Journal of Personality and Social Psychology*, **11**, 240–244.

Home Office (1984). *Police and Criminal Evidence Act: Codes of Practice*. London: HMSO.

Kruger, A. C. & Tomasello, M. (1986). Transactive discussions with peers and adults. *Developmental Psychology*, **22**, 681–685.

Lindner, K. C., Sarason, I. G. & Sarason, B. R. (1986). Assessed life stress and experimentally provided social support. In *Stress and Anxiety*, Vol. 11 (C. D. Spielberger & I. G. Sarason, Eds). Washington: Hemisphere.

Marin, B. V., Holmes, D. L., Guth, M. & Kovac, P. (1979). The potential of children as witnesses. *Law and Human Behavior*, **3**, 295–306.

Melamed, B. G. & Siegel, L. J. (1984). Children's reactions to medical stressors: an ecological approach to the study of anxiety. In E. M. Hetherington & R. D. Parke (Eds). *Contemporary Readings in Child Psychology*, third edition. New York: McGraw-Hill.

Metropolitan Police and Bexley Social Services (1987). *Child Sexual Abuse Joint Investigative Programme Bexley Experiment Final Report*. London: HMSO.

Moston, S. (1990). How children interpret and respond to questions: situational sources of suggestibility in eyewitness interviews. *Social Behaviour*, **5**, 155–167.

Moston, S. & Engelberg, T. (in press). The effects of social support on children's eyewitness testimony. *Applied Cognitive Psychology*.

Murray, K. (1988). *Research Paper on Evidence from Children: Alternatives to In-Court Testimony in Criminal Proceedings in the United States of America*. Edinburgh: Scottish Law Commission.

Nelson-LeGall, S. A. & Gumerman, R. A. (1984). Children's perceptions of helpers and helper motivation. *Journal of Applied Developmental Psychology*, **5**, 1–12.

Peters, D. P. (1987). The impact of naturally occurring stress on children's memory. In S. J. Ceci, M. P. Toglia & D. F. Ross (Eds). *Children's Eyewitness Memory*. London: Springer-Verlag.

Sandler, I., Wolchik, S. & Braver, S. (1985). Social support and children of divorce. In I. G. Sarason & B. R. Sarason (Eds). *Social Support: Theory, Research and Applications*. Dordrecht: Martinus Nijhoff.

Sarason, I. G. (1981). Test anxiety, stress and social support. *Journal of Personality*, **49**, 101–114.

Sarason, I. G. & Sarason, B. R. (1986). Experimentally provided social support. *Journal of Personality and Social Psychology*, **50**, 1222–1225.

Stephenson, G. M., Brandstatter, H. & Wagner, W. (1983). An experimental study of social performance and delay on the testimonial validity of story recall. *European Journal of Social Psychology*, **13**, 175–191.

Vernon, D. T. A., Foley, J. M. & Schulman, J. L. (1967). Effect of mother–child separation and birth order on young children's responses to two potentially stressful experiences. *Journal of Personality and Social Psychology*, **5**, 162–174.

Winstead, B. A. & Derlega, V. J. (1985). Benefits of same-sex friendships in a stressful situation. *British Journal of Social and Clinical Psychology*, **3**, 378–384.

Wortman, C. B. & Lehman, D. R. (1985). Reactions to victims of life crises: support attempts that fail. In I. G. Sarason & B. R. Sarason (Eds). *Social Support: Theory, Research and Applications*. Dordrecht: Martinus Nijhoff.

CHAPTER 4

Children as Witnesses in Sexual Abuse Cases: Investigative Interview and Assessment Techniques

Max Steller

Free University of Berlin

and

Tascha Boychuk

St Joseph's Hospital, Phoenix

While it is impossible to determine with certitude the exact numbers of children who are sexually abused, it is generally undisputed that sexual abuse is the fastest growing form of reported child abuse cases (Finkelhor, 1983). The increase of reported cases in the United States has obviously been represented by an increase in both truthful and questionable allegations of sexual abuse. Some authors express the view that there is widespread occurrence of false accusations of child sexual abuse (Eberle & Eberle, 1986; Wakefield & Underwager, 1988; Coleman & Clancy, 1990).

These contentions can be seen as a resurrection of an unfounded view of child sexual abuse allegations, which historically were dismissed as untrue. Children were described as "the most dangerous

Children as Witnesses. Edited by H. Dent and R. Flin
© 1992 John Wiley & Sons Ltd.

witnesses" (Whipple, 1911, p. 308). This position had its roots not only in scientifically unfounded notions about children's abilities to function as witnesses but also in unjustified generalizations from early eyewitness laboratory research. In spite of shortcomings in the early research, Stern (1902) concluded that erroneous statements of children are the rule and that accurate statements are exceptions. The negative biases regarding child witnesses were eventually countered by beliefs of the opposite extreme stating that "children do not make up stories asserting they have been sexually molested" (Faller, 1984, p. 475).

Either extreme position may lead professionals to use assessment techniques that corroborate their respective biases versus truly investigating the allegation. This may lead to circumstances in which children are returned to abusive situations or those in which innocent persons are falsely accused of abuse.

Impartial investigations of child sexual abuse allegations are essential to maximize the reliability of information obtained from children. Statement validity analysis (SVA) is a systematic method of obtaining and examining sexual abuse allegations by considering comprehensive case materials. Although SVA (in the form of less systematized precursors than described here) has been applied to child sexual abuse cases in Germany for decades, the procedure has been controversial in the United States. In the United States SVA has often been misconceptualized as a test and has also been characterized as a method that may be used to discredit children who have actually experienced abuse. This chapter addresses these misunderstandings. Statement validity analysis is described and its application is illustrated using a case example. Finally, the scientific basis of SVA is outlined.

STATEMENT VALIDITY ANALYSIS

Statement validity analysis is a method of structuring an assessment of child sexual abuse complaints by systematically collecting and examining information from children's interviews and other relevant case facts. Statement analysis originated in Germany and Sweden approximately four decades ago (Undeutsch, 1967; Arntzen, 1970; Trankell, 1972; Szewczyk, 1973). In order to differentiate between the content analysis of the statement and the complete overall credibility assessment, the terms criteria-based content analysis (CBCA) and statement validity assessment (SVA) were introduced.[1] CBCA refers to

[1]The authors acknowledge the contributions by Drs P. Esplin (Phoenix, AZ), D. Raskin (Salt Lake City, UT), and J. Yuille (Vancouver, BC) to previous joint efforts in systematizing SVA and CBCA for practical use and in developing training materials for workshops.

the analysis of the child's statement using a set of defined criteria. The term SVA refers to the overall diagnostic procedure that includes the results of CBCA. SVA in its current form includes: (a) careful review of relevant case information, (b) preserved semistructured interview of the child, (c) criteria-based content analysis of the transcribed interview, (d) validity checks of additional case information, and (e) a systematic summarization of content analysis and validity checks.

Review of Relevant Case Information

Relevant case facts are derived from all possible sources of information. This includes, but is not limited to, information from police records, child protective services files, psychosocial histories of all parties involved, diagnostic testing if available, court documents, and information from schools. The origin and progression of the allegation is examined throughout the sources of data.

As such, the data will allow the evaluator to form alternative hypotheses about the alleged sexual events. For example, the first and foremost hypothesis would be that the child is describing the events as they occurred. Another hypothesis might be that the child is accurately reporting the events but naming the wrong perpetrator. A third hypothesis might be that the child is accurately reporting the events and not all of the perpetrators were named. A fourth hypothesis might be that the child has been coerced to allege sexual abuse against an innocent person. The semistructured interview is designed to test the alternative hypotheses.

Semistructured Interview

The interview is structured with regard to principles of cognitive development in children. It is well recognized that free recall increases the likelihood of accuracy of information. The interview format, therefore, is designed to obtain as much information as possible in free narrative style from the child. The interview questions move from broad to specific as is necessary. The design of the questions can be visualized as a funnel, moving from those questions that are designed to produce free-recall information to those requiring specific responses.

Rapport is established by discussing neutral topics with the child. Possible topics include such things as hobbies, best friends, or favorite music. This discussion also provides a sample of the child's language capacity.

Free narratives are often obtained by the interviewer simply stating, "I understand something may have happened to you. Tell me as best you can about that so that I understand". Another way of obtaining free-recall information is to state, "I understand that you are having some problems. Tell me about those so I understand".

Open-ended questions are designed to assist the child in specifying information. In cases where children are describing chronic abuse, these questions generally include "Tell me about the very last time that something happened" and "Tell me about the very first time that something happened", thereby making use of primacy and recency effects. Another question that has been particularly useful is 'Tell me about the time you recall most clearly". This latter question is useful with the child who has formed a corresponding script to the abuse and has difficulty differentiating between chronic incidents. The question is meant to direct the child to episodic memory without including any suggestions in the question's wording.

Young children may provide less free-recall information than older children when asked open-ended questions (Saywitz et al, 1990). Cue questions are used to trigger a child's memory about an event. Retrieval cues are useful in those situations where children may not respond as well to abstract questions. Location cues appear to be particularly salient with children. Once a cue question such as "Where did something happen?" is asked, every attempt must be made to elicit free-recall information subsequent to the question. For example, if the child responded by stating "In the bedroom", the next directive would be "Tell me as much as you remember about what happened in the bedroom".

Direct questions are asked to obtain any other relevant investigatory information. This includes information such as the name of the accused, addresses (if age appropriate) and questions that aid a child with dating the events. It is important to remain sensitive to the child's development when assisting him or her in dating the events. Simply because a child can count it does not imply that he or she can count events in time (Kail, 1990). Events that are important to the individual child may be used to assist him or her in anchoring the sexual abuse events. For example, if a child was excited about attending a carnival or a party, such a cue could be used to assist the child in describing whether or not the sexual events occurred before or after the carnival activity. Again, this illustrates the importance of obtaining as much information as possible prior to commencing an interview of a child. It is helpful to obtain from the caretaker a list of activities that the child participated in during the period of time that the alleged abuse occurred.

Other direct questions may be asked near the end of the interview or if all other types of questions have been attempted with the child. Questions such as "Did anyone else do anything to any part of your body?" serve two purposes. One purpose is to check out all necessary case information. Secondly, the question serves as a suggestibility check of the child. For example, if the child responds "Yes" to such a direct question but is unable to provide any further information, one would need to test further for suggestibility. If the child states "Yes" and can provide additional information, one needs to examine whether or not there are multiple perpetrators of sexual abuse or perhaps if there is perpetrator substitution.

The interviewer always concludes the interview in a positive manner. Again, neutral topics are discussed with the child.

Criteria-Based Content Analysis

Pioneering work in the 1950s by Undeutsch led to the development of "reality criteria". These criteria were based upon what Steller (1989, p. 145) later termed the "Undeutsch hypothesis". The Undeutsch hypothesis asserts that statements about actually experienced events differ in content and quality from statements based upon fantasy, fiction or coercion (Undeutsch, 1967, p. 125).

The work of Undeutsch (1967), Trankell (1972), Arntzen (1983) and Szewczyk (1973) was organized and systematized by Steller and Koehnken (1989) into specific criteria that are referred to as content criteria as opposed to the more general reality criteria identified by pioneering authors. The content criteria are used to assess the content of the statement. The presence of the criteria would indicate an actually experienced event. The absence of criteria does not necessarily indicate that the statement is false. The 19 content criteria, grouped into five categories, are listed in Table 4.1.

The five major categories move from broad to specific aspects of the statement. The first major category, general characteristics of the statement, requires examination of the entire statement. Logical structure is present if the statement essentially makes sense. Unstructured production is present if the statement is not continuously structured but, rather, information is scattered throughout the statement. Quantity of details refers to the presence of details about time, place, persons and objects related to the crime.

The second and third major categories refer to specific aspects of the statement. They focus on cognitive capacities of the child. The criteria in these two categories are applied while asking the question, "Would a child be able to make up an allegation with qualities such as those

Table 4.1. Content criteria

General characteristics
1. Logical structure
2. Unstructured production
3. Quantity of details
Specific contents
4. Contextual embedding
5. Descriptions of interactions
6. Reproduction of conversation
7. Unexpected complications during the incident
Peculiarities of content
8. Unusual details
9. Superfluous details
10. Accurately reported details misunderstood
11. Related external associations
12. Accounts of subjective mental state
13. Attribution of perpetrator's mental state
Motivation-related contents
14. Spontaneous corrections
15. Admitting lack of memory
16. Raising doubts about one's own testimony
17. Self-deprecation
18. Pardoning the perpetrator
Offence-specific elements
19. Details characteristic of the offence

Adapted from Steller, M. & Koehnken, G. (1989). Criteria-based statement analysis. In D. C. Raskin (Ed.). *Psychological Methods in Criminal Investigation and Evidence.* New York: Springer, pp. 217–245.

described by the criteria?" (Steller, 1989, p. 138). For example, contextual embedding places the alleged event in time and space relative to the child's routine life experiences. Experiences do not occur in a vacuum and hence, the presence of contextual embedding indicates an actually experienced event. Descriptions of interactions, reproduction of conversations and reports of complications such as interruptions all indicate that a child is actively reconstructing memory of an experienced event. Unusual details are details unique to the child's experience. Superfluous details or accounts of the child's or perpetrator's mental state may be present in truthful accounts. Accounts of mental state include thoughts or feelings of the child or perpetrator at the time of the incident(s). Often young children who experience an event beyond the scope of their knowledge misinterpret an event that they describe correctly. For example, young children may describe semen as urine. Related external associations is present if the child describes a sexually toned conversation or relationship that is not part of the crime but refers to an "overlapping or interlocking of at least two relationships" (Arntzen, 1983, p. 38). For example, this criterion would be fulfilled if a child molested by her father reports conversations in which he repeatedly questions the child about peer-related sexual activity.

The fourth category of criteria addresses the motivation of the child to make a false allegation. These criteria are applied considering the question, "Would a child mention details that tend to be unfavorable to him or herself if the child were fabricating an account?" (Steller, 1989, p. 138). The criteria spontaneous corrections, admitting lack of memory, raising doubts about one's own testimony, and pardoning the perpetrator would not be expected in a fabricated statement.

The fifth major category, offense-specific elements, refers to elements of the actual crime. Empirical findings from research examining different categories of child sexual abuse are considered here. The progression of events in an incestuous relationship would be expected to be different from the dynamics surrounding a single-incident stranger assault. If a child describes events in a manner in which professionals know that certain crimes are perpetrated, "details characteristic of the offense" is considered present.

In praxis, CBCA is applied to a verbatim transcript of a recorded interview. CBCA consists of a sentence-by-sentence analysis of the child's statement. For this purpose the more extensive descriptions of the criteria (Steller and Koehnken, 1989) are helpful. A rating should be performed for each criterion ranging from absent through present to strongly present.

In evaluating a child's statement, only contents related to the alleged crime are considered for rating. Repeated information in the statement is only rated once. Additionally, certain information can fulfill more than one criterion. For example, "First he tickled me and then he said turn over on your stomach and then I said 'No I don't want to' and he pushed me over" would fulfill criterion 5, descriptions of interactions, and criterion 6, reproduction of conversation.

The statement must be rated with consideration for the child's verbal and cognitive capacities as well as the complexity of event being described. For example, a four-year-old child describing a single incident of fondling would be expected to produce a statement qualitatively different from a 10-year-old child describing a chronic incestuous relationship. The application of the content criteria is *not* a summation of the number of criteria present in a statement. Until CBCA is scrutinized scientifically with larger samples, cut-off scores, weighting of criteria or summation of any kind is not advised. Research is being conducted to assess the quantitative precision of CBCA in discriminating between actually experienced events and fictitious events (see later section on research findings).

After rating the content criteria in terms of the extent to which they are fulfilled in a given statement, one analyzes them to formulate an overall assessment of the quality (not credibility) of the statement. The quality of the statement, together with other case information, is used in SVA to assess the likelihood that the child witness has actually experienced the event he or she has described.

Validity Checks

The overall credibility assessment in a specific case combines a variety of information which leads to an evaluation of the probability that the witness refers to a real event or a product of fabrication or coercion. In addition to the content quality assessment (CBCA), other sources of information are used by the expert to come to an opinion regarding the credibility of a given statement. In order to organize and standardize this complex assessment, a validity checklist for this part of the overall assessment procedure was developed (see Table 4.2).

The validity checklist contains information to be considered in addition to the quality assessment of the statement by CBCA. The presentation of statement validity assessment in a checklist for purposes of organization must not obscure the fact that the judgement process of the investigator is a complex hypotheses-testing procedure with multiple feedback between data collection and psychological and

Table 4.2. Validity checklist

Psychological characteristics
 1. Appropriateness of language and knowledge
 2. Appropriateness of affect
 3. Susceptibility to suggestion
Interview characteristics
 4. Suggestive, leading, or coercive questioning
 5. Overall adequacy of the interview
Motivation
 6. Motives to report
 7. Context of the original disclosure or report
 8. Pressures to report falsely
Investigative questions
 9. Consistency with the laws of nature
10. Consistency with other statements
11. Consistency with other evidence

---

forensic inferences. The factors which have to be considered in the overall assessment of the validity of an accusation will now be briefly discussed.

First, certain psychological characteristics (validity checks 1–3) have to be considered.

1. Psychological characteristics which have to be evaluated include language style and specific knowledge which is beyond the developmental level of a person of the witness's age. If speech characteristics or descriptions are present which indicate a possible influence of adults in preparing and organizing the statement, one cannot definitely conclude that the statement is fabricated but, of course, this is important in order to investigate possible influences by third persons.

2. Although behavior signals cannot be unequivocally interpreted as to truthfulness or deception, the investigator continuously observes the witness's performance. Behavioral indicators of inappropriate affect during the interview, the absence of accompanying affect which would be expected to occur from the content of the report, and affect that is congruent with thought content are important and have to be taken into consideration in the overall credibility assessment procedure.

3. If the witness has shown susceptibility to suggestions during the interview, this, of course, is another important psychological factor which has to be considered in the validity assessment. High degrees of suggestibility of a witness may affect the accuracy of the statement, or even indicate a lack of concrete (episodic) memory because the allegation was fabricated. Resistance to suggestion is also noteworthy.

Interview characteristics (validity checks 4–5) are further sources to evaluate a given statement. Characteristics of the interview on which the credibility assessment is based as well as the techniques of prior interviews have to be assessed. Unintended suggestions, leading questions or coercion, as well as less obvious failures like premature direct questioning, interrupting or systematically reinforcing the witness, may limit the diagnostic power of criteria-based content analysis. The interview characteristics should be assessed in two steps.

4. As a first step, it should be registered whether the witness was ever interrogated by inadequate interview techniques in the case under investigation. Mistakes of prior interviews may influence the present statement although an adequate technique might now be employed.

5. Secondly, the technique of the interview which is used for the evaluation by CBCA should be evaluated separately.

Possible motives (validity checks 6–8) have to be explored and incorporated in the SVA.

6. There must be an assessment of whether the reporting witness possesses questionable motives to report. Important sources of information are the relationship between the witness and the accused and the possible consequences of the accusation for all individuals involved.
7. A main point to be considered in motivation analysis is the origin or "history" of the statement. The context surrounding the first report has to be thoroughly explored.
8. Thorough assessments must include an investigation of whether the witness or other persons have been pressured to report falsely.

The last section of the validity checklist (9–11) deals with investigative questions.

9. Descriptions which are contrary to laws of nature, of course, raise questions as to the validity of the allegation in spite of what may appear to be a high content quality of a statement.
10. A second question is whether major elements in the statement are contradicted by another statement made by the same witness or by another witness's statement. Comparisons with (prior) statements of the same witness have to be conducted by considering our knowledge about children's capacity to remember events and suggestive effects of prior interviews or the present interview. One would expect the central features of the event to remain the same. Peripheral details may change or be forgotten over time.

    Contradictions to statements of other witnesses which cannot be attributed to errors or lies on behalf of another person do not deliver an obvious indication of untruthfulness of the particular witness, but must be considered and explored in the overall validity assessment of a statement.
11. One must consider whether there are one or more major elements in the statement which are contradicted by substantial physical or other concrete evidence. This validity check is not of a psychological but rather a criminalistic nature. For example, contradiction of major elements of a statement by physical (eg medical) evidence, of

course, raises doubt as to the validity of the statement even if it possesses a high (content) quality.

Systematic Summarization of Content Analysis and Validity Checks

The separation of the overall procedure of statement validity assessment into different aspects through which the investigator can work step by step is useful for the analysis of practical cases. The results of CBCA and the validity checks are analyzed. The evaluator's process of combining all information, however, is a very complex one in which the different aspects and judgements are interconnected and their assessment cannot take place independently. Standardizing this procedure helps to organize facts and inferences as well as assist in weighting various data. All of this material is used in the complex assessment process to develop an estimation of the credibility of a given statement.

A CASE EXAMPLE

Relevant Case Information

The following is a real case example of the interview protocol. Tina, a 10-year-old white female, was referred by the local police department to a child abuse evaluation center for assessment of possible sexual abuse. Tina's 33-year-old mother was interviewed without the child present in the room. She informed personnel at the center that her daughter alleged sexual abuse by an adult male neighbor identified as Mike and expressed shock and disbelief at the child's allegations. The mother reported that the child had made the allegations earlier that evening, stating that the alleged events had occurred after school on that date.

Tina's mother reported that current household members include herself and her three female children aged two, nine and 10 and two male children aged six and three years. There is no adult male in the household. Tina has never had contact with her father, who left the home when she was an infant. Tina's mother is employed as a waitress. Tina attends fifth grade, achieving average academic reports. To the mother's knowledge, Tina has not been exposed to sexually explicit magazines or materials.

Investigative Interview

The following is the first interview conducted with Tina.

INTERVIEWER.   Hi Tina, my name is Tascha and I need to talk with you
for a bit. I'm recording us because I'm so bad at remembering things
... Now, I know your first name is Tina. What's your whole name?
TINA.   Tina——.
INTERVIEWER.   How old are you, Tina?
TINA.   I just turned 10 on Friday.
INTERVIEWER.   You did? My goodness. What did you do for your ...
What did you do for your birthday?
TINA.   Well, I just had like a party and my Mom was gonna get me a
cake but she didn't cause she didn't have time cause she was
working but we had icecream ... and I got a game and some ninja
turtles.
INTERVIEWER.   You did? Those turtles are pretty neat. Which ones did
you get?
TINA.   I got the one with the sword and ... I forget his name.
INTERVIEWER.   Oh well, I'm not sure of their names either. Well, Tina,
what led your Mom to bring you over to the emergency room?
TINA.   I got molested by this guy named Mike.
INTERVIEWER.   Tell me exactly what happened as best you remember so
that I can understand from the very beginning to the very end.
TINA.   I went to his house to use his phone cause we haven't got one
right now and he said I could so I used his phone and I called a guy
named Willy ... no I mean a guy named John cause ... cause my
Mom was gone ... and I wanted to see if she was there and nobody
answered at John's house so I told him "Thank you for letting me
use the phone" and he said "You're welcome" and he told me to sit
down and I sat down and he was undoing his pants and I told him
"No" and I was going to the door and he must have taken his pants
off cause he called me back and he had his underwear off and then I
tried to go but he locked the door and I said "What do you want" ...
like I said it kind of in a shaky voice cause I got scared and then he
grabbed my arms and threw me real hard on the bed. [pause]
INTERVIEWER.   And then what happened?
TINA.   He started licking my private.
INTERVIEWER.   And then what happened after that?
TINA.   He um ... took out his private and put it in the back of me ... no
first the front and then in the back of me and then I heard a knock on
the door and he told me ... he got up and I said "Someone's at the
door" and he said "I don't care they'll just leave" and I said "No"

and he put on his pants real fast and when he went to the door I put on my shorts ... these right here and I um ... jumped out his window and my sister ... that's how my sister found out ... when I was jumping out the window and then she told my Mom and my Mom said "Mike wouldn't never do a thing like that" and she didn't believe me and then she said she would take me to the hospital to find out ... and that's all.

INTERVIEWER. Anything else happen?

TINA. No.

INTERVIEWER. I need to ask you a couple more questions to help me understand some things better.

TINA. The things I said?

INTERVIEWER. Yes. You said something about Mike grabbing your arms. Tell me a little more about that so I understand better.

TINA. He um ... he just went like this and then he had the one hand holding me here real tight and then he had his other hand pulling down his underwear and then one time I started yelling and he put his other hand ... not the one he was holding my hands with but the other one ... he put it on my mouth and I could hardly breathe and then someone was knocking on the door.

INTERVIEWER. Now where did Mike do this to you?

TINA. It was in the bedroom at his house.

INTERVIEWER. Tell me a little more about the bedroom.

TINA. Well ... he like dragged me in there and then he threw me on the bed. He has this junky bed and there's like a TV and he has a goldfish in there and the water smells bad cause I don't think he changes it too much.

INTERVIEWER. Now you said Mike was licking your private. What was he licking it with?

TINA. His mouth ... it was gross.

INTERVIEWER. When you say he was licking your private, where exactly do you mean?

TINA. Right here in my front ... and that's where he put his private in the front ... but he couldn't get it right in cause I had my legs shut and then here ... right here in the back ... he put it in my butt and it really hurted and I was crying.

INTERVIEWER. Did he touch your front private with anything else?

TINA. No ... just his ... he was licking and his private.

INTERVIEWER. Did he touch your back private with anything else?

TINA. No.

INTERVIEWER. Did anything come out of his private?

TINA. White stuff and it was all sticky and I got it on my shorts but I wanted to get out the window so I just left it on there ... see ...

INTERVIEWER.   I see that spot. Now Tina, help me understand a little more about that white stuff.

TINA.   It was like ... he was going like up and down like that and it came out on me here and at first I thought it was pee but it wasn't and that's when someone was knocking at the door and then I wanted to get out of there so I put my shorts on top and it was all squishy but I just jumped out of the window anyway ... cause I was scared and see ... it got on my shorts.

INTERVIEWER.   I see. Now where does Mike live?

TINA.   He lives in our apartments in 3D. ... just like you go this way and then there's this bush and then the stairs to his place are right there.

INTERVIEWER.   Has anyone else besides Mike ever done anything to any part of your body?

TINA.   No ... just Mike.

INTERVIEWER.   When we first started, you used the word "molested". Where did you learn that word?

TINA.   We had this guy come to our class and he talked to us about it and he said if you ever get molested you should tell the police ... but I didn't tell the police yet cause I just told my Mom.

INTERVIEWER.   When was it that Mike licked your private and put his private in the front and back part of you?

TINA.   Um ... it was just a while back ... like right after my Mom went out cause I went to use the phone to try and find her ... and then when my sister saw me jumping out the window she found her and then my Mom brought me here and I was scared to tell cause I shouldn't have been at his house.

INTERVIEWER.   I'm sorry, I'm kind of confused. What day was it that this happened with Mike?

TINA.   Today ... it was just like right after school.

INTERVIEWER.   What is your sister's name ... the one that saw you jumping out the window?

TINA.   Rebecca ... she's 12.

INTERVIEWER.   Anything else that you can remember that would help me understand what happened?

TINA.   That's all ... but you know he's so weird, he would say like one time he told me he loved me and I don't know why he says that and he wants to know if I have boyfriends. Yuk ... I hate boys. ... They're always pulling my hair!

INTERVIEWER.   I see. Well you're going to visit with the doctor in a minute and she's going to check you from the top of your head down to your toes. If you remember anything that you forgot to tell me, please tell her, OK?

TINA. OK.

INTERVIEWER. Do you have any questions?

TINA. No.

INTERVIEWER. Well, I noticed that your little sister in the waiting room had her swimsuit on. Do you have a pool at your apartment complex?

TINA. Yeh ... and we have like a jacuzzi too.

INTERVIEWER. Do you like to swim?

TINA. Yeh ... and my Mom said maybe I could take swimming lessons this year but I have to go to a different place to take them.

INTERVIEWER. A different place?

TINA. Yeh ... it's like a girls' club or something cause we ... my Mom can't afford to get us lessons.

INTERVIEWER. I see. Well what other favorite things do you like to do?

TINA. I like to read and sometimes I like to play video games. We have these video games in our place.

INTERVIEWER. I bet you're good at video games. Well, let's go see if the doctor is ready to visit with you.

Application of CBCA

Once the interview is completed the tape is transcribed and criteria-based content analysis is applied to the transcribed statement. Described below are some examples of the criteria found in the interview with Tina. These examples are meant to illustrate the criteria, which are organized under the five general categories of CBCA. Each criterion is italicized and accompanied by examples of its presence in Tina's statement.

General Characteristics of Tina's Statement

Logical structure is present because the statement makes sense when one reads it from beginning to end. The content is logical. The criterion *unstructured production* is present as there are pieces of information scattered throughout the statement. Tina shifts focus from the sexual acts to discovery by her sister to disbelief by her mother. Information about the sexual acts is scattered throughout the interview. There is *quantity of details* throughout the statement that identifies time, place, person and events. Tina specifically describes Mike sexually assaulting her after school in the bedroom of his apartment. There is a wealth of detail about the location and sexual acts (eg descriptions of ejaculation, furnishing of the room in which the assault occurred).

Specific Contents of Tina's Statement

Contextual embedding is present as illustrated by Tina placing the events in the routine of her life, for example "I went to his house to use his phone cause we haven't got one right now ..." or "cause my Mom was gone and I wanted to see if she was there". There are *descriptions of interactions* with many examples of actions and reactions. Tina states, "*I* tried to go but *he* locked the door and *I* said what do you want ...", "*I* said no and *he* put on his pants real fast and when he went to the door *I* put on my shorts ...". *Reproductions of conversation* occur several times throughout the interview. Some examples include "I told him thank you for letting me use the phone", "I said what do you want", "I said someone's at the door" and he said "I don't care they'll just leave ...". Tina describes an *unexpected complication during the incident* when she states ... "then I heard a knock on the door ...".

Peculiarities of Content in Tina's Statement

Tina's explanation of "I pulled on my shorts ... these right here and I um ... jumped out his window ... and that's how my sister found out" is an example of an *unusual detail*. There are *superfluous details* scattered throughout the statement as illustrated by the italicized portion of these examples. I said "What do you want ... *like I said it in kind of a shaky voice cause ...*" and "I put on my shorts ... *these right here* and I um ...". An *accurately reported detail misunderstood* is Tina's description of ejaculation. She states, "... it came out on me here and at first I thought it was pee but it wasn't and then ...". *Related external associations* are present when Tina describes a conversation between herself and the accused. Tina states, "... he told me he loved me and I don't know why he says that and he wants to know if I have boyfriends ...". There are *accounts of subjective mental state* when Tina describes her fear. For example, "... I said it in kind of a shaky voice cause I got scared ..." and "... I just jumped out the window anyway cause I was scared ...". Tina does not reference the perpetrator's thoughts or feelings so the criterion *attribution of perpetrator's mental state* is not fulfilled.

Motivation-Related Contents in Tina's Statement

Tina adds information to previously provided information such as her descriptions of ejaculation. *Spontaneous corrections* include '... I called a guy named Willy ... no I mean a guy named John ..."; "... took his private and put it in the back of me ... no first the front and then back ...". A second criterion under this category of motivation-related contents, *admitting lack of memory*, is not fulfilled in this statement. However, *raising doubts about one's own testimony* is present. Tina states, "... my Mom said Mike wouldn't never do a thing like that and she didn't believe me ...". Tina also expresses *self-deprecation* by stating, "... and I was scared to tell cause I shouldn't have been at his house ...". Not present in this statement is the criterion *pardoning the perpetrator*.

Offense-Specific Elements in Tina's Statement

There are *details characteristic of a sexual offense* perpetrated by someone outside of the home. The assault was committed by someone known to the child. There was a progression of events that started with the alleged perpetrator telling the child he loved her and eventually ending in an assault.

Sixteen of the 19 possible criteria were fulfilled when CBCA was applied to Tina's statement. That means that the statement is of considerably high content quality. As stated above, there are no exact rules as to how many criteria would have to be present in a truthful statement. The credibility assessment is dependent upon the incorporation of additional information as systematized in the validity checks.

Validity Checks

The following is a short summary of the validity checks. First, *psychological characteristics* are considered. Tina used *appropriate language* for a 10-year-old. She described sexual knowledge that is inappropriate for a 10-year-old but not beyond what she would glean from the alleged abuse. Tina's *affect* was congruent with her thought content. Tina did not appear *susceptible to suggestion*. In fact, she resisted suggestion during the interview. She did not take the opportunity to elaborate or embelish upon the allegations.

Evaluation of the *interview style* revealed that suggestive, leading, or coercive questions were not present in this interview. The technique progressed from rapport building to obtaining a narrative, open-ended questions, direct questions, suggestibility checks and ended with a neutral topic.

There did not appear to be *questionable motives to report*. There were no arguments between Tina and her neighbor. In fact, Tina became acquainted with the accused during the previous week as he was a new resident in the complex. There was no *questionable context of disclosure*. The disclosure arose when Tina's sister witnessed her jumping out of the neighbor's window. The sister stated Tina was crying and screaming for help. There is no indication that Tina was *pressured to falsely report*. To the contrary, her mother expressed shock and disbelief.

Investigative questions indicated that Tina's descriptions of the sexual acts fit with our understanding of human anatomy. There were no acts described that are *contrary to the laws of nature*. No formal preserved statements of Tina were obtained by other professionals. Therefore, there were no *contradictory statements*. Tina's spontaneous utterances to her sister were consistent with the information in this interview. There is no *physical evidence* that contradicts what Tina has reported. To the contrary, medical evidence and evidence gathered by law enforcement at the crime scene support her allegations. The rape kit results and Mike's bedsheet collected by the police provided corroborating physical evidence.

Summary

The validity checks of Tina's allegations did not raise any other issues that require further investigations. In the final step of statement validity assessment the evaluation of the content quality using CBCA and the results of the validity checks are summarized to form an overall validity assessment of the allegations. In the case example, Tina, a 10-year-old white female, provided descriptions of penile–genital contact with descriptions of ejaculation, penile–anal contact, and oral–genital contact by an adult male neighbor identified as Mike. Based upon the above findings and taking into consideration the age and competencies of the child, it is highly likely that Tina has actually experienced the events she described. The content quality of the statement makes it a highly improbable hypothesis that Tina has invented the accusations. Indeed, Mike confessed to law enforcement subsequent to viewing the videotaped interview of Tina. He was sentenced to 15 years in prison. Tina commenced therapy following complaints of post-traumatic stress symptoms.

SCIENTIFIC BASIS FOR STATEMENT VALIDITY ANALYSIS

In spite of the fact that SVA has a high degree of face validity, little empirical analysis has been conducted to assess its validity and reliability. One component of statement validity analysis that has received some scientific scrutiny is criteria-based content analysis.

The first simulation studies to examine the validity of content criteria conducted by Koehnken and Wegener (1982) and Yuille (1988; cited in Steller, 1989) lack external validity as to the situation of child witnesses in alleged sexual abuse cases. Therefore, Steller et al (1988) attempted to approximate sexual abuse experiences by categorizing children's experiences that included the circumstances of: (a) direct involvement by a child, (b) loss of control, and (c) negative emotional tone. The researchers identified giving a blood sample, being physically beaten by another child, being attacked by an animal, receiving dental work, and undergoing surgery as having the three necessary elements to best approximate sexual abuse in an analogue study.

The aim of the study was to assess the validity of the Undeutsch hypothesis which is the basis for CBCA. In the context of a story-telling competition children from first and fourth grades were asked to produce two stories about the aforementioned group of experiences. One story was to be about an actually experienced event. The second story was to be fictitious. Three blind raters applied CBCA to 88 true and 88 fictitious stories. The raters used a four-point scale ranging from 0 = not present to 3 = strongly present.

The differences between the mean scores for each criterion over the three raters and over all 88 true versus all 88 untrue stories were calculated (the possible range of mean scores per criterion was 0–9). t-tests for dependent samples were calculated between the mean scores per criterion. Due to the underlying one-sided hypotheses, differences on a 10% level were considered as significant. Table 4.3 shows the mean degrees of strength per criterion over the 88 true and 88 untrue stories.

Table 4.3 shows that the Undeutsch hypothesis could be corroborated by nine criteria: namely criterion 1 (logical consistency), criterion 3 (quantity of details), criterion 4 (contextual embedding), criterion 7 (unexpected complications during the incident), criterion 8 (unusual details), criterion 9 (superfluous details), criterion 10 (accurately reported details misunderstood), criterion 11 (related external associations), and criterion 12 (accounts of subjective mental state).

Criterion 5 (descriptions of interactions) and 6 (reproduction of conversation) only slightly missed significance (also due to a low frequency of occurrence of these criteria in the analyzed stories), but the difference is in the expected direction.

Other data show that criterion 2 (unstructured production) was obviously misunderstood by the raters. It is negatively correlated with criterion 1 in this sample, which means that the raters did not follow the instruction given. The failure of significance with criterion 13 (attribution of perpetrator's mental state) might also be due to low frequency of occurrence.

Table 4.3. Means and standard deviations for the criteria in 88 true (t) and 88 fictitious (f) accounts; based upon three ratings on a four-point rating scale from 0 (absent) to 3 (strongly present)

	t	σ_t	f	σ_f	t_{emp}	p
General Characteristics						
1. Logical structure	6.61	1.56	5.59	1.80	4.93	0.00
2. Unstruct. production	Definition was misunderstood by raters					
3. Details	6.05	2.05	4.88	1.96	5.74	0.00
Specific contents						
4. Embedding	4.65	2.13	4.02	2.09	2.61	0.01
5. Interactions	3.26	1.74	2.95	1.80	1.42	0.16
6. Conversation	3.69	2.90	3.17	2.80	1.51	0.13
7. Complications	2.27	2.18	1.26	1.73	3.56	0.00
Peculiarities of the content						
8. Unusual details	2.89	1.92	1.57	1.77	5.35	0.00
9. Superfluous details	5.28	2.07	4.07	2.21	4.28	0.00
10. Misunderstood details	1.58	1.82	0.64	1.14	4.09	0.00
11. Associations	0.81	1.61	0.33	0.85	3.05	0.00
12. Subject's feelings	4.72	2.73	4.10	2.73	1.68	0.10
13. Perpetrator's feelings	1.27	2.02	1.11	1.82	0.68	0.50
Motivation-related contents						
14. Corrections	2.06	1.62	1.89	1.53	0.79	0.43
15. Lack of memory	2.70	2.64	2.67	2.57	0.10	0.92
16. Doubts	Was not assessed as present in any account					
17. Self-deprecation	0.67	1.12	1.09	1.57	-2.11	0.04
18. Pardoning	1.17	1.70	1.23	1.54	-0.24	0.81
Offense-specific elements						
19. Characteristic details	Does not qualify for type of stories told					

Overall, the category of motivation-related contents failed to differ significantly in true versus untrue stories. For the interpretation of this result the different psychological situations of a lying witness during police interrogations or court hearings and a child in a story-telling competition have to be considered. Criterion 17 (self-deprecation) reached significance in the opposite direction than expected. A closer look revealed that this significance is almost exclusively due to the occurrence of criterion 17 in those stories where the children described an attack by a dog. Most of the children described failures of action on their part prior to the attack of the dog which they felt caused the dog to attack them.

Altogether, the external validity of this simulation study for the category of motivation-related content criteria can well be questioned. Therefore, the results of this study do not exclude those criteria from further consideration in research and practice, especially if the results of the field study (see below) are taken into account.

Basically, Undeutsch's hypothesis about qualitative differences between true accounts and fictitious stories can be looked upon as strongly supported by this simulation study. The psychological characteristics of experiencing sexual abuse should be further defined for future research in order to enhance the ecological validity of simulation studies. Additionally, field studies using actual statements of children in sexual abuse cases are needed.

Esplin et al (1988) conducted the first field study of criteria-based content analysis. Forty statements about sexual abuse were examined using CBCA. The statements were obtained from children aged three to 15 years. Twenty of the statements were from cases where the abuse had been confirmed and twenty from cases where the abuse was considered highly doubtful.

The confirmed category was established by the case meeting at least two of the following criteria: (a) confession prior to plea bargain, (b) extreme physical evidence, (c) witness to the event, (d) deceptive polygraph of the accused. Eighteen of the 20 cases included a confession prior to plea bargain. Sixteen cases met the medical evidence requirement, 11 cases included a witness to the event, and one case had a deceptive polygraph. No other polygraphs were available in the cases.

Placement in the highly doubtful group was more difficult. This group consisted of 20 cases with no confession by the accused, 19 cases with no corroborating evidence, 14 nondeceptive polygraphs of the accused, 15 recantations of the allegation, 10 specific findings by civil court that the abuse was unlikely to have occurred. Each case in this group met at least three of these criteria and 10 met all five criteria. There were only 14 polygraphs available in this group.

Transcripts of all 40 children were rated using CBCA. The evaluator was blind to group placement. Score was calculated by assigning 0 if the criterion was not present, 1 if it was present and 2 if the criterion was strongly present. Per cent presence of the criteria is presented in Table 4.4.

The confirmed group had a mean score of 24.8 while the mean score for the highly doubtful group was 3.6. This differed significantly, $t(38) = 16.53$, $p < 0.001$. The range of scores for each group did not overlap. Scores in the confirmed group ranged from 16 to 34. Scores in the highly doubtful group ranged from 0 to 10. The mean age in the confirmed group was 9.1 years compared to a mean age of 6.9 years in the doubtful group. This difference is statistically not significant ($t(38) = 1.95$, $p > 0.05$), suggesting that age cannot account for the variation of the findings between the two groups. The results of this study, therefore, show promise for the use of CBCA as part of an

Table 4.4. Per cent presence of criteria in confirmed and doubtful statements

Criterion	Confirmed	Doubtful
General characteristics		
1. Logical structure	100	55
2. Unstruc. production	95	15
3. Details	100	55
Specific contents		
4. Embedding	100	35
5. Interactions	100	30
6. Conversation	70	0
7. Complications	70	0
Peculiarities of the content		
8. Unusual details	95	0
9. Superfluous details	100	5
10. Misunderstood details	5	5
11. Associations	5	0
12. Subject's feelings	90	30
13. Perpetrator's feelings	40	0
Motivation-related contents		
14. Corrections	100	10
15. Lack of memory	75	35
16. Doubts	10	0
17. Self-deprecation	25	0
18. Pardoning	55	5
Offense-specific elements		
19. Characteristic details	100	30

overall assessment procedure for the evaluation of children's allegations of sexual abuse.

The Esplin et al study was criticized by Wells and Loftus (1991), who pointed out that the findings are based on the rating of only one evaluator. Sample size and problems of defining independent outer criteria for the classification of truthful and fabricated statements in field studies were also addressed in their commentary. In a study where CBCA was applied to 75 transcribed statements of child sexual abuse, validity and interrater reliability were examined (Boychuk, 1991). These results support further study and refinement of CBCA, although Boychuk (1991) cautions against their premature use in American courtrooms.

CONCLUSION

Statement validity analysis has been applied to sexual abuse cases in Germany for the past four decades. In the United States, SVA has generated controversy. The greatest concern has been that SVA will be used to discredit children who have actually experienced abuse. SVA has also been misconceptualized as being equivalent to a test. SVA, however, simply provides a systematic approach to obtaining and analyzing facts relevant to a sexual abuse allegation. Even criteria-based content analysis has not yet reached the status of a psychometric method. Results of recent empirical investigations, however, are encouraging, indicating that CBCA is capable of being further refined.

There is agreement that obtaining reliable information from child witnesses in a developmentally appropriate manner is essential to the integrity of child abuse cases. Until recently, interview methodology and the basis for professional opinions about child sexual abuse have been determined by clinical judgement. These issues are only now being empirically investigated. SVA offers a semistructured method of systematically obtaining information from children.

As of this date, field examination of SVA with adequate sample sizes does not exist. Large-scale analyses of CBCA are currently underway at the National Institute of Child Health and Human Development in Bethesda (Maryland) under the direction of Dr Michael Lamb as well as in Canada under the direction of Dr John Yuille (University of British Columbia). Given that the existing data are encouraging, it is critical that further research projects explore SVA particularly in the context of field validation studies. It would also be desirable to enhance our knowledge about the differential weights of individual criteria in CBCA as well as about cut-off scores affected by variables such as age and complexity of sexual events. Research that addresses the theoretical and empirical underpinnings of individual criteria is also needed (Bekerian & Dennett, 1990). For this purpose analogue studies can be useful. Additionally, the interview methods suggested in this chapter must continue to be refined.

Although SVA and its core component CBCA originate in forensic-psychological practice and research, their application is not restricted to psychologists. The interview and assessment techniques described in this chapter have been taught by the authors to professionals of various backgrounds such as law enforcement, social work, mental health, and psychology. The value of SVA and CBCA lies in the systematization of the interview and evaluation procedure. Personal biases, therefore, are less likely to interfere with the investigative goal of the interview. Finally, we wish to point out that an investigative attitude (ie a neutral position as to the outcome of the evaluation) is compatible with a child-oriented perspective. SVA and CBCA are most often used to corroborate children's statements in cases where abuse actually did occur. At the same time, the process enables the interviewer not to overlook indicators of possible false accusations. CBCA has also assisted in differentiating truthful from invented parts within the same statement and in evaluating the validity of recantations of abuse. These more complex constellations that frequently occur in praxis could not be addressed extensively in this introductory chapter.

REFERENCES

Arntzen, F. (1970). *Psychologie der Zeugenaussage*. Goettingen: Hogrefe.

Arntzen, F. (1983). *Psychologie der Zeugenaussage: Systematik der Glaubwuerdigkeitsmerkmale*. Muenchen: Beck.

Bekerian, D. A. & Dennett, D. (1990). The truth in content analysis of a child's testimony. Paper presented at the 2nd European Conference on Law and Psychology in Nuremberg.

Boychuk, T. (1991). Criteria-Based Content Analysis of children's statements about sexual abuse. Unpublished dissertation, Arizona State University, Tempe (AZ).

Coleman, L. & Clancy, P. E. (1990). False allegations of child sexual abuse. Why is it happening? What can we do? *Criminal Justice*, Fall, 14–47.

Eberle, P. & Eberle, S. (1986). *The Politics of Child Abuse*. Secaucus, NJ: Lyle Stuart.

Esplin, P., Boychuk, T. & Raskin, D. C. (1988). A field validity study of Criteria-Based Content Analysis of children's statements in sexual abuse cases. Paper presented at the NATO Advanced Study Institute on Credibility Assessment in Maratea, Italy.

Faller, K. C. (1984). Is the child victim of sexual abuse telling the truth? *Child Abuse and Neglect*, **8**, 473–481.

Finkelhor, D. (1983). Removing the child–prosecuting the offender in cases of sexual abuse. *Child Abuse and Neglect*, **7**, 195–205.

Kail, R. (1990). *The Development of Memory in Children*. New York: W. H. Freeman.

Koehnken, G. & Wegener, H. (1982). Zur Glaubwuerdigkeit von Zeugenaussagen: Experimentelle Ueberpruefung ausgewaehlter Glaubwuerdigkeitskriterien. *Zeitschrift fuer experimentelle und angewandte Psychologie*, **29**, 92–111.

Saywitz, K. J., Goodman, G. S. & Meyers, J. B. (1990). Can children provide accurate eyewitness reports? *Violence Update*, September.

Steller, M. (1989). Recent developments in statement analysis. In J. Yuille (Ed.). *Credibility Assessment. A Unified Theoretical and Research Perspective*. Dordrecht: Kluwer Academic Publishers, pp. 135–154.

Steller, M. & Koehnken, G. (1989). Criteria-Based Statement Analysis. In D. Raskin (Ed.). *Psychological Methods in Criminal Investigation and Evidence*. New York: Springer, pp. 217–245.

Steller, M., Wellershaus, P. & Wolf, T. (1988). Empirical validation of Criteria-Based Content Analysis. Paper presented at the NATO Advanced Study Institute on Credibility Assessment in Maratea, Italy.

Stern, W. (1902). Zur Psychologie der Aussage. *Zeitschrift fuer die gesamte Strafrechtswissenschaft*, **22**, 315–370.

Szewczyk, H. (1973). Kriterien der Beurteilung kindlicher Zeugenaussagen. *Probleme und Ergebnisse der Psychologie*, **46**, 47–66.

Trankell, A. (1972). *Reliability of Evidence*. Stockholm: Beckmans.

Undeutsch, U. (1967). Beurteilung der Glaubhaftigkeit von Aussagen. In U. Undeutsch (Ed.). *Handbuch der Psychologie, Band 11: Forensische Psychologie*. Goettingen: Hogrefe, pp. 26–181.

Undeutsch, U. (1982). Statement Reality Analysis. In A. Trankell (Ed.). *Reconstructing the Past*. Stockholm: Norstedt & Soners, pp. 27–56.

Undeutsch, U. (1984). Courtroom evaluation of eyewitness testimony. *International Review of Applied Psychology*, **33**, 51–67.

Undeutsch, U. (1989). The development of Statement Reality Analysis. In J. Yuille (Ed.). *Credibility Assessment. A Unified Theoretical and Research Perspective*. Dordrecht: Kluwer Academic Publishers, pp. 101–119.

Wakefield, H. & Underwager, R. (1988). *Accusations of Child Sexual Abuse*. Springfield: Charles Thomas.

Wegener, H. (1989). The present state of statement analysis. In J. Yuille (Ed.). *Credibility Assessment. A Unified Theoretical and Research Perspective*. Dordrecht: Kluwer Academic Publishers, pp. 121–133.

Wells, G. L. & Loftus, E. F. (1991). Is this child fabricating? Reactions to a new assessment technique. In J. Doris (Ed.). *The Suggestibility of Children's Recollections: Proceedings of the Cornell Conference*. Washington, DC: American Psychological Association.

Whipple, G. W. (1911). The psychology of testimony. *Psychological Bulletin*, **8**, 307–309.

CHAPTER 5

The Perceived Credibility of Child Eyewitnesses

C. A. Elizabeth Luus

and

Gary L. Wells

Iowa State University

How credible are children as eyewitnesses? There are two ways to interpret this question. First, how are child eyewitnesses perceived by jurors? Secondly, how well are children able to remember and truthfully recount a witnessed event? Our primary focus is the *perceived credibility* of child eyewitnesses. Nevertheless, some of our discussion will also focus on the actual capabilities of child witnesses although not on the truthfulness component of their testimony. That is, we will restrict our discussion to situations where it can be assumed that the child is not intending to deceive the listener. This is not to say that children do not lie. But our emphasis is the perceived and actual abilities of children to recall prior events and communicate their recollections to other people, rather than children's propensities to be truthful or deceptive.

A number of studies have addressed the question of how children's eyewitness testimony is perceived by adults. The issue is important for several reasons. First, we need to know whether there is an age below which a child is perceived to have little or no credibility. Prosecutors are quite interested in this question as it tells them something about

Children as Witnesses. Edited by H. Dent and R. Flin
© 1992 John Wiley & Sons Ltd.

the likelihood of obtaining convictions based on testimony from young children. Also, we need to know something about why adults might discount young children's eyewitness testimony. Is it the manner or style in which children testify or is it merely the fact of their age that would lead adults to discount their testimony? These are important questions because they help us address the validity of adults' reasons for discounting children's testimony. And, because it is adults who serve as triers of fact (eg as prosecutors, judges, jurors), adult perceptions of children's testimony are critical to our understanding of trial outcomes.

ADULTS' STEREOTYPES OF CHILDREN'S EYEWITNESS CAPABILITIES

The competence of child eyewitnesses has been doubted for many years by the criminal justice system largely because of the legal community's skepticism of children's capacity to provide accurate testimony, particularly in response to leading questions (Whipple, 1911). Considerable research suggests that jurors' opinions are in tune with this pessimistic view of the child eyewitness (Ross et al, 1991; Leippe & Romanczyk, 1987; Yarmey & Jones, 1983). For example, Ross et al asked respondents to evaluate the eyewitness capabilities of hypothetical 6, 8, 21 and 74 year old witnesses and found that children were perceived as less accurate and more suggestible than adults.

Empirical studies of stereotypes of children's eyewitness capabilities complement these survey results. Goodman et al (1987), for example, presented mock jurors with one of three versions of a mock trial that differed only with respect to the supposed age of the key eyewitness for the prosecution. The three versions of the trial, including the testimony given, were identical except for the stated age of the witness (written version of the trial) or the age of the individual playing the role of eyewitness (videotaped version of the trial). In every case, the young child was judged to be significantly less credible than the adult.

HOW IMPORTANT ARE STEREOTYPES IN EVALUATING CHILDREN'S TESTIMONY?

The findings of the studies described above suggest that jurors enter the courtroom with a negative bias toward child eyewitnesses. What rule does such bias play in judgements of perceived eyewitness credibility? We have already reviewed research that suggests that jurors' stereotypes of children's eyewitness capabilities play a central role when jurors are asked to evaluate transcribed testimony or view actors reciting a testimony script. However, in actual cases jurors view authentic witnesses using their own words to describe what they saw. Such an experience allows the juror to note the child's mannerisms, apparent confidence in testifying, and his or her speech style. What the child says might be tempered by how he or she says it. Research suggests that the power of an eyewitness's speech style plays an important role in jurors' assessments of adults' eyewitness credibility such that witnesses who deliver testimony in a powerful style are perceived as more credible than witnesses with a less powerful speech style (eg Erickson et al, 1978). Whereas the powerless style is marked by verbal hedges (eg "I think so"), hesitations (eg "uhm", "uh"), intensifiers (eg "definitely"), and inflection that causes statements to be uttered as questions, the powerful style includes few of these characteristics (Conley et al, 1978; Erickson et al, 1978; Lind & O'Barr, 1979; O'Barr, 1982).

To the extent that children's testimony is more powerless than adults', we can expect child eyewitnesses to be perceived as less credible than adults. Research that provides jurors with an opportunity to view actual child eyewitnesses testifying can assess the fit between jurors' stereotypes of children's eyewitness capabilities and their perceptions of the child's actual eyewitness capabilities. Goodman et al's (1987) use of a videotaped trial is a step in the right direction. However, it falls somewhat short of what is required because it included only one child actor reciting a testimony script. That one child might not have been representative of his or her age group. Furthermore, the scripted testimony might not be representative of how that child (or others the same age) would recount the event had he or she actually seen it happen. In fact, it might be very difficult to find one child who is typical of his or her same-age peers. Research indicates that, just as there is considerable variation in the believability of adults' eyewitness testimony (Wells et al, 1979), so too is there variation within samples of children's testimony (Wells et al, 1989).

This variation in children's testimony probably accounts for the divergent findings of Goodman et al (1987) and Ross et al (1987). Whereas Goodman et al found that an eight-year-old eyewitness was perceived as less credible than an adult who provided the same testimony, Ross et al found no age differences in credibility. Moreover, Ross et al found that the eight-year-old witness was rated as *more* accurate, forceful, consistent, truthful, confident, and intelligent than the 21-year-old, whereas the ratings of the 21-year-old witness and a 74-year-old witness did not differ. Perhaps the child or adult in one or both of these studies was unrepresentative of his or her age (eg the child actor in the Ross et al study might have been especially believable for his age or the adult especially unbelievable).

We recommend the use of *samples* of child and adult eyewitnesses, rather than the use of one child or adult, because the testimonies of a given child and adult might differ for numerous reasons other than their ages. Furthermore, we suggest that the child and adult eyewitnesses actually observe an event and then provide testimony in their *own* words rather than recite a testimony script. This methodology captures the variance of adults' and children's testimony and allows us to assess how children testify orally when relying on their memory for something they personally witnessed.

EVALUATING CHILDREN'S EYEWITNESS TESTIMONY

One of the fundamental assumptions of our work on children's testimony is that any questions concerning the competence or perceived competence of child witnesses must be placed in a comparative framework. It does not make sense to ask the question, "How credible are young children as witnesses?" without establishing a referent or comparison. In our work the referent typically is the adult witness. There are other possible referents. For example, we could ask "How credible is the child eyewitness compared to an error-free recording device such as a videotape system?". Inevitably, however, comparisons of the latter type are not particularly useful or informative. We already know that human perception and memory are not like a videotape system. The relevant comparison for children's testimony is adult testimony, for two main reasons.

First, there already exists a relatively large research literature on adult eyewitnesses (eg see volumes by Clifford & Bull, 1978; Loftus, 1979; Wells & Loftus, 1984; Yarmey, 1979). From this research we know that adults can give wrong answers about events they witnessed as a function of misleading questions (Loftus, 1979), accuracy of responding and eyewitness certainty are related only weakly (eg Wells & Murray, 1984), lineups can be biased in ways that promote false identifications (eg Lindsay & Wells, 1980), short temporal events tend to be overestimated (eg Schiffman & Bobko, 1974), eyewitnesses tend to be believed by subject-jurors if they give confident testimony (eg Wells et al, 1981), and so on. If research with child witnesses revealed these same problems, would we be discovering something about child eyewitnesses or would we be discovering something about human witnesses in general? Our argument for using adult witnesses as the comparison goes even further; we believe that adult samples should be included in the *same* experiment as the children sample. Otherwise, we could not detect some critical interactions. For example, a researcher might use a child-only sample and find that the children were easily influenced by misleading questions. What does this mean? We can't be sure. With the inclusion of an adult sample for comparison, our interpretation is highly dependent on whether the children were more influenced, equally influenced, or less influenced than were the adults by the misleading questions. Although we might wish that we had the technology to make statements about the absolute competencies of witnesses, we are still largely a discipline that requires comparative or relative statements about differences between samples.

Adult witnesses are the most relevant sample for comparison to child witnesses for yet another reason. Specifically, adult witnesses have an already-established status in the legal system. Thus, the child–adult witness comparison is the nexus for bridging research findings with legal policy regarding child witnesses. For example, if children are as competent as adults in certain witness domains, and if adults are allowed to give testimony in that domain, then we have a clear argument for what policy should be regarding child testimony in that same domain. On the other hand, if children have a special problem with certain kinds of testimony or certain types of question techniques, then we have reason to advocate alternative techniques for child witnesses. Again, however, the issue is not whether children have difficulty with leading questions, feel stress when reporting a violent event, and so on that we think to be critical. Instead, it is a question of whether these things are more true of children than they are of adults.

For the purposes of this chapter, where our principal question concerns the *perceived* credibility of child witnesses, the adult–child comparison is a critical one. Although there is much more work to be done, we believe that we have preliminary answers to the following questions. Are child eyewitnesses perceived to be less credible eyewitnesses than adults when they give testimony in a courtroom-like setting? What are the cues that people use in judging whether or not to believe a child's account of a witnessed event? Are these the same cues that are used to judge adult testimony?

EXPERIMENT 1

The paradigm we used was modelled upon that used by Wells and his colleagues to examine adults' eyewitness testimony (eg Lindsay et al, 1981; Wells et al, 1979). In the first phase of this research, all witnesses viewed a simulated crime (a videotape that depicted an 11-year-old boy being abducted from a playground) and one day later responded to direct- and cross-examination questioning. The examinations were videotaped and, in the second phase, were presented to subject-jurors who evaluated the accuracy, believability, and confidence of the eyewitnesses. Actual testimony accuracy (as scored by the experimenters) was compared with subject-jurors' estimates of testimony accuracy.

Phase 1

Both elementary/junior high school aged children and introductory psychology students participated in phase 1. Fourteen male and female grade 3 students (mean age = 7.9 years) and 14 male and female grade 7 students (mean age = 11.8 years) were recruited from a Canadian elementary school following approval of the research by the school board. In addition, 14 male and female introductory psychology students participated in partial fulfillment of a course requirement.

Each of the 42 eyewitnesses viewed the staged abduction on a 152.4 cm videoscreen. Participants were not told prior to viewing the film that their memory for it would later be tested. Rather, they were told that the study was concerned with people's impressions of filmed material. In keeping with this cover story, participants were first shown a videotaped tennis match and were then asked to estimate such things as the effort and ability of each player. Thus, whatever subject-witnesses remembered about the abduction tape that was shown next was (as is the case in actual eyewitness situations) the result of incidental, rather than intentional, memory encoding. The abduction video depicted an 11-year-old boy playing at a playground with a 13-year-old friend. A man sat on a bench and observed the children play, then approached the 11-year-old, persuaded him to go with him to his car, ushered him in, and then sped away. After viewing this abduction, the child eyewitnesses received a "safety message" advising them to say "no" to rides from strangers. At the conclusion of this session all participants scheduled a follow-up interview for the following day. They were told only that they would be doing "something similar to what you did today".

At this follow-up session, participants were greeted by the same experimenter who had conducted the previous day's session. The experimenter explained that he or she would first ask some questions about the playground abduction and that afterwards a second experimenter (who had yet to interact with the witness) would ask several more questions. Subject-witnesses were asked for their permission to be videotaped while responding to questions; all witnesses agreed.

The first experimenter then posed 10 straightforward questions to the witness (eg "How many children were at the playground?"). Following this direct examination, the second experimenter posed a series of 10 cross-examination questions to the eyewitness. In contrast to the direct examination, this series of questions was less straightforward and more adversarial, typically designed to undermine the witness's credibility and/or elicit inconsistent testimony. For example, one of the cross-examination questions was, "You claimed before that the playground was fairly crowded, is that correct?". The majority of the witnesses had previously noted correctly under direct examination that only two children and the abductee were on the playground. Both the direct- and cross-examination questions were cast in a way that allowed the questioners to follow their examination form regardless of how the witness responded.

Phase 2

Two hundred and ninety-four introductory psychology students participated in partial fulfillment of a course requirement. Two to four individuals participated at any given experimental session. Each participant was seated alone in a cubicle with a television monitor and headset and was asked to watch four of the phase 1 testimony videotapes. In every case the four witnesses were from the same age group.

After viewing the direct examination of each witness, the videotape was stopped and participants were asked to estimate the number of questions the witness had answered correctly and to rate the believability and confidence of the witness on seven-point scales. Similarly, after viewing the cross-examination of each witness, participants were asked to assess the accuracy, confidence, and believability of the witness under cross-examination. After viewing the testimony of each witness in its entirety, participants were asked to estimate the "overall" believability and confidence of the witness (on seven-point scales). After viewing four testimony videotapes, participants were thanked for their participation and fully debriefed.

Results

Phase 1: Accuracy of Testimony

Two accuracy scores were calculated for each of the 42 witnesses, one based on 10 direct-examination questions and the other on 7 cross-examination questions. The mean accuracy scores of witnesses as a function of age and type of examination are presented in Figure 5.1. (Note that these scores have been converted to percentages to control for the different numbers of questions contained in the direct vs cross-examinations.) A two-way mixed ANOVA (with age as the between-subjects factor and examination type as the within-subjects factor) revealed a main effect for age, $F(2,39) = 10.03$, $p = 0.003$. A subsequent Newman–Keuls analysis indicated that the 8-year-olds were significantly less accurate than both the 12-year-olds and adult witnesses. The latter two groups did not differ from each other at the 0.01 level. The ANOVA also indicated a main effect for examination type such that all witnesses were more accurate under direct examination than under cross-examination, $F(1,39) = 31.07$, $p < 0.0001$.

Although the predicted interaction between age and examination type was only marginally significant, $F(2,39) = 2.69$, $p = 0.08$, simple effects analyses were conducted to test the hypothesis that age differences in accuracy exist only under direct examination and not under cross-examination. These analyses supported the hypothesis in that direct-examination accuracy did not differ among the three age groups, $F(2,39) = 2.23$, $p = 0.12$, but cross-examination accuracy did vary as a function of age, $F = (2,39) = 8.91$, $p < 0.001$. A subsequent Newman-–Keuls analysis indicated that the 8-year-olds were significantly less accurate than their 12-year-old and adult counterparts, whose cross-examination accuracy did not differ from each other at the 0.01 level.

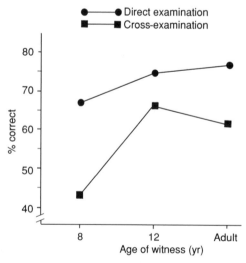

Figure 5.1. Actual accuracy scores under direct and cross-examination as a function of witness age

Phase 2: Perceived credibility and confidence

Eight preliminary univariate ANOVAs for each of the credibility and confidence measures were conducted to test the influence of presenting multiple eyewitnesses to participants. There was a significant main effect for order of presentation on seven of these measures ($0.001 < p < 0.004$) and a marginally significant effect on the believability ratings under direct examination ($p = 0.067$). Therefore, all subsequent analyses have been conducted only on the data for the first witness viewed by each subject-juror.

Credibility and confidence ratings by the 294 subject-jurors were averaged (over approximately 7 subject-jurors who evaluated each witness) to yield a stable estimate of the perceived credibility and confidence for each of the 42 eyewitnesses. Table 5.1 presents the average ratings on each dimension for each of the three age groups. The age of the eyewitness proved to be unrelated to any of the five credibility measures (direct and cross-examination accuracy, direct and cross-examination believability, and overall believability) or any of the three confidence measures (direct and cross-examination, and overall). Univariate, one-way ANOVAs for each measure, with age as the between-subjects variable, failed to produce any significant effects. Eight bivariate regression analyses (one for each measure), with age as the predictor variable, also failed to produce a significant effect for age of the eyewitness.

The correlations among measures employed in phase 2 are displayed in Table 5.2. Despite the lack of a significant effect for eyewitness age on any of the measures, the significant intercorrelations attest to the

Table 5.1. Subject-jurors' mean credibility and confidence ratings of witnesses as a function of witness age

	Witness age (yr)		
	8	12	Adult
Credibility			
Perceived accuracy/direct	6.73	8.87	6.87
Perceived accuracy/cross	6.10	6.16	6.35
Belief/direct	4.96	4.99	5.08
Belief/cross	4.52	4.44	4.59
Belief/overall	4.64	4.73	4.65
Confidence			
Confidence/direct	4.33	4.43	4.81
Confidence/cross	3.96	3.99	4.06
Confidence/overall	4.30	4.22	4.33

Table 5.2. Correlations among measures

		PAD	PAC	BD	BC	BO	CD	CC	CO
Credibility									
Perceived accuracy/direct	(PAD)	×	0.45	0.81	0.36	0.67	0.66	0.38	0.58
Perceived accuracy/cross	(PAC)		×	0.54	0.72	0.63	0.29	0.71	0.64
Belief/direct	(BD)			×	0.59	0.79	0.75	0.59	0.73
Belief/cross	(BC)				×	0.67	0.34	0.79	0.67
Belief/overall	(BO)					×	0.58	0.77	0.79
Confidence									
Confidence/direct	(CD)						×	0.52	0.77
Confidence/cross	(CC)							×	0.87
Confidence/overall	(CO)								×

reliability of the measures. These correlations illustrate, for example, that the subject-jurors tended to believe strongly eyewitnesses who were perceived as confident, and that high-confident witnesses were assigned higher accuracy estimates than were low-confident witnesses. The internal coherence of these correlations can be observed in the fact that measures of perceived accuracy, believability, and confidence correlate more highly *within* cross-examination and *within* direct examination than they do across these tasks. The perceived accuracy of cross-examination correlates more strongly with other cross-examination measures (eg $r = 0.72$ and 0.71 for believability and confidence) than with those same measures taken under direct examination (eg $r = 0.54$ and 0.29 for believability and confidence). This is the type of pattern and magnitude of correlations that would be expected from a set of reliable measures, and thus seems to rule out unreliable measures as an explanation for the lack of differences between ages on these measures.

Actual vs perceived accuracy

Subject-jurors' estimates of eyewitness accuracy were fairly close to the witnesses' actual accuracy in all cases except for the eight-year-olds' cross-examinations. Figure 5.2 compares actual and perceived accuracy for direct and cross-examination as a function of age.

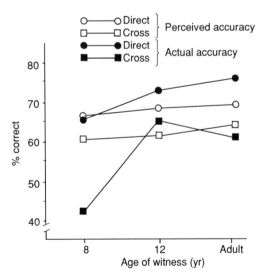

Figure 5.2. Actual and perceived accuracy under direct and cross-examination as a function of witness age

Recall that the 8-year-old witnesses were significantly less accurate than the 12-year-old and adult witnesses under cross-examination. Subject-jurors were not sensitive to this difference and thus perceived the eight-year-olds' cross-examinations as much more accurate than they actually were.

Discussion

Are children perceived to be less credible eyewitnesses than adults when they give testimony in a courtroom-like setting? Within the range of ages that we tested, our results suggest that children are not perceived to be less credible than adults. Although some of the eight-year-old witnesses were in fact perceived to be relatively inaccurate and not believable, this was also true of an approximately equal proportion of the adult witnesses.

The tendency to perceive an eyewitness as accurate and believable seems to be closely related to the confidence of the eyewitness. Although confidence was merely a correlated variable in this study, previous work that has experimentally manipulated eyewitness confidence has shown that confidence plays a major *causal* role in affecting jurors' perceptions of eyewitness credibility (eg Luus & Wells, 1991; Wells & Murray, 1984; Wells et al, 1981). Accordingly, it makes sense to construe the confidence of eyewitnesses as a major cue that our subject-jurors used to make their estimates of accuracy and believability, rather than a mere correlate of perceived accuracy and believability. Construed in this fashion, we can speculate that the reason that the average eight-year-old was as readily believed as the average adult witness was because these two groups were perceived as equally confident on average. And, the relation between the perceived confidence of the eyewitnesses and the perceived accuracy and believability of the eyewitnesses was equally strong regardless of whether the subject-jurors were viewing 8-year-old, 12-year-old or adult eyewitnesses. This suggests that the subject-jurors used the same credibility cues and that they used these cues to the same extent regardless of the age of the eyewitness.

Although it might be tempting to take solace in the finding that 8-year-old eyewitnesses were perceived to be as credible as the adult eyewitnesses, we cannot ignore the fact that the 8-year-old eyewitnesses were less accurate than the adults in their answers to the cross-examination questions. In this sense, subject-jurors erroneously perceived the 8-year-olds as being as equally credible as the adults.

We do not feel that the young children necessarily had a poorer recollection of the witnessed event than their adolescent and adult counterparts. Rather, we suspect that the children's low accuracy under cross-examination stems from a need or desire to conform to the requests of an adult authority figure. The results of a recent study by Ceci et al, (1987) support this interpretation. Recall that, whereas our direct examination consisted of straightforward probes for "facts", the cross-examination contained a number of misleading questions. Ceci et al found that children's susceptibility to misleading information was reduced (but not eliminated) when another child, as opposed to an adult, provided the misleading information.

Subject-jurors were sensitive to the main effect difference between direct- and cross-examination performance (appropriately estimating lower accuracy for cross- than for direct examination), but were not sensitive to the interaction between type of question and age of eyewitness. The failure of subject-jurors to appreciate the difficulties that the 8-year-old eyewitnesses had with cross-examination resulted in their overestimating the 8-year-olds' cross-examination accuracy. It might be premature to conclude that jurors are likely to overestimate the accuracy of young children's cross-examination accuracy in actual cases, but these results strongly suggest that the interaction between age and type of question is not intuitive.

Our results, showing children and adults to be perceived as equally credible eyewitnesses, do not contradict earlier studies that have shown a stereotypic bias by jurors as a function of eyewitness age. In some of those studies, jurors were not permitted to actually observe the child's testimony. Thus, they did not have a concrete individual to evaluate, but rather they were being asked to respond to an age category, which is a condition that is more likely to allow stereotypes to surface in human judgement than when an individual, vivid member of that category is shown in detail. Jurors might enter the courtroom with such a stereotype; however, the present findings suggest that qualities of the witness's testimony play a more important role than does the witness's age in judgements of eyewitness credibility. That is, people might imagine children to be incapable of delivering accurate, convincing testimony, but these preconceived negative views of child eyewitnesses seem to be quickly discarded upon actually observing a child testify. It is important to note that there was considerable variability in the credibility and confidence scores *within* ages but that the means were functionally equivalent *across* ages. So, the inconsistencies in previous studies (eg Goodman et al (1987) found their child witness to be less credible than the adult witness whereas Ross et al (1987) found their child witness to be more credible than the adult) are likely attributable to witness sampling. Indeed, given the variance within each age group in terms of overall credibility (the range for

8-year-olds was 4.1–6.0; for 12-year-olds, 4.15–5.75; for adults, 3.9–5.7), there is approximately a 50% chance that a randomly selected 8-year-old will be perceived as less credible than a randomly selected adult and a 50% chance that the 8-year-old will be perceived as more credible than the adult. It should not be surprising that studies using only one witness from each age group have yielded inconsistent results.

EXPERIMENT 2

There are at least two general interpretations as to why the eight-year-old eyewitnesses were judged to be as credible as the adult eyewitnesses in study 1. First, perhaps jurors judge both adult and child eyewitnesses' credibility on the basis of their speech presentation style. That is, age *per se* plays no role in a juror's decision to believe or question the testimony of an eyewitness. Rather, the eyewitness's apparent confidence in testifying is what counts. Alternatively, perhaps the children did give discernibly weaker testimony than the adults and the jurors had anticipated that this would be the case. Therefore perhaps they evaluated the children differently, more leniently than the adults, in accordance with the lesser expectations they had for the eyewitness performance of children as compared to adults. Recent research supports this latter interpretation (Leippe & Romanczyk, 1989). Leippe and Romkanczyk (1989) presented subject-jurors with either a *description* of a case involving a child or adult witness or they had the subject-jurors read a *transcript* of the child or adult witness's testimony. In general, their results showed that subject-jurors tended to show a bias against the child's testimony in the description cases, where they merely knew the child's age, but a bias favoring the child's testimony when they read the testimony transcript. "It seems that adults' negative preconceptions about children's memory will not dispose them to reject a child's memory message if the message's quality is sufficiently 'mature' to belie the stereotype" (Leippe & Romanczyk, 1989, p. 127).

We designed a second experiment to partial out experimentally the credibility effects due to content of the testimony from people's stereotypes with regard to the source of the testimony. In this second study we used written transcripts from a sample of eight-year-olds and a sample of the adults to see if subject-jurors could discern differences in the verbal portions of the testimony. By using transcripts rather than videotapes, we were able to manipulate the ostensible age of the witnesses independently of the actual age of the witnesses. Thus, for each of the six transcripts, three versions were created: one with the witness described as 8 years old, one with the witness described as 12 years old, and the third with the witness described as 25 years old.

Method

Subjects and design

Two hundred and sixteen introductory psychology students, participating in partial fulfillment of a course requirement, were randomly assigned to one of 18 conditions in a 3 (actual age of eyewitness: 8 years old vs adult) × 3 (ostensible age of eyewitness: 8 vs 12 vs 25 years old) × 3 (testimony credibility: high vs medium vs low) between-subjects factorial design. This latter factor, testimony credibility, is a categorical classification of the transcripts based on the composite credibility score of the witnesses as obtained in experiment 1. The purpose of this factor was to allow us to sample from the transcripts (rather than use all 42) while at the same time performing an ANOVA test to see if the subjects who were most and least credible in experiment 1 (based on evaluations of their videotaped testimony) were also the most and least credible when subject-jurors were evaluating only written transcript versions of their testimony.

Procedure

Participants were asked to read one of 18 testimony transcripts provided by eyewitnesses who participated in the first phase of experiment 1. Three transcripts were selected from grade 3 students who had been assigned a high, medium, or low credibility score by the subject-jurors in experiment 1. Three transcripts were selected from adult witnesses from experiment 1 who were similarly judged to be either high, moderate, or low in terms of credibility. Three versions of each testimony were created by the written assertion that the witness was either 8, 12, or 25 years old. Participants were asked to respond to eight questions concerning: (a) the number of questions answered correctly by the witness under direct examination, (b) number correct under cross-examination, (c) the believability of the witness under direct examination, (d) believability under cross-examination, (e) the confidence of the witness under direct examination, (f) confidence under cross-examination, (g) the overall believability of the eyewitness, and (h) the overall confidence of the eyewitness. All confidence and believability assessments were made on seven-point scales.

Results and Discussion

Univariate ANOVAs were conducted on each of the eight measures. A significant main effect for the credibility classification emerged on seven of the eight measures ($0.01 < p < 0.045$). The only measure that did not show significant differences for the credibility classification variable was the measure of believability of direct examination ($p = 0.40$). Recall that the credibility classification variable refers to the perceived overall credibility of the witnesses as evaluated by subject-jurors in experiment 1 based on their videotaped testimony. This result, therefore, shows that subject-jurors in experiment 2 were able to see the same kinds of credibility differences between witnesses based merely on the transcripts that the subject-jurors in experiment 1 saw in the videotaped testimony from which these transcripts were drawn.

There were no interaction effects associated with the credibility classification variable. There also were no main effects or interaction effects associated with actual age (all $p > 0.4$). Thus, the 8-year-olds' transcripts were judged to be just as credible as the adults' transcripts.

Importantly, there were also no main or interaction effects associated with ostensible age (all $p > 0.5$). Subject-jurors did not judge the witness to be less credible when described as 8 years old than when described as 12 or 25 years old. This is an important observation bearing on our interpretations of experiment 1. Specifically, these results suggest that subject-jurors were not giving the 8-year-olds "extra credit" because they believed them to be less capable eyewitnesses than adults. If the 8-year-olds were being judged more leniently by subject-jurors in experiment 1 owing to their age, then there should have been an ostensible age effect in experiment 2.

We are led to conclude, therefore, that the absence of an age effect on perceived credibility in experiment 1 derives from a true lack of mean differences in the perceived credibility of the different aged witnesses. Subject-jurors were not compensating for the age of the witnesses by giving the younger children higher credibility scores because of their age.

GENERAL DISCUSSION

The results of the two studies reported here attest to the credibility of child eyewitnesses relative to adult eyewitnesses. First, with respect to the adequacy of children's memories, we found no age differences in the actual accuracy of the witnesses' direct examination testimony.

Thus, children *can* recall witnessed events with the same degree of accuracy as adults. However, they will only *report* their memories with the same degree of accuracy as adults if questioned in the direct, straightforward manner characteristic of direct examination. As expected, cross-examination presented more problems for the 8-year-old witnesses than for the 12-year-old or adult eyewitnesses on measures of actual testimony accuracy. The non-leading aspect of direct examination versus the leading aspect of cross-examination seems to account for this interaction between age and type of examination.

The errors that the young children made under cross-examination cost them little in terms of perceived credibility. Indeed, despite the difficulty our 8-year-old witnesses had in providing accurate testimony under cross-examination, they were perceived as no less confident or believable than their more accurate adolescent and adult counterparts. Moreover, this finding does not reflect an insensitivity on the part of subject-jurors to differences in the witnesses' testimonies. In fact, the subject-jurors were highly discriminating in the way they evaluated the eyewitnesses. There was considerable variance across the 42 witnesses in the ways that subject-jurors perceived the confidence, believability, and accuracy of the witnesses. And, as evidenced in experiment 2, there was good interjudge reliability and cross-modal (ie video vs transcript only) reliability as to which witnesses were thought to be the most confident, believable, and accurate.

There is some cause for concern, perhaps, that subject-jurors found the 8-year-old witnesses to be as credible as the 12-year-old and adult witnesses in their cross-examination testimony when in fact the 8-year-olds were significantly less accurate. This is yet another example of the difficulty subject-jurors seem to have in evaluating the accuracy of eyewitness testimony (eg Wells & Leippe, 1981: Wells et al, 1979). In part, the difficulty stems from the fact that eyewitness confidence does not closely track eyewitness accuracy (eg Brigham & Cairns, 1988; Leippe et al, 1978; Parker & Caranza, 1989; Wells & Murray, 1984), whereas the believability of eyewitness testimony tracks eyewitness confidence closely (eg Wells et al, 1979). Similar results were found in the current study in that the perceived confidence of the 8-year-olds' testimony under cross-examination was equal to that of adults', whereas accuracy was lower and the overall believability of the witnesses corresponded closely to the witnesses' overall confidence.

Why did we not find an effect for the age of the eyewitnesses on perceived credibility when previous research found such effects? As we have noted previously, some studies have found children to be perceived as less credible than adults (eg Goodman, 1984), but others have found the opposite (eg Ross et al, 1987). We believe that these inconsistent findings can be explained by the fact that these previous studies used the testimony of only one child actor whereas we sampled a number of witnesses from each age group. Selecting any one child and any one adult could lead to results suggesting that either the adult is more credible or the child is more credible. Our data clearly demonstrates that there is enough variation in perceived credibility *within* ages to preclude the assumption that any one person could represent the perceived credibility of that age group.

Although we believe that our results show that characteristics of eyewitnesses other than their age (eg confidence of testimony) are responsible for attributions of credibility to eyewitness testimony, we can only make this conclusion within the boundaries of the ages that were used in these studies. Had we used four-year-olds or even six-year-olds, we might have found some robust differences in perceived confidence, accuracy, and believability as a function of age.

Nevertheless, our results support the views of Leippe and Romanczyk (1989) that there might be a stereotyped bias against the child eyewitness, but the provision of actual children's testimony seems sufficient to overcome these preconceptions. In other words, our findings do not contradict the results of previous studies that evidenced a negative stereotype of eight-year-olds' eyewitness capabilities. Jurors might very well enter the courtroom with a negative stereotype of an eight-year-old's eyewitness capabilities but then lay that stereotype to rest upon actually hearing the eight-year-old provide much better testimony than they had anticipated.

REFERENCES

Brigham, J. C. & Cairns, D. L. (1988). The effect of mugshot inspection on eyewitness identification accuracy. *Journal of Applied Social Psychology*, 18, 1394–1410.

Ceci, S. J., Ross, D. F. & Toglia, M. P. (1987). Age differences in suggestibility: narrowing the uncertainties. In S. J. Ceci, M. P. Toglia & D. F. Ross (Eds). *Children's Eyewitness Memory*. New York: Springer-Verlag, pp. 79–91.

Clifford, B. R. & Bull, R. (1978). *The Psychology of Person Identification*. London: Routledge & Kegan Paul.

Conley, J. M., O'Barr, W. M. & Lind, E. A. (1978). The power of languages: presentational style in the courtroom. *Duke Law Journal*, 1375–1399.

Erickson, B., Lind, E. A., Johnson, B. C. & O'Barr, W. M. (1978). Speech style and impression formation in a court setting: the effects of "powerful" and "powerless" speech. *Journal of Experimental Social Psychology*, 14, 166–179.

Goodman, G. S. (1984). Children's testimony in historical perspective. *Journal of Social Issues*, 40, 9–31.

Goodman, G. S., Golding, J. M., Hegelson, V. S., Haith, M. M. & Michelli, J. (1987). When a child takes the stand: jurors' perceptions of children's eyewitness testimony. *Law and Human Behavior*, 11, 27–40.

Leippe, M. R., Wells, G. L. & Ostrom, T. M. (1978). Crime seriousness as a determinant of accuracy in eyewitness identification. *Journal of Applied Psychology*, 63, 345–351.

Leippe, M. R. & Romanczyk, A. (1987). Children on the witness stand: a communication/persuasion analysis of jurors' reactions to child witnesses. In S. J. Ceci, M. P. Toglia & D. F. Ross (Eds). *Children's Eyewitness Memory*. New York: Springer-Verlag, pp. 155–177.

Leippe, M. R. & Romanczyk (1989). Reactions to child (versus adult) eyewitnesses. *Law and Human Behavior*, 13, 101–132.

Lind, E. A. & O'Barr, W. M. (1979). The social significance of speech in the courtroom. In H. Giles & R. N. St Clair (Eds). *Language and Social Psychology*. Baltimore: University Park Press, pp. 66–87.

Lindsay, R. C. L. & Wells, G. L. (1980). What price justice? Exploring the relationship of lineup fairness to identification accuracy. *Law and Human Behavior*, 4, 303–314.

Lindsay, R. C. L., Wells, G. L. & Rumpel, C. (1981). Can people detect eyewitness accuracy within and across situations? *Journal of Applied Psychology*, 63, 345–351.

Loftus, E. F. (1979). *Eyewitness Testimony*. Cambridge, MA: Harvard University Press.

Luus, C. A. E. & Wells, G. L. (1991). Unpublished manuscript, Iowa State University.

O'Barr, W. M. (1982). *Linguistic Evidence*. New York: Academic Press.

Parker, J. F. & Caranza, L. E. (1989). Eyewitness testimony of children in target-present and target-absent lineups. *Law and Human Behavior*, 13, 133–149.

Ross, D. F., Dunning, D., Toglia, M. & Ceci, S. J. (1991). The child in the eyes of the jury: assessing mock jurors' perceptions of the child witness. *Law and Human Behavior*, 14, 5–23.

Ross, D. F., Miller, B. S. & Moran, P. B. (1987). The child in the eyes of the jury: assessing mock jurors' perceptions of the child witness. In S. J. Ceci, M. P. Toglia & D. F. Ross (Eds). *Children's Eyewitness Memory*. New York: Springer-Verlag, pp. 142–154.

Schiffman, H. R. & Bobko, D. J. (1974). Effects of stimulus complexity on the perception of brief temporal durations. *Journal of Experimental Psychology*, 103, 156–159.

Wells, G. L., Lindsay, R. C. L. & Ferguson, T. J. (1979). Accuracy, confidence, and juror perceptions in eyewitness identification. *Journal of Applied Psychology*, 64, 440–448.

Wells, G. L. & Leippe, M. R. (1981). How do triers of fact infer the accuracy of eyewitness identification? Using memory for detail can be misleading. *Journal of Applied Psychology*, 66, 682–687.

Wells, G. L., Ferguson, T. J. & Lindsay, R. C. L. (1981). The tractability of eyewitness confidence and its implications for triers of fact. *Journal of Applied Psychology*, 64, 440–448.

Wells, G. L. & Loftus, E. F. (Eds) (1984). *Eyewitness Testimony: Psychological Perspectives*. New York: Cambridge University Press.

Wells, G. L. & Murray, D. M. (1984). Eyewitness confidence. In G. L. Wells & E.

F. Loftus (Eds). *Eyewitness Testimony: Psychological Perspectives.* New York: Cambridge University Press, pp. 155–170.

Wells, G. L., Turtle, J. W. & Luus, C. A. E. (1989). The perceived credibility of child eyewitnesses: what happens when they use their own words? In S. J. Ceci, D. F. Ross & M. P. Toglia (Eds). *Perspectives on Children's Testimony.* New York: Springer-Verlag.

Whipple, G. M. (1911). The psychology of testimony. *Psychological Bulletin,* 8, 307–309.

Yarmey, A. D. (1979). *The Psychology of Eyewitness Testimony.* New York: Free Press.

Yarmey, A. D. & Jones, H. P. T. (1983). Is the study of eyewitness identification a matter of common sense? In S. Lloyd-Bostock & B. R. Clifford (Eds). *Evaluating Witness Evidence.* Chichester: Wiley.

CHAPTER 6

Opinions Held by Professionals Who Work with Child Witnesses

John C. Brigham

and

Stacy A. Spier

Florida State University

Children are currently being called upon to render testimony in the US legal system more than ever before. They may be called to identify others (as in sexual assault cases involving a stranger) or to recall complex events (as in child custody hearings, domestic violence cases and sexual assault cases involving a person familiar to the child). As the number of reports of child maltreatment have risen dramatically in recent decades (Bulkley, 1989), numerous psycholegal researchers have attempted to assess the accuracy of children's memories and their susceptibility to social influence factors. The research outcomes have been summarized in several books and conferences (eg Ceci et al, 1987b, 1989; Doris, 1991).

The relationship between age, quality of memory, and suggestibility is not a simple one. Some studies using forensically relevant stimuli have found an absence, or only small effects, of age on memory (eg Goodman & Reed, 1986; Zaragoza, 1987). However, some developmental

Children as Witnesses. Edited by H. Dent and R. Flin
© 1992 John Wiley & Sons Ltd.

differences in eyewitness identifications, event memory, and suggestibility have been observed (eg Ceci et al, 1987a). Overall, research
results seem to suggest that the memory performance of children as
young as five may approach that of adult subjects if they are questioned in a manner sensitive to their verbal and conceptual abilities,
one which avoids leading questions and concentrates on familiar
witnessed events (Berliner & Barbieri, 1984; Melton & Thompson,
1987).

Other factors may interact with age in influencing suggestibility.
Goodman et al (1990) found no age differences in accuracy on open-
ended questions, but on the specific questions older children were both
more accurate and more resistant to misleading suggestions. Child
subjects who were bystanders were less resistant to general misleading
information compared to participants.

In contrast to these results, Clarke-Stewart et al (1989) found
children were suggestible when a situation was difficult to understand.
After a set of two adult interrogations, one or both of which were
inconsistent with the actual witnessed events, a large majority of
children changed their version to match the adults'. Studying questioning styles meant to minimize children's suggestibility, Dent (1991)
found that children who received the maximal prompting questions
gave the most complete but the least accurate answers; those with
minimal prompting questions responded least completely but most
accurately. Additionally, children appeared more suggestible when
asked about descriptive details. Dent (1982) also found that the skills of
the interviewer affected children's suggestibility. Less suggestivity
occurred when the interviewer used cognitive context reinstatement
and did not phrase questions in such a way as to obtain only information consistent with the interviewer's version of what occurred.

Several studies have found that highly aroused children were more
susceptible to misleading postevent information (Peters, 1991). Another study that observed memory of an arousing, anxiety-provoking
event (Bottoms et al, 1989) found that when interviewers were kind to
the subjects, interviewing them several times and providing the
children with practice, children's reports were more accurate.

Perceptions of child witnesses are important at two phases of the
criminal justice process, at the investigative stage and at trial. At the
investigative stage, attitudes of child protection workers and law
officers may affect the extent to which a child's allegations are taken
seriously, while prosecuting attorneys' attitudes may determine
whether or not criminal charges are filed. At trial, jurors' attitudes,
schemas, and age-related stereotypes will affect how a child's testimony is evaluated and remembered.

As positive findings regarding children's memory have become better known, and as society attempts to ensure that child abusers are brought to justice, demands for greater openness to child testimony have been made (Altman & Lennon, 1986). For instance, in US courts competency evaluations, which were once required to admit the testimony of children as old as 14, are no longer routinely required (Goodman, 1984). In the US, the requirement that a child's testimony be corroborated by additional evidence before allowing it has been removed in cases of sexual abuse (Myers, 1987). Some states have changed testimony procedures to make them more accommodating to children's special needs (Leippe et al, 1989). The courts in the United Kingdom have also recommended procedures amenable to the needs of children (*Report on the Evidence of Child and Other Potentially Vulnerable Witnesses*, 1990; *Report of the Advisory Group on Video Evidence*, 1989).

Although these developments have resulted in part from recent empirical findings regarding children, there are few studies on the perception and treatment of child witnesses by those in the judicial system. Legal scholars and professionals working with child victims of sexual assault (eg Berliner & Barbieri, 1984) have maintained that prosecutors are often unwilling to try cases that rely mainly on the eyewitness testimony of a young child, supposedly due to burden-of-proof difficulties and to the assumption that jurors entertain negative stereotypes of children's memory skills. Others have assumed, without substantial empirical support, that prosecutors hesitate to seek juried trials in child sex abuse proceedings, that the average child will find serving as a witness traumatic, and that defense attorneys will handle child witnesses harshly on the witness stand (Leippe et al, 1989). Hence, attorneys' biases regarding the accuracy of children's testimony and the credibility of children as assessed by juries may affect decisions about going to trial and the strategies they use when in court.

There has also been little effort to ascertain what other groups of professionals who deal with child witnesses think about these crucial issues. Among the first professionals to have contact with child witnesses in physical or sexual abuse cases are child protection workers and law enforcement personnel. In Florida, any person who knows, or has reason to suspect, that a child has been abused must report it to the Department of Health and Rehabilitative Services (HRS), which contains a division of Children's Medical Services. HRS professionals conduct a preliminary investigation of the charges and may call in a regional Child Protection Team (CPT). The multidisciplinary teams include physicians, psychologists, nurses, attorneys, and case coordinators (social workers). The CPT's primary goal is to provide the child with medical and related care, including diagnosis, evaluation, and treatment.

In light of conflicting recent research results involving the suggestibility of children and the importance of pretrial interviews performed by professionals, it is important to learn what professionals who perform most of the initial interviewing (child protection workers and law officers) believe about the memories of child witnesses. Child protection workers, for example, may tend to believe that children almost never lie about sexual abuse (Faller, 1984). Since both the accuracy and credibility of a child witness may depend to a great extent on the interviewing technique used, the beliefs of these professionals regarding child witnesses may directly affect the accuracy of a child's memory that is elicited.

Past research has led us to expect some inaccuracy in the belief of the professionals regarding the recall and recognition skills of child witnesses, since some inaccuracy has been noted in surveys dealing with opinions about adult eyewitnesses (Brigham & WolfsKeil, 1983; Yarmey & Jones, 1983). To assess evaluations of child witnesses, we conducted a state-wide survey of four groups of professionals (defense attorneys, prosecuting attorneys, child protection workers, and law enforcement personnel), assessing four general issues relating to child witnesses: beliefs about a child's memory and communication skills, beliefs about the truthfulness of children's testimony, beliefs about jurors' perceptions of child witnesses, and ways of eliciting and presenting child witness evidence.

METHOD

Procedure

The survey was conducted in two stages: responses were first gathered from attorneys, after which the questionnaire was revised slightly and sent to child protection workers and law enforcement personnel. During the first stage, we sent packets of six questionnaires to the central Public Defender's office and the central State Attorney's office (prosecutors) in each of Florida's 20 judicial circuits. Follow-up letters were sent approximately six weeks later to those offices from which no reply had been received. About four weeks after the second mailing, phone calls were made to those offices that had not yet responded, encouraging them to complete and return the questionnaires. (The results of the attorney survey are also reported in Leippe et al, 1989.)

After consulting with both child protection workers and law enforcement personnel, the questionnaire was revised to make the contents more pertinent to the experiences of these groups. Packets of six questionnaires were then sent to each of the 19 central Child Protection Team (CPT) offices, 13 central Health and Rehabilitative Services (HRS) offices, 50 city police departments (located in Florida's 50 largest cities), and 67 county sheriff departments. A cover letter was enclosed in each packet requesting that the questionnaires be distributed to those persons in the agencies that had the most experience working with child victims or child witnesses. We used the same sequence of follow-up letters and phone calls as in the attorney survey.

Subjects

Packets of questionnaires were returned by 85% (17/20) of the Public Defender's offices and 50% (10/20) of the State Attorney's offices; 58% (11/19) of the CPT offices, 100% (13/13) of HRS offices, 60% (40/67) of sheriff departments, and 78% (39/50) of police departments. Completed questionnaires were received from a total of 74 defense attorneys, 47 prosecuting attorneys, 42 CPT workers, 60 HRS workers, 223 police offices, and 140 sheriff's department personnel.

Our samples were similar to each other in some demographic respects and quite different in others. Mean age was similar across samples (35–36 years), while educational levels differed. While all attorneys had advanced law degrees, 32% of the child protection workers (CPW) had earned advanced degrees (28% masters, 4% doctorate). The vast majority (85%) of the law officers had attended at least some college; 24% had bachelor's degrees and another 7% reported some academic work beyond the bachelor's level. The law enforcement personnel had longer average on-the-job experience (mean $11\frac{1}{2}$ years) than did the attorneys or the CPW samples (means of 5–7 years). The majority (60%) of the child protection workers were women, while women comprised 24%, 32%, and 24% of the law enforcement, defense attorney, and prosecutor samples. Twenty per cent of the CPW sample and 23% of the law enforcement respondents were nonwhite, as compared to only 2% of the defense attorneys and 7% of the prosecutors.

Involvement in physical abuse cases where a child is an important witness was a common experience for child protection workers and those law enforcement personnel who work with child witness cases. These respondents reported working on a mean of 107 and 81 such cases, respectively, in the past two years. Attorneys encountered these cases less often—an average of 58 cases for prosecutors and 32 for defense attorneys over a two-year period. The most common types of cases were family violence and physical abuse by a parent. Child protection workers, law enforcement personnel, and prosecutors all encountered alleged sexual abuse cases fairly often (means of 59, 32, and 46 cases in two years), while defense attorneys saw fewer cases (a mean of 13).

RESULTS

Survey results will be presented in terms of the four general categories of issues addressed: the prevalence of beliefs about a child's memory and communication skills, beliefs about the truthfulness of children's testimony, beliefs about jurors' perceptions of child witnesses, and methods of eliciting and presenting child witness evidence in court.

Beliefs About Children's Memory and Communication Skills

In order to provide a frame of reference for comparing perceptions of children's and adults' memories, we asked our respondents to imagine a situation in which a 5–9-year-old child, or an adult, is a witness to a 15-second episode where an acquaintance is assaulted by a stranger. The stranger flees the scene, leaving the acquaintance unharmed but robbed and shaken up. The next day the witness is asked to recall as much as possible about the event and try to identify the assailant from a six-person photo lineup. Respondents were asked to compare child and adult witnesses' likely performance on: amount recalled, ability to identify the assailant from the lineup, suggestibility, sincerity, and inconsistencies in the description of the event. Survey responses are summarized in Table 6.1; responses were analyzed in terms of five response categories but have been collapsed to three categories for ease of interpretation in Table 6.1.

Almost all of the defense attorneys (96%) thought that child witnesses would recall less than an adult, but only 50–57% of respondents of the other three types agreed ($\chi^2(12) = 94.63$, $p < 0.001$; eta = 0.357). In these analyses, the proportion of variance accounted for by group membership is represented by eta squared, also known as the correlation ratio. The eta-squared value of 0.127 indicates that 13% of the variance in responses was accounted for by the group to which respondents belonged. The defense attorneys' greater pessimism about child witnesses was also evident on the second question, as 82% felt

Table 6.1. Competency of child witnesses. Ratings of 5–9-year-old children's characteristics compared to those of adults

Compared to adults, child witnesses are:		Defense attorneys (N = 74)	Prosecuting attorneys (N = 47)	Child prot. workers (N = 104)	Law enforcement (N = 356)
likely to recall ___	Less/much less	96%	57%	55%	50%
	About the same	4	36	30	28
	More/much more	0	7	14	22
___ likely to identify an assailant who is present in the lineup	Less/much less	82	41	49	41
	About equally	16	50	38	39
	More/much more	3	9	11	21
___ suggestible	Less/much less	1	11	20	17
	About as	3	20	13	18
	More/much more	96	70	67	65
___ sincere when communicating to a police officer, attorney, or jury	Less/much less	23	4	1	4
	Just as	41	33	25	29
	More/much more	36	63	74	67
apt to give accounts of a witnessed criminal event that include ___ inconsistencies	Fewer/many fewer	6	9	31	34
	About the same no.	7	36	25	36
	More/many more	87	55	44	30

that child witnesses would be less likely than an adult witness to correctly identify the assailant from a photo lineup, while fewer than half of the other respondents agreed. They were about equally split between those who felt that children and adults were equally likely to identify the assailant and those who thought children would do less well. As with the previous question, between-group differences were highly significant ($\chi^2(12) = 85.78$, $p < 0.001$; eta = 0.321).

The four groups were in somewhat more agreement about suggestibility, as a majority of all groups thought that children are more suggestible than adults. the defense attorneys thought this most strongly (96%), and between-group differences were again significant ($\chi^2(12) = 118.30$, $p < 0.001$; eta = 0.324). Most child protection workers (74%), law enforcement personnel (67%), and prosecutors (63%) believed that children are likely to be more *sincere* than adults when communicating to a police officer, attorney, or jury; only 41% of defense attorneys agreed ($\chi^2(12) = 64.06$ $p < 0.001$; eta = 0.279).

Defense attorneys' greater skepticism about child witnesses was again reflected in the final question in this series, as 87% of them felt that children are apt to include more inconsistencies in their accounts of a witnessed criminal event than adults are. Slightly over half of the prosecutors (55%), and fewer child protection workers (44%) and law enforcement personnel (30%), agreed. Once again, between-group differences were significant ($\chi^2(12) = 135.04$, $p < 0,001$; eta = 0.386).

Responses to these five questions demonstrated the chasm between defense attorneys' perceptions and the perceptions of members of the other three groups. Some law enforcement personnel appeared to have especially high confidence in child witnesses, as over 20% of them responded that children would recall more than adults, would include fewer inconsistencies, and would be more likely than adults to identify correctly an assailant from a lineup.

Perceived Truthfulness of Children's Testimony

To assess perceptions of children's truthfulness in sexual abuse cases, respondents were asked to envision instances in which a 5–9-year-old child reports that she or he was sexually abused and the situation comes to the attention of law enforcement personnel and/or an attorney. They were asked to estimate the percentage of the time that the child's description was thought to be quite accurate, distorted or exaggerated, completely inaccurate or fabricated, or inaccurate because the child *underestimated* the extent of sexual abuse. Responses are presented in Table 6.2.

Table 6.2. Perceived inaccuracy in cases of alleged sexual abuse. Respondents' evaluations of "instances in which a 5-9-year-old child reports that she or he was sexually abused and the situation comes to the attention of law enforcement personnel and/or an attorney"

	Estimated % age of time where child's description was thought to be:			
	Quite an accurate description	Significantly distorted or exaggerated although sexual abuse did take place	Completely inaccurate or fabricated; no sexual abuse took place	Inaccurate because child underestimated extent of sexual abuse
Defense attorneys	43.9_a	43.5_a	18.5_a	9.5_a
Prosecutors	67.4_{bcd}	12.67_b	5.6_b	20.2_{bcd}
Child protection workers	58.0_c	19.7_b	7.1_b	25.7_c
Law enforcement personnel	68.1_d	20.1_b	8.2_b	15.3_d
$F =$	11.13^{***}	15.47^{***}	18.26^{***}	9.67^{***}
$df =$	3,553	3,542	3,535	3,539

Notes
Respondents made percentage estimates for each outcome and often the percentages given totaled more than 100%.

Groups in the same column that do not share the same subscript differ from each other at the $p < 0.05$ level according to the Newman–Keuls procedure.

$^{***}f < 0.001$

Defense attorneys estimated significantly lower levels of accuracy than did the other three groups $(F (3,553) = 11.13, p < 0.001)$. The child protection workers' mean estimate was significantly lower than the law enforcement officers' estimate, according to the Newman–Keuls procedure. The likelihood that the description would be distorted or exaggerated was seen as much greater by defense attorneys than the other three groups $(F (3,542) = 15.47, p < 0.001)$. The defense attorneys, on average, felt that almost one-fifth (18.5%) of the child witness cases they encountered involved children's testimony that was completely inaccurate or fabricated! Members of the other three groups felt that such occurrences were much rarer (6–8% of the time) $(F(3,535) = 18.26, p < 0.001)$.

We also asked our respondents to consider situations in which a child retracts an allegation of sexual abuse. Mean estimates of the prevalence of retractions ranged from 18% (law enforcement) to 29% (child protection workers) $(F(3,557) = 8.25, p < 0.001)$. Child protection workers estimated a significantly higher retraction rate than did the other three groups. Respondents also evaluated seven reasons why retractions might occur; Table 6.3 summarizes our subjects' views on the prevalence of each of these reasons. Between-group differences were significant on all items; the defense attorney-vs-others dichotomy was most evident for the statement that a child's retraction could stem from her/his knowledge that the previous testimony was false. One-quarter of the defense attorneys responded that this was often or very often the reason for a retraction, but few of the other respondents (3–10%) agreed $(\chi^2(12) = 57.73, p < 0.001;$ eta $= 0.289)$.

Because law enforcement personnel and child protection workers are the groups most likely to encounter children's statements or retractions at the early investigatory phase, we asked them whether they could "personally tell whether a child witness is telling the truth or not". Most (79% of child protection workers and 76% of law enforcement personnel) responded that they "usually" could tell; very few (3% of each group) responded that they could always tell. An open-ended question then asked, "What information or cues do you use in deciding if a child witness is being truthful?". Factors that were listed by 3% or more of either sample are presented in Table 6.4.

The consistency of the child's statement was the cue mentioned most often by both groups. The behavioral cues of body language and eye contact were the next most frequently listed factors. Largest between-group differences occurred for "extent of sexual knowledge compared to peers" and heightened affect (nervous, emotional, afraid), both of which were cited more than twice as often by child workers than by law officers.

Table 6.3. Reasons for retraction of testimony. Percent of respondents reporting that each is "often" or "very often" a reason why a child may report sexual abuse then later retract her or his statement

	Defense attorneys	Prosecuting attorneys	Child prot. workers	Law enforcement	$\chi^2_{(12)}$	Eta
Pressure from parent or family member	65	82	94	82	38.82***	0.250
Embarrassment about incident(s)	45	31	48	39	42.32***	0.179
Feeling responsible for, or guilty about, the incident	34	42	57	41	28.30***	0.157
Fear of retaliation or harm	28	45	73	55	52.41***	0.285
Fear of being on the witness stand	27	15	30	33	19.81***	0.120
Knowledge that the previous testimony was false	25	2	3	10	57.73***	0.289
Desire to protect other family members	[a]	[a]	77	53	23.49***	0.232

[a]This option was not included in the attorneys' survey.
*** $f < 0.001$

Table 6.4. Cues to deception. "What information or cues do you use in deciding if a child witness is being truthful?" (free response)

	Law enforcement	Child protection workers
Verbal presentation:		
Content		
Consistency of statement	36%	49%
Memory of detail, knowledge, amt. info.	13	16
Sexual knowledge vs peers	6	17
Language, vocabulary	4	6
Plausibility, believability	3	8
Verbal: style		
Affect: nervous, emotional, afraid	10	21
"Child's attitude"	5	0
Sincerity, conviction	2	5
Behavioural cues		
Body language	28	27
Eye contact	22	15
Eye movement	3	0
Facial expression	3	0
Other factors		
General background, history	6	5
Concept of truth, knowing right from wrong	6	3
Consistency with other evidence, family info.	5	5
Age	5	5
Medical history/evidence	2	3

Perceptions of Jurors' Reactions to Child Witnesses

Respondents were asked to estimate typical jurors' reactions to child witnesses as compared to their reactions to an adult witness. They were asked about jurors' beliefs about child witnesses' suggestibility, sincerity, ability to remember events, and the extent to which inconsistencies in testimony would lower a child's or an adult's credibility in the courtroom, as well as whether a jury is more likely to convict if the eyewitness is a child or an adult. More than the other groups, defense attorneys asserted that jurors are influenced by child witnesses. Most defense attorneys (67%) felt that a child's credibility is less damaged by inconsistencies than an adult's would be, a sentiment shared by only 33–46% of the members of the other groups. A substantial number of defense attorneys (37%) believed that a jury is *more* likely to convict if the eyewitness is a child than if it is an adult; fewer members of the other groups (18–24%) felt this way. In sum, defense attorneys, whose task may often be made difficult by child witnesses for the prosecution, are more likely to see these children as able to strongly influence a jury.

When asked to estimate the age at which a child becomes as believable to jurors as an adult, the groups differed significantly ($F(3,554) = 3.66, p < 0.02$). Both prosecutors and law officers gave mean estimates of 11.6 years old, while defense attorneys' and child workers' mean age estimates were higher (12.9). The defense attorneys' relatively high age estimate, implying that younger children will not be believed as readily as adults, seems to contradict their other assertions that jurors are highly influenced by child witnesses.

Alternative Ways of Eliciting and Presenting Children's Testimony

We listed eight methods that have been proposed as alternative ways to admit testimony from or about children who are victims or witnesses in alleged crimes of sexual abuse. The methods are generally intended to spare the child the trauma of live courtroom testimony and cross-examination. When asked how acceptable, in principle, each alternative method was, enormous differences appeared between the defense attorneys and the other three groups. Over 80% of the defense attorneys disapproved of all but one of the methods: a slight majority (51%) approved of testimony with the aid of anatomically correct dolls and other props. In contrast, the other three groups of subjects strongly approved of a range of alternative methods. In descending order of approval rate, the methods (with percentage of these respondents approving of it) were: testimony with the aid of anatomically correct dolls (89%), hearsay evidence of medical doctor (89%), hearsay evidence of psychologist (83%), videotaped testimony (82%), hearsay evidence of teacher (77%), hearsay evidence of parents (72%), hearsay evidence of other children (62%), and written testimony of child's account (50%). Values of eta-squared ranged from 0.30 to 0.37 across the four groups for seven of the eight methods.

In order to ascertain how attorneys react to disputed child witness testimony, the attorneys were asked to consider a trial in which their *opponent's* case included a child witness as an important component. They were given a list of six possible strategies and asked the extent to which they would employ each strategy (on a five-point scale from "never" to "always"). The defense attorneys estimated greater use of each of the strategies than did the prosecutors ($p < 0.001$ for four of the six strategies). The most widely endorsed techniques (attorneys said they would use each technique "often" or "always") were pointing out weaknesses in the child's testimony (97% of defense attorneys vs 76% of prosecutors) and, in closing arguments, stressing the youth of the witness and reasons to distrust the child's testimony (91% vs 51%). Stressing these same two factors in opening arguments (65% vs 31%) and stressing the child's vulnerabilities during cross-examination (67% vs 34%) were also favored by most of the defense attorneys. Interestingly, the two strategies that most directly involve psychology —citing psycholegal research (13% vs 10%) or bringing in a psychologist as an expert witness (12% vs 13%)—were not popular with either set of attorneys. In part, the unenthusiastic responses to the latter strategy may have reflected attorneys' knowledge that in Florida expert testimony by psychologists on such matters has usually not been admitted by trial judges.

We looked at several demographic variables—age, race, gender, and educational level—to see if they consistently influenced responses. No consistent differences emerged for age, education, or race, but gender had some consistent effects. Within the child protection worker sample, males gave significantly higher estimates than females ($p < 0.001$) of the likelihood that a child witness's account would be exaggerated or fabricated. Across all samples combined, males saw a significantly greater likelihood ($p < 0.05$) that child witnesses' testimony would be distorted or exaggerated. Across all samples, women saw a greater likelihood that children would retract allegations of sexual abuse ($p < 0.01$). Women also saw several of the possible reasons for retraction as significantly more likely than men did: family pressure, fear of retaliation, embarrassment about the incident(s), feelings of responsibility or guilt, and the desire to protect other family members.

DISCUSSION

Professionals' views of child witnesses in the legal arena appear to be strongly related to professional role. Defense attorneys evaluated child witnesses very differently from prosecuting attorneys, child protection workers, and law enforcement personnel. For most issues the latter three groups, despite differences in level of education, gender representation, and professional duties, viewed child witnesses in similar ways. In general, these groups had more confidence in child witnesses' ability to remember accurately, testify appropriately, and resist suggestion than did the defense attorneys. The defense attorneys stated that children are likely to give completely inaccurate or distorted testimony about sexual abuse almost one-fifth of the time but the other three groups believed this to be a rare occurrence. The child protection workers were particularly sensitive to the possibility that children might underestimate the extent of sexual abuse.

In recent years there has been growing concern about children who are caught in the midst of acrimonious divorce or child custody or visitation disputes and may be pressured to invent, exaggerate, or deny instances of sexual abuse. Benedek and Schetky (1985) were unable to confirm allegations of sexual abuse in 55% of a sample of cases involving custody or visitation disputes. Raskin has noted that his polygraph examinations on persons accused of sexual abuse of children during the period 1983-87 indicated 79% truthful outcomes (denials), a substantial increase from a 50% truthful rate observed from 1974 to 1982 (Raskin & Yuille, 1989). Given this concern with the truthfulness of child witnesses in these situations, professionals' abilities to tell if a child is lying become particularly salient. Most of our child protection workers and law officers felt that they could "usually" tell when a child was telling the truth. But there was little consensus about useful cues to deception. Body language and eye contact were second and third most frequently mentioned cues, after consistency of the child's statement. Respondents generally did not specify what aspects of body language they noticed, so it is not possible to compare their assumptions with the research findings regarding bodily cues to deception (Ekman & O'Sullivan, 1989). The frequent use of eye contact as a cue is interesting, inasmuch as research suggests that eye contact may not be a valid indicator of deception (DePaulo et al, 1985).

The gender difference on possible reasons for retracting an allegation of sexual abuse, where women saw several reasons for retraction as more likely than men did, might reflect cultural differences. One might speculate, as did Leippe et al (1989), in line with overall gender differences observed in western culture (Eagly & Wood, 1991), that most female professionals might have warmer, more empathic styles of working with child witnesses than their male counterparts. They might, as a result, evoke a greater degree of self-disclosure from children, revealing a more complete picture of the reasons for a retraction. In addition, given the research findings that women tend to read nonverbal cues better than men (Hall, 1984), they might be more likely to infer fear or embarrassment from the nonverbal behavior of child witnesses who are recanting than men would. These explanations must remain at the level of speculation until they can be tested empirically.

Our results indicate that professionals have different views of the problems with child witness evidence and ways of eliciting that evidence in courts of law with minimal trauma to the child. The US Supreme Court struck down a procedure that had permitted placing a screen between the defendant and his alleged sexual abuse victims, two teenaged girls, while each of the girls testified (Coy v. Iowa, 1988). The Supreme Court opined that the screen violated the defendant's Sixth Amendment right to confront his accuser and also might have set up a presumption of guilt in the jurors' minds. However, the Court recently approved the use of one-way closed circuit television with child witnesses if it is established that the child would otherwise suffer serious emotional distress such that the child could not reasonably communicate in court (Maryland v. Craig, 1990). Use of a videotaped recording in place of live testimony by the child is now allowed in England (*Report of the Advisory Group on Video Evidence*, 1989) and encouraged in Scotland (*Report on the Evidence of Children and Other Potentially Vulnerable Witnesses*, 1990). Our results suggest that, with the exception of defense attorneys, most US professionals involved with child witnesses in the legal system will welcome alternative procedures.

Professionals' attitudes undoubtedly play an important role in their treatment of child witnesses. In discussing the attorneys' response in the current survey as reported by Leippe et al (1989), Bulkley (1989) commented on defense attorneys' skepticism about child witnesses, suggesting that "The situation however, may be much worse than the [attorney] survey indicates. Not only may defense attorneys be more likely to view children with greater skepticism, but some are disseminating erroneous information despite awareness of current research" (p. 217). Bulkley cited two articles devoted to false allegations of child sexual abuse in legal magazines for defense attorneys (Renshaw, 1986; Slicker, 1986) that appeared to misuse and overstate the research findings in the direction of discrediting child witnesses.

We can speculate that the significant differences in attitudes between defense attorneys and prosecutors may have resulted from the different job demands involved in these careers. Defense attorneys are often called to defend alleged perpetrators against the incriminating accounts of eyewitnesses. Perhaps the skepticism needed for this role generalizes to attitudes regarding eyewitness memory, while the necessity to believe eyewitnesses that support one's case may result in prosecutors trusting eyewitness testimony to a greater extent. If attorneys' behavior and roles affect their opinions of child witnesses, these opinions probably in turn affect the way the attorneys act toward witnesses and jurors, which may influence the performance and believability of the witness.

Since professionals often have to deal with accusations that a child is lying, particularly in cases of alleged sexual abuse and acrimonious divorce, custody, and visitation disputes, forensically relevant studies on this issue will be of great value. Thus far, the results of the few studies that have attempted to mimic the major situational pressures inherent in such situations have not been clear-cut and, further, are not well known in the professional community. Thus, for example, in a recent chapter on children and deception written for clinicians, Quinn (1988) cited none of the experimental work discussed in the present chapter. She concluded that, "As a general guideline, children under the age of 6 have been shown to be unable to lie successfully" (p. 116). This conclusion appears both oversimplified and premature.

SUMMARY

In conclusion, the results of this survey have provided a great deal of information on the attitudes and opinions of the chief groups of professionals called upon to work with child witnesses. Each of the groups, defense attorneys, prosecuting attorneys, child protection workers, and law enforcement personnel, have a different role and therefore potentially different opinions. By far the most striking difference was that defense attorneys were much more skeptical of a child witness's ability to remember accurately, testify appropriately, and resist suggestion than were the other professionals. Child protection workers and law enforcement personnel felt they could "usually" tell if a child is lying, though little consensus on useful clues to deception was found. A gender difference was observed, as women viewed several reasons for retractions of accusations of sexual abuse as more likely. The use of alternative procedures for eliciting and presenting child testimony is becoming more common and was supported by all the groups but the defense attorneys. The survey results enable us to evaluate the beliefs and behaviors of professionals who encounter child witnesses in an attempt to further understand these witnesses' current treatment, as this treatment will surely affect the children's witness skills.

ACKNOWLEDGEMENTS

We are grateful to Catherine C. Brandt and Lori Merchant for their help in the data-gathering and analysis phase of this study. We would also like to thank Casey Schmidt for his comments on earlier drafts.

REFERENCES

Altman, M. J. & Lennon, D. (1986). Child witnesses in felony trials—competency and protection. *New York Law Journal*, 1–3.

Benedek, E. P. & Schetky, D. H. (1985). Allegations of sexual abuse in child custody and visitation disputes. In D. H. Schetky & E. P. Benedek (Eds). *Emerging Issues in Child Psychiatry and the Law*. New York: Brunner Mazel.

Berliner, L. & Barbieri, M. K. (1984). The testimony of the child victim of sexual assault. *Journal of Social Issues*, 40(2), 125–137.

Bottoms, B. L., Goodman, G. S., Rudy, L., Port, L., England, P., Aman, C. & Wilson, M. E. (1989). Children's testimony for a stressful event: improving children's reports. Paper presented at the American Psychological Association, New Orleans, La, August 1989.

Brigham, J. C. & WolfsKeil, M. P. (1983). Opinions of attorneys and law enforcement personnel on the accuracy of eyewitness identifications. *Law and Human Behavior*, 7(4), 337–349.

Bulkley, J. A. (1989). The impact of new child witness research on sexual abuse prosecutions. In S. J. Ceci, D. F. Ross & M. P. Toglia (Eds), *Perspectives on Children's Testimony*. NY: Springer–Verlag, pp. 208–229.

Ceci, S. J., Ross, D. F. & Toglia, M. P. (1987a). Age differences in suggestibility: narrowing the uncertainties. In S. J. Ceci, M. P. Toglia & D. F. Ross (Eds). *Children's Eyewitness Memory*. New York: Springer-Verlag, pp. 78–91.

Ceci, S. J., Ross, D. F. & Toglia, M. P. (Eds). (1989). *Perspectives on Children's Testimony*. New York: Springer-Verlag.

Ceci, S. J., Toglia, M. P. & Ross, D. F. (Eds). (1987b). *Children's Eyewitness Memory*. New York: Springer-Verlag.

Clarke-Stewart, A., Thompson, W. & Lepore, S. (1989). Manipulating children's interpretations through interrogation. Symposium at the meeting of the Society for Research in Child Development, Kansas City, MO, April 1989.

Coy v. Iowa (1988). 56 U.S.C.W. 4931.

Dent, H. R. (1982). The effects of interviewing strategies on the results of interviews with child witnesses. In A. Trankell (Ed.). *Reconstructing the Past*. Stockholm: Nordstedts, pp. 279–298.

Dent, H. R. (1991). Experimental studies of interviewing child witnesses. In J. L. Doris (Ed.). *The Suggestibility of Children's Recollections*. Washington, DC: APA, pp. 138–146.

DePaulo, B. M., Stone, J. I. & Lassiter, G. D. (1985). Deceiving and detecting deceit. In B. R. Schlenker (Ed.). *The Self in Social Life*. New York: McGraw-Hill, pp. 323–370.

Doris, J. L. (Ed.) (1991). *The Suggestibility of Children's Recollections*. Washington, DC: APA.

Eagly, A. H. & Wood, W. (1991). Explaining sex differences in social behavior: a meta-analytic perspective. *Personality and Social Psychology Bulletin*, 17, 306–315.

Ekman, P. & O'Sullivan, M. (1989). Hazards in detecting deceit. In D. C. Raskin (Ed.). *Psychological Methods in Criminal Investigation and Evidence*. New York: Springer, pp. 297–332.

Faller, K. C. (1984). Is the child victim of sexual abuse telling the truth? *Child Abuse and Neglect*, 7, 473–481.

Goodman, G. S. (1984). Children's testimony in historical perspective. *Journal of Social Issues*, 40(2), 9–32.

Goodman, G. S. & Reed, R. S. (1986). Age differences in eyewitness testimony. *Law and Human Behavior*, **10**, 317–332.

Goodman, G. S., Rudy, L., Bottoms, B. & Aman, C. (1990). Children's memory and concerns: issues of ecological validity in the study of children's testimony. In R. Fivush & J. Hudson (Eds). *Knowing and Remembering in Young Children*. New York: Cambridge University Press.

Hall, J. A. (1984). *Nonverbal Sex Differences: Communication Accuracy and Expressive Style*. Baltimore: Johns Hopkins University Press.

Leippe, M R., Brigham, J. C., Cousins, C. & Romanczyk, A. (1989). The opinions and practices of criminal attorneys regarding child eyewitnesses: a survey. In S. J. Ceci, M. P. Toglia & D. F. Ross (Eds). *Children's Eyewitness Memory*. New York: Springer-Verlag, pp. 100–130.

Maryland v. Craig (1990). 110 S. Ct. 3157 111 LED 2d. 666.

Melton, G. B. & Thompson, R. A. (1987). Getting out of a rut: detours to less travelled paths in child-witness research. In S. J. Ceci, M. P. Toglia & D. F. Ross (Eds). *Children's Eyewitness Memory*. New York: Springer-Verlag, pp. 209–229.

Myers, J. E. B. (1987). The child witness: techniques for direct examination, cross-examination, and impeachment. *Pacific Law Journal*, **18**(3), 801–942.

Peters, D. P. (1991). The influence of stress and arousal on the child witness. In J. L. Doris (Ed.). *Suggestibility of Children's Recollections*. Washington, DC: APA, pp. 60–76.

Quinn, K. M. (1988). Children and deception. In R. Rogers (Ed.). *Clinical Assessment of Malingering and Deception*. New York: Guildford, pp. 104–119.

Raskin, D. C. & Yuille, J. C. (1989). Problems in evaluating interviews of children in sexual abuse cases. In S. J. Ceci, M. P. Toglia & D. F. Ross (Eds). *Children's Eyewitness Memory* . New York: Springer-Verlag, pp. 184–207.

Renshaw, D. C. (1986). When sex abuse is falsely charged. *The Champion*, **5**(1), 8–10.

Report of the Advisory Group on Video Evidence (1989). London: Home Office.

Report on the Evidence of Children and Other Potentially Vulnerable Witnesses (1990). Edinburgh: HMSO.

Slicker, W. D. (1986). Child sex abuse: the innocent accused. *Case and Comment*, **12**, 12–20.

Yarmey, A. D. & Jones, H. P. T. (1983). Is the study of eyewitness identification a matter of common sense? In S. Lloyd-Bostock & B. R. Clifford (Eds), *Evaluating Witness Evidence*. Chichester: Wiley, pp. 13–40.

Zaragoza, M. (1987). Memory, suggestibility, and eyewitness testimony in children and adults. In S. J. Ceci, M. P. Toglia & D. F. Ross (Eds). *Children's Eyewitness Memory*. New York: Springer-Verlag, pp. 53–78.

CHAPTER 7

Reforming the Law on Children's Evidence in England: The Pigot Committee and After

J. R. Spencer

University of Cambridge

BACKGROUND

In recent years the rules of criminal evidence in England have been attacked for making it needlessly hard for children to be heard as witnesses, or if they are heard believed. The following matters, in particular, have been the subject of repeated comment.

The Competency Requirement

On principle, all evidence in criminal proceedings in England must be given on oath, and no one is permitted to take an oath unless they understand what is meant by one. Whereas an adult is presumed to have this level of understanding, a child under the age of 14 is not, and must be questioned on the subject by the judge before being permitted to give evidence. If questioning shows that a child "of tender years" does not understand the nature of an oath, section 38 of the Children

Children as Witnesses. Edited by H. Dent and R. Flin
© 1992 John Wiley & Sons Ltd.

and Young Persons Act 1933 allows the court to receive the child's evidence unsworn, provided "he is possessed of sufficient intelligence to justify the reception of the evidence, and understands the duty of speaking the truth". On the face of it, this test does not look particularly onerous. In practice, however, this competency test as interpreted in England has imposed a very severe restriction on the ability of the courts to receive the evidence of little children, because in the case of *Wallwork* (1958) 42 CrApR 153, the Court of Criminal Appeal held that it was not proper for a judge to allow a child as young as five to give evidence.

Taken together with the hearsay rule, which prevents the court hearing a young child's account of an incident from the mouth of an adult to whom she told it, the competency requirement as glossed in this case made it almost impossible to prosecute anyone for a sexual offence against a little child, unless he was foolish enough to abuse the child in the presence of an older witness or to confess what he had done.

In 1990 there was an important change of judicial tune in the case of *R v Z* [1990] 3 WLR 113, where the Court of Appeal condemned the idea of a fixed age below which a judge may not find the competency requirement satisfied. The reason such a limit had been imposed, they said, was the fear that the stress of giving evidence would be bad for the child, and the fear that a young child's evidence was so untrustworthy that to admit it would invariably be bad for justice, but recent changes had made these two fears obsolete. The live videolink had now made the process of giving evidence less stressful for the child, and there was "an increasing belief that the testimony of young children, when all precautions have been taken, may be just as reliable as that of their elders". The Court of Appeal made it clear that if the judge in a case is satisfied with the answers a young child gives in the course of a competency examination he may allow the child to give evidence.

The decision in *R v Z* makes the competency requirement less of an obstacle to children giving evidence, but it certainly does not remove it altogether. The judge is still obliged to question the child, and must reject him as a witness if he fails to show that he "understands the duty of speaking the truth". And it is probably significant that in the course of its judgment the Court of Appeal said "It may be very rarely that a five-year old will satisfy the requirements of section 38 (1)".

Open Court – Adversarial Examination

Where the child passes the competency examination, the next problem has always been that on principle he has to give evidence under the same conditions as an adult—testifying live, on the day of the trial, in open court, in the presence of the defendant, and then subjecting himself to an adversarial cross-examination. These conditions are stressful for many adults. They prevent many children giving evidence at all.

In the last few years some significant changes have been made, and it is no longer true that children must give their evidence under exactly the same conditions as adults. Starting with a case at the London Central Criminal Court in 1987, the practice has grown up of allowing a child witness to give evidence from behind a screen that stops her having to look at the defendant as she does so, a practice that eventually received the formal approval of the Court of Appeal in 1990 (*R v X, Y & Z* (1990) 91 CrApR 36). Meanwhile, Parliament had passed the Criminal Justice Act 1988, section 32 of which permits children under the age of 14 to give evidence in trials in the Crown Court for offences of sex and violence by means of a live videolink. During 1989 this provision was brought into force in certain courts experimentally and a team of researchers appointed to monitor progress (see Davies and Westcott, Chapter 13, this volume).

To a limited extent, the courts have also tried to address the problem that a child witness sometimes finds the adversarial procedure so stressful that she breaks down in the course of giving evidence. In two recent decisions the Court of Appeal has held that it is proper for the judge to intervene and stop the examination, and where this is done it does not have the legal effect of making the evidence of that witness inadmissible (*Stretton* (1988) 86 CrApR 7, *Wyatt* [1990] Crim LR 343).

At present, however, the child, like the adult witness, is still expected to give evidence live on the day of trial. This is the source of a number of serious problems, particularly if the child was the victim of a serious and unpleasant offence. The prospect of giving evidence may hang over the child disturbingly, and at the trial she will inevitably be reminded of an experience that she ought to be allowed to forget. Furthermore, the need to give evidence may seriously hinder the start of treatment for the victim. If the child is allowed to talk the matter through with a "counsellor", there is the risk that her evidence becomes "contaminated"—or at any rate the risk that the defence will say that this has happened; and if the counselling enables the child to put the incident behind her, she may then prove an inefficient witness at the trial. And at the trial, which may be many months afterwards, the child is expected to tell the tale afresh, unaided by any previous statement she or he has made, which means that the evidence the court receives may be diminished in value by the effect of time on the child's memory, or the fact that she has been discussing the case with others (Flin & Spencer, 1991).

For these reasons, therefore, there seems much to be said for a system under which the evidence of children is routinely taken in advance of trial. In fact, a procedure to allow this to be done already exists, theoretically, in sections 42 and 43 of the Children and Young Persons Act 1933. These provide that where a court appearance would involve serious danger to the child's life or health, a magistrate may examine the child in advance of trial, and, provided the defence were given an opportunity to put their questions, a written transcript of this examination may then be used as a substitute for live testimony from the child. Although these sections have been on the statute book since 1894, however, they are rarely if ever used. The various reasons for this have been explained elsewhere (Spencer & Flin, 1990, ch. 4).

The Rule Against Hearsay

A prominent feature of the law of criminal evidence in England is the rule against hearsay. This provides that a fact may not be established by calling A, who did not see or hear it, to tell the court that he heard B, who did, describe it; either B must be called to describe it to the court or the incident must be proved by other means. The rule, surprisingly, extends not only to oral statements which those who heard them repeat from memory, but also to statements preserved in documents, and even to statements recorded on audio or videotape. (As far as the law is concerned a tape-recorder is not a mechanical device enabling an absent human witness to communicate with the court, but a mechanical witness who is trying to repeat from memory what somebody else has told it.)

There are a number of important exceptions to the hearsay rule and these have been widened considerably in recent years. The courts have recently decided to accept hearsay evidence of what the victim of a serious and frightening offence said immediately after it took place (*Andrews* [1987] AC 281), and Parliament has enacted sections 23–26 of the Criminal Justice Act 1988, one of the effects of which seems to be that a criminal court may now receive the written or tape-recorded statement of a witness who is too frightened to give live evidence at trial (*R v Acton J. J.* (1991) 92 Cr Ap R 98). Despite these exceptions, however, the hearsay rule still largely prevents adults repeating to the court what a child has told them about a criminal offence. This, when taken in conjunction with the competency requirement, causes great difficulties in child abuse cases. The competency requirement prevents the court from hearing an account of the incident from the mouth of the child itself, and the hearsay rule stops the court hearing an account second-hand from an adult. The usual result, inevitably, is that a child molester goes unjustly free, but as these rules apply equally to the defence they can also cause an innocent person to be wrongly convicted.

The leading case in this area is *Sparks v R* [1964] AC 964, where a white man was prosecuted for indecently assaulting a little girl of three—and he was not permitted to call evidence that immediately after the incident the child had described her assailant as black.

The hearsay rule bars not only evidence of out-of-court statements by non-witnesses, but evidence of previous out-of-court statements made by those who do give evidence at trial. This extension to the hearsay rule is odd, because the previous statements of those who give evidence at trial are not open to the main objection to hearsay evidence in general: that the maker of the statement is not before the court and so not available for cross-examination. The other risk with hearsay evidence is that the person giving evidence of what was said misreports it. With previous statements by witnesses this risk may indeed be present, but even where the previous statement is accurately preserved on videotape, with every nuance of tone and gesture, it is still excluded by the hearsay rule.

An exception to the rule excluding evidence of previous statements that is sometimes helpful to the child witness involves what are known as "recent complaints". Where the complainant gives evidence in a sex case, the prosecution is permitted to supplement the complainant's evidence in court with evidence of what he or she said to bring the incident to light. This exception is limited in scope, however, because it only applies where the statement was made spontaneously and at the earliest possible moment. Furthermore—for no intelligible reason—it only covers complaints of sexual offences.

In contrast, a hearsay exception that can be very damaging for child witnesses involves previous inconsistent statements. Although the party calling a witness is usually forbidden to lead evidence of any previous consistent statement to supplement or support what his witness says in court, his opponent is permitted to make use of any previous inconsistent statement to undermine credibility.

Thus, to summarize, the position with the hearsay rule and previous statements of child witnesses is this. A child who has told her tale to the police or to the social services, even several times, is expected to repeat it in the witness-box from memory afresh, probably under stress; her previous statement may neither replace her courtroom evidence nor supplement it; but if it differs in some way from what she says in court, as it probably will, it may be used to destroy her in cross-examination.

Corroboration

If, despite the difficulties just mentioned, a child's evidence is put before a criminal court, the rules about corroboration reduce the chance of its being accepted and acted upon.

Until 1988 there were three related and interlocking rules. First, by section 38 Children and Young Persons Act there could be no conviction on the uncorroborated evidence of a child who gave evidence unsworn, however convincing his or her evidence might be. Secondly, by a judicial gloss on that statute, the corroboration had to consist of something other than the unsworn evidence of other children. Thirdly, there was a judge-made rule that whenever a child gave evidence— even when on oath—the trial judge must utter a warning about the danger of accepting it without corroboration.

Following widespread public criticism of these rules, and a review of the psychological evidence by the Home Office Research and Planning Department (Hedderman, 1987), the rules were abolished by section 34 of the Criminal Justice Act 1988.

As far as the unsworn evidence of children is concerned this section makes a major change. As regards the judicial duty to warn about the danger of accepting the evidence, however, the change is more apparent than real. This is because there is still in existence another judge-made rule which requires the trial judge to utter a warning against the danger of accepting the uncorroborated evidence of a sexual complainant. When children give evidence against adults, they commonly do so, unfortunately, as complainants in sexual cases, and consequently when most children give evidence it is still legally necessary to utter a warning about the danger of accepting their evidence.

Nobody knows exactly how warnings of this sort affect the willingness of juries to accept a piece of evidence, but the assumption, reasonably enough, is that it increases their reluctance to do so.

Suppression of the Fact that the Accused has Paedophile Tendencies

In England it is black-letter law that in a criminal trial the prosecution may not use against the defendant either the fact that he has a criminal record or any other evidence that shows that he merely has a tendency to break the criminal law. If evidence that happens to reveal the defendant's criminal record or criminal tendencies shows something else in addition to this, then in principle it is admissible although it incidentally reveals his general tendencies. This important qualification to the rule is easier to state than to apply, and a large and complicated body of case-law surrounds it. To cut a long story short, evidence that the defendant has paedophile tendencies was at one time regularly admitted in paedophile cases, but since the House of Lords decision of *DPP v Boardman* [1975] AC 421 it is now usually inadmissible unless it consists of incidents that are "strikingly similar" to what he is alleged to have done on the occasion the court is investigating. If the evidence "merely" reveals that he has sexual lusts of a particular and peculiar kind, that is not enough to make it admissible. Thus, for example, where a headmaster was on trial for buggering his teenage pupils it was not permissible for the prosecution to put before the court the fact that he had in his possession a videotape of two men committing buggery, plus a guide to the homosexual "meat-racks" of Paris (*Wright* (1990) 90 CrApR 325).

This rule is distinctly generous to defendants because in the nature of things evidence of paedophilia on a paedophile charge tells us something more important and more directly relevant than, say, evidence of previous dishonesty in a trial for theft or of previous violence in a trial for wounding or assault. Any competent child psychiatrist or paediatrician would want to discover whether any members of the child's family are known to have sexual tendencies towards children before giving an opinion on whether a child has been sexually abused, and a civil court would also wish to know this before making a decision on custody or access. The argument for the near total ban on such evidence in criminal cases, however, is that it is likely to inflame the hatred of the jury against the defendant.

If this is really the effect such evidence would have on a jury in a child-abuse case, however, it is surely as much an argument against using juries to try child abuse cases as it is against suppressing evidence of tendency.

(As this chapter goes to press, the recent House of Lords decision in *DDP v P* [1991] 3 WLR 161 adopts a more liberal approach to "similar fact evidence". The problems mentioned in this section may be less severe in future as a result.)

THE FORMATION OF THE PIGOT COMMITTEE

When in the autumn of 1986 the Bill was introduced which eventually became law as the Criminal Justice Acts 1987 and 1988, it contained a clause to introduce the live videolink. Encouraged by this, a number of pressure groups began to press for additional changes in the law relating to children's evidence. One of these—alterations to the rules about corroboration—the Government conceded, and these duly found their way into the Criminal Justice Act 1988. A proposal to amend the rules about hearsay to make videotapes of earlier interviews with child witnesses admissible was not acceptable to the Government, however. It nevertheless attracted a large amount of influential support, and in June 1988—when the Criminal Justice Bill was in its final stages—this moved the Government to set up an official committee to look into videotaping further. The proper name of this committee was the Home Office Advisory Group on Video Evidence. It is usually known, after its chairman, as the Pigot Committee.

The chairman was the Common Serjeant, Judge Tom Pigot QC, the experienced Old Bailey judge who had first sanctioned the use of screens for child witnesses in October 1987. The other members of the group were a senior officer in the Metropolitan Police, a senior social worker, a barrister in practice at the criminal bar, and Jennifer Temkin, an academic lawyer who had recently published *Rape and the Legal Process*, a book which voices criticism of the way in which the legal system treats the victims of rape. The group had, in addition, the services of a secretary from the civil service, and observers from the Home Office and from the Crown Prosecution Service.

In theory, the Committee was tied down by terms of reference which were distinctly narrow. Their brief was:

> to look in greater depth than has so far been possible at the idea that video recordings of interviews with child victims (and possibly other victims of crime) should be readily admissible as evidence in criminal trials.

Furthermore, a public statement from the Minister, Mr John Patten, at the time the Committee was set up, made it clear that no proposals would be acceptable to the Government which trenched upon the defendant's right to cross-examine his accuser (para 2.22). Thus they were restricted not only as to the problems they were at liberty to examine, but also on the solutions they were free to offer.

However, this did not prevent the Committee taking a broad view of their task. They received oral and written evidence from a wide range of people, among whom child psychiatrists and psychologists, paediatricians and social workers and police officers were as prominently represented as people from the legal profession, and they studied how foreign legal systems cope with child witnesses by attending an international conference on children's evidence at Cambridge in June 1989 (Spencer et al, 1990). The breadth of the Committee's approach is shown in the closing words of Chapter one of their report.

> In this report we are concerned with aspects of the law which, in a democracy, cannot safely be left to politicians and lawyers alone.

Members of the general public have a deep significant and legitimate interest in these questions. We have attributed considerable weight to the views expressed to us by representatives of many organisations dedicated to the welfare of children. Their opinions are based upon wide experience and should not be lightly dismissed or stigmatised as anecdotal.

The Committee acted quickly: although the Home Office did not publish their Report until the end of December 1989, it was submitted to the Home Secretary in the autumn of that year. The initial 1000-copy print-run was soon exhausted, and the Report was hastily reprinted.

THE PIGOT COMMITTEE'S PROPOSALS

Competency

Competency, like most other issues, was not directly included in the Pigot Committee's terms of reference. It was immediately clear to them, however, that any proposals to make it easier for little children to give evidence by using videotape would be a waste of breath if they were still legally ineligible to give evidence once it had become practically possible for them to do so. This thought moved the Committee to examine the competency requirement. The Committee were convinced that the competency rule as interpreted in *Wallwork* (and as not yet reinterpreted *R v Z* [1990] 3 WLR 113—see above) made it impossible to prosecute for a number of serious offences of sex and violence committed against young children. The competency requirement, they decided, served no useful purpose whatsoever; and they recommended, not its revision, but its total abolition.

> A competence requirement is evidently only useful if by reference to the test which imposes it is possible to ascertain whether a child is likely to subsequently give a truthful and accurate account. We have failed to find any evidence that the existing requirement achieves this. Indeed it seems logical to suppose that a child who is not able to explain what the oath signifies, or what concepts like truth and duty mean, is rather less likely to be sophisticated enough to invent and consistently and successfully sustain falsehoods than other witnesses. Alternative formulations of the requirement are open to the same objection .... In principle it seems wrong to us that our courts should refuse to consider any relevant and understandable evidence. (para 5, 11–5, 12)

In their view, the court should listen to a witness of any age without first subjecting them to any test of eligibility. As the law stands, the judge can stand an adult witness down if it becomes clear in the course of his evidence that he is of unsound mind, incoherent or unable to communicate his evidence in some way that makes sense, and having done so he may direct the jury to disregard any evidence he has given. This, they said, is all that is needed to deal with child witnesses as well. But they did think that it might be a good idea if English judges, like their counterparts in Scotland, routinely warned child witnesses of the need to tell the truth.

Open Court – Adversarial Examination

The Pigot Committee was set up to consider whether videotapes of previous interviews with witnesses should be made more widely admissible.

This question they answered with a resounding "yes". And going much further, they said that videotaping makes it possible to create a radical new method of dealing with child witnesses which would do much to solve the problems caused by the need for evidence to be given in open court and under adversarial examination.

The scheme they put forward is most easily explained with the help of a simple diagram (see Figure 7.1).

The Committee proposed that when an allegation is made on which the evidence of a child is needed, the child should be examined, once only, under cooperative arrangements made between the police and the local social services department. The interview should be informal, but under controlled conditions. There should be an official Code of Practice incorporating the best methods of obtaining reliable information from children by questioning and the interviewers should be trained to follow it. This interview should be videotaped.

If at this interview the child accused someone of committing a criminal offence, and the police wanted to prosecute, the next stage would normally be for the person accused to be invited to view the tape of the interview at the police station. At the subsequent trial, if there was one, the videotape of the original interview would be admissible in evidence, and would replace the child's evidence "in-chief", unless a judge ruled it inadmissible because he felt that in all the circumstances the videotape was "more prejudicial than probative". Thus, if the police decided to prosecute after having interviewed the suspect, the next stage would be for the tape of the initial interview to be shown to a circuit judge to decide the question of admissibility. (The Committee envisaged child abuse cases being handled by a panel of specially selected judges, and the same judge being in charge of a case from start to finish.) The defence would be allowed to see the videotape, and

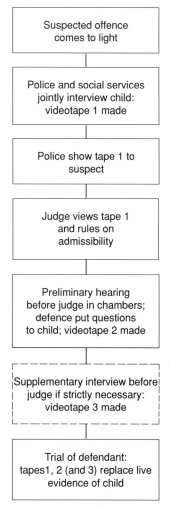

Figure 7.1. The Pigot Committee scheme. (Reproduced from Spencer & Flin, 1990 by permission of Blackstone Press Ltd)

would be able at this point to require a cross-examination. This would take place before the judge, in chambers, and with as much informality as possible. The only people present would be the judge, prosecution and defence counsel, the child, and the child's "support person". The defendant would not be present, but would be permitted to watch the proceedings from an adjoining room by means of a one-way mirror or a live videolink, and to communicate with his lawyer by means of a microphone in the lawyer's ear. The cross-examination session would also be recorded on videotape, and the tape would be shown to the court in place of the traditional in-court cross-examination. The cross-examination would be carried out as early as possible, in order to get around the problems of stress and fading memory caused by delay. If further matters then came to light which the defence wished to put to the child, the judge in charge of the case would have a discretion to hold a supplementary cross-examination, under conditions similar to the first, the tape of which would also be admissible in evidence.

Under the Pigot Committee scheme the child would still have to undergo an adversarial cross-examination, albeit in what would probably be less terrifying surroundings. On a number of measures designed to make this less of an ordeal for the child the Committee were unanimous: that the judge and the lawyers should not wear their wigs and robes, that defendants who refuse the services of counsel should not be able to insist on carrying out a cross-examination in person, and that the judge "should control the cross-examination with special care" (para 2.29).

There was disagreement, however, on the more radical idea of giving the judge the power, where children are very young or seriously disturbed, to order the defence to put their questions through some neutral person who enjoys the child's confidence (and who might, presumably, be the person who conducted the initial examination). The majority of the Committee were in favour of this proposal, but Anne Rafferty, the barrister, dissented, arguing that the right solution was to allow counsel to meet the child before the hearing—something which is at present forbidden by the Code of Practice of the Bar to avoid suspicion of advocates "sandpapering" the evidence (Miss Rafferty's dissent on this one point was the only disagreement in the whole Report).

The Committee proposed that the new scheme should be available where any witness aged under 14 gives evidence in a trial for an offence of violence, and where any witness under 17 gives evidence in a trial for a sexual offence. They also thought it should be available whether or not the young witness is alleged to be the victim of the offence. It should, they said, be the routine method, available whenever the prosecution wishes to use it, rather than an optional alternative available at the discretion of the judge.

The Committee recommended that initially the new scheme should apply in the Crown Court only, and that it should only be used in the magistrates' courts where a juvenile offender is tried for an offence against another child which would be serious enough to go to the Crown Court if the defendant was an adult; later on, consideration should be given to extending the scheme to summary trials.

As the law stands, a trial in the Crown Court is almost always preceded by "committal proceedings" in the magistrates' courts, at which the defendant has the legal right to insist on the prosecution producing their witnesses for a preliminary dose of adversarial examination. Committal proceedings in child abuse cases the Committee anathematized as "cumbersome, expensive, time-consuming", adding that "on occasions they are abused by the defence to deter witnesses from appearing at the subsequent trial or to undermine their confidence". Where child witnesses are involved they proposed that committal proceedings should be abolished altogether.

Hearsay

The Committee proposed no further exceptions to the hearsay rule proper. As their new scheme would have enabled most children to give evidence to the court in person by means of videotape, there was little need for them to propose further exceptions to the hearsay rule covering statements made by children who do not give evidence. They recognized there was something to be said for admitting in evidence the previous statements of those children who do give evidence, but felt this took them into general questions of criminal evidence which were beyond their terms of reference (para 2.8), and made no recommendation on the matter.

Corroboration – Evidence of Tendency

Although the question of corroboration lay nearly as far outside the Committee's terms of reference as evidence of a witness's previous statements, they felt that this was a matter, like competency, which had to be addressed if their main proposals were to have a chance of working properly. The duty to warn the jury of the "danger" of accepting the evidence of a sexual complainant is based, they said, on wholly outmoded views about the extent to which people make false complaints of sexual assault. The legal technicalities that surround the rule are such, they added, that "We suspect that many jurors find the whole exercise quite impenetrable" (para 5, 24). They therefore recommended that the duty to warn should be abolished. The Committee also noted that "where the only issue is the identity of the defendant it is sometimes suggested that there is an argument for allowing any previous convictions for similar offences against children to be put in evidence", but they felt this was too far removed from their terms of reference for them to consider it.

REACTION TO THE PIGOT COMMITTEE REPORT

On publication the Report evoked a leading article in the *Guardian* which was generally favourable—though doubting whether cross-examination at a preliminary hearing would really be much more relaxing for the child than cross-examination at the trial. Articles in the professional journals followed later, and these too were favourable (Sood & Stevenson, 1990; McEwan, 1990). As far as I am aware, no one then publicly attacked the Report, or even made more than minor public criticisms of it. The Home Secretary invited comments on the proposals, as a result of which the Home Office received something over 100 comments, roughly half from organizations. The Home Office does not publish such comments, but some of the commentators did so. Thus we know that the NSPCC was in favour, and also the Law Society, subject to certain reservations. The Report was also discussed at a number of conferences open to the public. At those that I attended the general reaction was certainly favourable. In the course of parliamentary debates, it was later revealed that both the Criminal Bar Association and the Council of Her Majesty's Circuit Judges were also in favour of the scheme.

In November 1990 the Government introduced a Criminal Justice Bill, which contained a number of important clauses about the evidence of children. These embody the Government's reaction to the Pigot Report.

In a number of important respects the Government accepted the arguments of the Pigot Committee in their entirety. There was a clause in the Bill intended to wipe out the competency requirement (although it may not achieve the desired effect: Spencer, 1990). Other clauses enabled committal proceedings to be bypassed in certain child abuse cases, and deprived the defendant of his right to give the child a "baptism of fire" at such committal proceedings as will remain. There was nothing in the Bill about corroboration; this was because the Law Commission was examining the whole question of corroboration (Law Commission, 1991).

However, the idea of using videotechnology to set up a new scheme relieving child witnesses of the need to give evidence in court—in other words, the central recommendation of the Pigot Committee—proved too radical for the Government, despite the widely based support the idea received. Instead of the Pigot scheme, the Bill contained a proposal to make videotapes of earlier interviews with children admissible in evidence in criminal cases—but strictly on condition that the child then comes to court on the day of trial to undergo a live cross-examination.

The Pigot scheme, it will be recalled, provided for the evidence of the child to be taken in two stages: stage one, the preliminary interview by a trained examiner, operating under an official Code of Practice, and stage two, a cross-examination carried out before a judge in chambers. On the face of it, the Bill did not even provide for stage one, because it contained nothing to make the videorecording of an initial interview with the child a routine procedure in a child abuse case—or to provide for the use of trained examiners, or for an official Code of Practice. All we found in the Bill was a clause saying that in a child abuse trial a videorecording—if one happens to have been made—shall be admissible; provided the judge gives leave, and provided it appears that the child will be available for cross-examination at trial. However, the Government has not abandoned stage one of the Pigot scheme as well as stage two. The Home Office is planning to organize an official set of instructions for conducting preliminary interviews with children, but means to do this informally by issuing an administrative direction—a "Home Office circular"—rather than by the more formal method of obtaining statutory powers to promulgate an official Code of Practice. From the Home Office point of view, the informal method has the advantage of flexibility: an unworkable provision in a Home Office circular can be revoked by merely issuing a new circular—an administrative step within the control of the Home Office itself—whereas it is impossible to amend a Code of Practice except by following the more complicated procedure for amendment that an Act of Parliament usually lays down. Another and an unofficial reason for proceeding in this informal manner may be a desire to avoid giving too much ammunition to defendants. At present, a Code of Practice made under the Police and Criminal Evidence Act 1984 governs the conduct of police interviews with suspects, and there is a feeling—at least among the police—that the courts too readily exclude evidence of what defendants said at interview because of fairly minor breaches of the Code. It may be felt that this is less likely to happen with breaches of a code that exists at a purely administrative level. The Government may also have it in mind to introduce the other features of stage one of the Pigot scheme by similar informal methods.

Stage two of the Pigot scheme—removing the cross-examination of the child from the trial itself to a private session taking place in chambers beforehand—was bound to be politically controversial. The vision of a barrister, fearless in the pursuit of truth, intervening at the last minute to save his client from a miscarriage of justice by means of a dramatic cross-examination that forces the prosecution witness to break down and admit his lies at trial has a powerful hold over the imagination of the public—and not least of that section of it which practises at the Bar, or did before it entered politics. Thus, if the Government decided to drop this part of the Pigot scheme it was not particularly surprising. But the reason it gave for doing so was depressingly defeatist. It said that if we have a scheme under which children are cross-examined at a preliminary hearing, provision would have to be made for a supplementary hearing to enable the defence to put to the child any new matters that came subsequently to light—and in practice this would mean a long series of such supplementary hearings, worse in total than a single helping of cross-examination conducted on the day of trial. As many people pointed out, this would not be the case if both the prosecution and the defence in a child abuse case could be persuaded to get their tackle in order early, although this would mean a significant change in the way in which business is conducted at the criminal Bar—which might be reflected in higher costs and a bigger bill for legal aid.

As supporters of the Pigot scheme made repeated attempts to get the bill amended in Parliament, it became clear that its real opponents were the Home Office; and that the main reason for their opposition was that they either agreed with, or were not prepared to argue with, a group of ultra-traditionalist barrister peers in the House of Lords who claimed it would undermine the position of the defendant. This was first, because it would make him disclose his defence ahead of trial, and secondly, because a child accuser is more likely to retract if cross-examined in the traditional way at trial than if this is done in chambers earlier. The answer to the first objection should have been that the only defendant to lose by revealing his defence ahead of trial is the guilty one. And the same answer should have been given to the second objection if, as is widely suspected, a traditional cross-examination can pressure a truthful child to retract a genuine accusation.

In the end, the attempt to get the Bill amended failed, and the Criminal Justice Act 1991 enacts the truncated version of the Pigot scheme as presented in the original Bill.

While it is pleasing that the Government decided to implement any part of the Pigot recommendations, the decision to reject this central feature of the Pigot scheme is disappointing. If making videotapes of early interviews with child witnesses is sufficient to increase the chance of convicting the guilty, only a change that enables the child to drop out of criminal proceedings early is significantly likely to reduce the stress that children suffer. Speaking broadly, and at the risk of some oversimplification, it means that the Government has pressed ahead with those parts of the Pigot scheme which make it easier to prosecute and punish child molesters but ditched those parts that would make it easier for the child.

REFERENCES

Flin, R. & Spencer, J. (1991). Do children forget faster? *Criminal Law Review*, March, 189–190.

Hedderman, C. (1987). *Children's Evidence: The Need for Corroboration.* London: Home Office Research and Planning Unit Paper 41.

Law Commission (1991). Law Commission No. 202, *Criminal Law – Corroboration in Criminal Trials*, Cm 1620. London: HMSO.

McEwan, J. (1990). In the box or on the box? The Pigot Report and Child Witnesses. *Criminal Law Review*, 363–370.

Report of the Home Office Advisory Group on Video Evidence (1989). (Pigot Committee Report). London: Home Office.

Sood, U. & Stevenson, K. (1990). Pigot: the need for a good look at videos. *Law Society Gazette*, **87**, 23.

Spencer, J. R. (1990). Children's evidence and the Criminal Justice Bill, *New Law Journal*, **140**, 1750.

Spencer, J. R. & Flin, R. H. (1990). *The Evidence of Children: The Law and the Psychology.* London: Blackstone.

Spencer, J., Nicholson, G., Flin, R. & Bull, R. (Eds) (1990). *Children's Evidence in Legal Proceedings – An International Perspective.* Cambridge Law Faculty.

Temkin, J. (1987). *Rape and the Legal Process.* London: Sweet and Maxwell.

CHAPTER 8

The Child Witness in Scotland

Gordon Nicholson

Sheriff Court House, Edinburgh

and

Kathleen Murray

University of Glasgow

INTRODUCTION

For more than 20 years the Scottish legal system has had a curious anomaly. During this time children who have committed offences or are in need of care and protection have been dealt with in a sympathetic, understanding and constructive manner, whereas children who appear as witnesses in the criminal courts have often had scant attention paid to their needs or their fears. The reason for this is that, in 1971, a new system of juvenile justice was introduced in Scotland to deal with children who are, for whatever reason, in trouble. That system, whose central principle is the promotion of the child's best interests, is described in detail later in this chapter. By contrast, the criminal justice system has tended, until comparatively recently, to treat child witnesses much like any other witness, and has made little attempt to alleviate the fear and anxiety which, as is now widely recognized, tend to be significantly more pronounced in child witnesses than in adult witnesses. The first part of this chapter will describe the place of child witnesses within the Scottish criminal justice system,

Children as Witnesses. Edited by H. Dent and R. Flin
© 1992 John Wiley & Sons Ltd.

and will show how significant changes have taken place in recent times, or are being contemplated for the future.

CHILD WITNESSES WITHIN THE CRIMINAL JUSTICE SYSTEM

Before considering how the position of child witnesses in Scotland has changed, and is changing, there are certain special features of the Scottish system which require to be mentioned. These relate to competency, to the need for corroboration, and to hearsay evidence.

Competency

Unlike the position in some other countries, where children below a certain age (often around seven) are never permitted to give evidence in criminal proceedings, there has never been any such restriction in Scotland, and it is by no means unknown for a child as young as three to give evidence in a criminal trial. It is, however, necessary for the trial judge to satisfy himself, by appropriate questioning of the child, that he or she can give evidence intelligibly and can understand the difference between truth and falsehood.

Corroboration

It is a general requirement of Scots law that every material fact which has to be proved in order to secure a conviction must be established by corroborated evidence, that is to say evidence coming from more than a single source. Unlike the position in some jurisdictions, this rule applies not only in respect of evidence given by children but in respect of all evidence. Although the corroboration requirement has recently been removed in relation to children in some countries (for example England and Wales), the view has been taken in Scotland that to remove the requirement only in relation to children would be unprincipled and anomalous. If the corroboration requirement is to be removed in Scotland, it would have to be removed across the board, but many Scottish lawyers would regard that as an unwise move.

Hearsay Evidence

Although hearsay evidence has recently become generally admissible in civil proceedings in Scotland (Civil Evidence (Scotland) Act, 1988), it is as a rule inadmissible in criminal proceedings. There are only two significant exceptions to that rule. A hearsay statement may be admitted in evidence where the maker of the statement is dead; and, where a witness gives evidence, an inconsistent prior statement made by him may be admitted, but only for the limited purpose of adversely affecting his credibility. As a result of these rules, a videorecorded interview with a child would not at present be admissible in Scotland in criminal proceedings unless it contradicted evidence given by the child in the course of a trial.

Moves Towards Reform

By the 1980s many people in Scotland were becoming increasingly concerned about the possible distress and trauma which could be occasioned to a child who was required to appear in open court and to recount distressing and embarrassing events not only in front of a judge, lawyers and court officials, but especially in front of the accused. As well as concern for the child, there was growing anxiety that in at least some cases, where children were simply unable to give their evidence in these circumstances, guilty people were managing to escape conviction. Consequently, when the Home Secretary, in 1987, proposed the introduction in England and Wales of a procedure to enable children to give evidence through the medium of a live closed circuit television link, there was a clamour for similar provision to be introduced in Scotland. However, the Lord Advocate, who is the senior law officer for Scotland, took the view that it would be preferable to have a comprehensive review of all the issues relating to child witnesses in Scotland, and he accordingly asked the Scottish Law Commission to carry out that review. (The Scottish Law Commission is a full-time statutory body responsible for providing government with proposals for law reform.)

The Scottish Law Commission made a detailed study of existing law and practice in relation to child witnesses both in Scotland and in other jurisdictions around the world and consulted widely on a series of preliminary, provisional proposals. Thereafter the Commission reassessed all the information before them and, in Feburary 1990, they published their final report (*Report on the Evidence of Children and Other Potentially Vulnerable Witnesses*, 1990).

In making recommendations for reform both in law and in practice, the Commission made several preliminary observations of a general nature. They recognized the need to offer children as much protection as possible from the more upsetting and traumatic aspects of giving evidence, but at the same time they regarded it as imperative that any new measures should not prejudice an accused person's right to a fair trial. In that connection they were particularly mindful of the provisions of Article 6 of the European Convention on Human Rights, which seeks to ensure that an accused person will be entitled to examine or have examined all witnesses against him. The Commission also expressed the general view, based largely on American experience, that, although special and sophisticated measures and techniques might be required in order to enable some children to give evidence confidently and without undue distress, the likelihood was that most children could probably give evidence in court by conventional means provided that they were suitably prepared in advance and that they were sensitively and helpfully dealt with in the courthouse itself.

Improvements in Existing Practices

For some years it was fairly common for judges and lawyers to try to reduce the formality of court proceedings while a child was giving evidence, for example by removing formal dress and by sitting together around a table rather than having the judge in an elevated position on the bench. Furthermore, in recent years prosecutors in Scotland have been paying more and more attention to the need to prepare a child for an appearance in court in the sense of explaining in advance what will be involved, and in some instances taking the child on a pretrial visit to the courtroom.

While applauding such initiatives, the Scottish Law Commission took the view that more could, and should, be done to reduce worry and anxiety for children giving evidence by conventional means. They accordingly recommended that:

(a)   The Lord Justice General (the most senior Scottish judge) should issue guidance to judges to promote greater consistency and uniformity of practice in relation to the removal of formal dress, allowing a child to give evidence from an informal position rather than from the witness-box, allowing a relative or other supporting adult to sit alongside a child while giving evidence, and clearing the court of non-essential persons while a child is giving evidence.

(b)   Cases where children are witnesses should be allocated to a courtroom which is as non-intimidating as possible.

(c)   Existing practices for preparing a child in advance for the experience of being a witness should be encouraged and extended.

(d)   Steps should be taken to ensure that children can be heard in court without having to be asked to speak up. This may involve the installation of appropriate sound amplification equipment, or it may involve allocating cases to courtrooms which are acoustically efficient.

(e) So far as practicable, children attending court as witnesses should be accommodated in waiting rooms from which all adults, other than those accompanying the children, are excluded. Waiting rooms should be supplied with a quantity of suitable furniture, toys, books and games for use by children.

In July 1990, following publication of the Commission's recommendations, the Lord Justice General of Scotland issued a memorandum to judges offering guidance as to the use of discretionary measures in cases where children are witnesses. (see Appendix)

Identification of an Accused

One ever-present problem in a criminal trial is that a child may at some stage be required to point to the accused and to identify him as, perhaps, her attacker or abuser. This, of course, is likely to be particularly traumatic for an already frightened child. In an attempt to meet this problem, and having in mind that in many instances a child will be doing no more than identifying someone who is very familiar and well known, the Scottish Law Commission recommended a notice procedure under which formal identification of an accused would not be necessary unless that were demanded by the accused. It was thought that an accused who demanded a visual identification without good cause would be unlikely to commend himself either to a judge or jury.

More Radical Reforms

Although accepting, as noted above, that many children would probably be able, without undue distress, to give evidence by conventional means, particularly if handled sensitively and constructively, the Scottish Law Commission none the less concluded that more radical measures were likely to be desirable in some cases. They took the view, however, that, unlike the position in some other jurisdictions, such radical measures should not be restricted only to children below a particularly young age or only to children who had been the victims of particular offences. In their view, any child required to give evidence might, depending on his or her circumstances, be likely to benefit from special measures. Accordingly, what they recommended were in effect three new techniques for taking evidence from children of any age and regardless of what it was that had brought about the need for the child to give evidence. Moreover, they concluded that it would be unwise to attempt to stipulate in advance the circumstances which would justify the selection of any one technique rather than another. Instead, they proposed that all of the techniques should be available on cause being shown, and it would then be for the judge to select the one which seemed likely to be most beneficial in the particular case. The three proposed techniques were as follows.

Pretrial Deposition

The Scottish Law Commission recommended that in future it should be possible to take a child's evidence in advance of a trial. While this would still be formal in the sense that there would be examination and cross-examination by lawyers, the proceedings would be in informal surroundings, possibly even in the child's own home. These proceedings would be videorecorded and the videorecording would be used at trial in place of live evidence by the child. This technique has been used for some years in some states in the USA, and experience there appears to suggest that it can be effective in some cases.

Screens in Court

At the moment screens are sometimes used in Scottish courts to shield a child from the sight of the accused. However, their use is at present unregulated, and the Scottish Law Commission took the view that some regulation is desirable. They recommended, so as to clear up any uncertainty, that it should be expressly provided that a court can order the use of screens despite any objection by an accused. However, they also recommended that, where screens are used, they should not prevent an accused from being able to watch the witness and to observe his or her demeanour while giving evidence. In practice, that means that either screens will have to be constructed of one-way glass, or alternatively a closed circuit television arrangement will have to be installed so that the accused can watch the witness on a screen.

Closed Circuit Television

Originally the Scottish Law Commission were not very enthusiastic about introducing into Scotland a system whereby a child could give live evidence from a separate room through the medium of closed circuit television. Their main concern was that feelings of isolation, coupled with exposure to a mass of electronic equipment, would be likely to be at least as distressing as appearing in court. Ultimately, however, it became clear that the equipment required for closed circuit television transmissions can be quite unobtrusive. Moreover, recent experience in England and Wales, where closed circuit television had been in use for about one year, suggested that in at least some cases it could be positively helpful in enabling a child to give evidence. Consequently, the Scottish Law Commission recommended that facilities for giving evidence through the medium of closed circuit television should be introduced in Scotland.

Prior and Videorecorded Statements

Mention has been made earlier of the restrictive nature of the rule against hearsay evidence in Scotland. As noted, one consequence of that rule is that, despite the increasing use being made elsewhere of videorecorded interviews with children, such videorecordings cannot at present be used in criminal proceedings in Scotland. The Scottish Law Commision took the view that it would not be desirable to admit such videorecordings, or indeed any other earlier statements by a child, as a substitute for live evidence by the child. However, they carefully considered the possibility of allowing prior statements, including videorecordings of interviews, to be used in order to supplement or confirm evidence given by a child either in court or by means of one of the other techniques described above.

Of course, one of the inherent problems about admitting hearsay evidence, even in the form of a prior statement by a person giving evidence, is that it may be inaccurately reported. Another difficulty is that the witness may deny having made the earlier statement, or may assert that he said something different.

To meet those difficulties the Scottish Law Commission recommended that, for a prior statement to be admissible, two requirements should be satisfied. First, the statement should be in a form, such as writing or a video- or audiorecording, from which it can reasonably be inferred that it accurately and completely records what was said on the previous occasion. Secondly, the statement should in effect be adopted by the witness as being true. Where these requirements were satisfied, the statement would be admissible not only in relation to credibility but also as evidence of any facts contained in the statement. The Scottish Law Commission took the view that this proposal would in future admit much valuable and reliable evidence, and might in some cases make it much easier to put the whole of a child's evidence before a court.

It should also be mentioned that the Commission realized that, in some cases where a prior statement has been given in the course of an interview, answers may have been in response to leading questions. It was recommended that this should not prevent the admissibility of the evidence, but should merely be a matter which a judge or jury could take into account when assessing the weight to be attached to the evidence.

Recent Reforms and Future Prospects

The report of the Scottish Law Commission did not of itself change the law in Scotland. The Government, having considered the recommendations contained in the report, introduced into a legislative bill clauses which would give effect to some of the Commission's proposals. The Law Reform (Miscellaneous Provisions) (Scotland) Act 1990, sections 56–60, now contains provision to enable the evidence of children to be given in Scottish courts through the medium of a live television link. The necessary equipment having now been installed in a selection of courthouses, that provision has been brought into effect. Where a child is giving evidence by means of a live television link the Act makes provision (section 58) to allow the accused to be identified by reference to a prior identification made by the child rather than identification in open court. It remains to be seen whether any or all of the Commission's other recommendations will be implemented in the future.

THE CHILDREN'S HEARINGS SYSTEM

The Origins

In April 1971, responsibility for dealing with children and young people in trouble was transferred under the terms of the Social Work (Scotland) Act, 1968, from the courts to a new and largely welfare-orientated system of "children's hearings". The new arrangements differed quite sharply from those prevailing in England and Wales as well as from the system that had previously been in force in Scotland. The plan had been proposed in 1964 in the report of the Kilbrandon Committee (as it came to be called, after the title of the High Court judge who chaired it) (*Report of the Committee on Children and Young Persons*, 1964). The Committee rejected the formality and stigma of criminal courts as providing an appropriate forum for dealing with young people in trouble with the law. Instead, it recommended bringing lay members of the community into the process of reaching disposition decisions about the children in question, establishing "the best interests of the child" as the criterion of good decision-making and giving responsibility for providing supportive social services to a group of specialist social workers attached to the local authority education department.

The 1966 White Paper, *Social Work and the Community*, stated the Government's intentions to implement the Kilbrandon proposals and at the same time to reshape quite fundamentally the personal social services of Scottish local authorities. Instead of a specialized family casework service being set up within the education authority, the White Paper proposed the creation of a comprehensive social work department which would among many other functions provide support for the children's panels. The new method for dealing with children in need of compulsory measures of care appeared in part III of the Social Work (Scotland) Act, 1968. A few amendments have been made by subsequent legislation but the legal and administrative framework remains in all important respects that of the 1968 Act and the Children's Hearings (Scotland) Rules, 1971 made under it.

The system was not designed to deal with all offenders; the small proportion (5% or less) who commit serious crimes appear before the sheriff courts. At the same time, the hearings system also responds to the problems of children who have not broken the law but are judged to be in need of care and protection because of neglect or injury by their parents.

Entering the System

Access to the system of children's hearings is controlled by reporters to children's panels employed by the regional and island authorities. Children are brought to the attention of the reporter by the police and procurator fiscal, by the education or social work department of the local authority, or indeed by any statutory or voluntary body or private individual who has reasonable cause to believe that a child may be in need of compulsory measures of care (which include protection, control, guidance and treatment). The conditions on which a child may be made the subject of compulsory measures of care are described in the statute as "grounds for referral". They are:

(a)   the child is beyond the control of his/her parents; or
(b)   the child is falling into bad associations or is exposed to moral danger; or
(c)   lack of parental care is likely to cause the child unnecessary suffering or to seriously impair the child's health or development; or
(d)   any of the offences mentioned in Schedule 1 to the Criminal Procedure (Scotland) Act 1975 has been committed in respect of

the child or in respect of a child who is a member of the same household; or

(dd) the child is, or is likely to become a member of the same household as a person who has committed any of the offences mentioned in Schedule 1 to the Criminal Procedure (Scotland) Act 1975; or

(e) the child, being a female, is a member of the same household as a female in respect of whom an offence which constitutes the crime of incest has been committed by a member of that household; or

(f) the child has failed to attend school regularly without reasonable excuse; or

(gg) the child misused a volatile substance by deliberately inhaling, other than for medicinal purposes, that substance's vapour; or

(g) the child has committed an offence; or

(i) the child is in the care of a local authority and his/her behaviour is such that special measures are needed for his/her adequate care and control.

(Ground gg came into effect in July 1983; and ground i was introduced in January 1984.) Social Work Scotland Act 1968, Section 32(2) as amended.

The pattern of referrals to reporters has changed dramatically in recent years. A reduction in the number of young people entering the system on the basis of delinquency has been counterbalanced by a sharp increase in referrals on non-offence grounds, particularly child abuse and neglect (Social Work Services Group, 1989). Referrals alleging that the child lacks parental care or is at risk of harm increased steadily through the 1970s and 1980s, accounting in 1988 for 20% of all referrals. Indeed, "at risk" referrals increased by more than threefold between 1980 and 1988.

Having been informed of a child, the reporter alone decides what steps should next be taken. After considering the information provided by the referring agent, the reporter may conclude that no further action is required because there is insufficient evidence, and may therefore decide not to request any further reports. In most cases, however, the reporter will ask for a social background report from the social work department and a school report where relevant; less frequently, reports may be requested from more specialized sources. On the basis of the information made available the reporter must determine the best course of action: to take no action; to ask the social work department to advise, guide and assist the child and family on a voluntary basis; or to bring the child before a children's hearing (if the reporter is satisfied that there is sufficient evidence of at least one ground for referral, and if it appears to the reporter that the child is in need of compulsory measures of care).

Additional powers can be brought into play when a child is believed to be in imminent danger. A social worker (or a police officer, or an official of the Royal Scottish Society for the Prevention of Cruelty to Children) may apply to a Justice of the Peace or to a sheriff for an order by which a child may be removed from home to a place of safety. When such an order is executed, the reporter must be notified immediately and must convene an emergency hearing within seven days to confirm or discontinue the place of safety order.

When functioning as the system's intake official, the reporter exercises considerable discretion. This was recently commented upon by the Lord Chancellor of England: "Parliament has entrusted him (the reporter) with a very very wide discretion indeed, and I think it very unusual to have a provision of that kind for a public official, namely that he should have power to take no action at all on what has been referred to him. It is a discretion that is exercised actively and frequently" (Lord MacKay, 1988). Of the 37 545 referrals made to reporters in 1988, no action was taken in almost half of the cases. The proportion, however, varied between offence referrals and the remainder. No formal action was taken on 64% of offences but only on 49% of other referrals. The reasons commonly given for taking no action on non-offence grounds are that there is insufficient evidence on which to proceed to a hearing, or a compulsory supervision requirement is currently in force (Social Work Services Group, 1989).

What emerges clearly from studies of reporters' discretion (Martin et al, 1981) is their constant attempt, in child abuse cases, to strike a balance between excessive interference with the rights of parents to determine their child's upbringing and protecting the child who may be at risk of future harm. Incomplete and unstandardized though the information at their disposal undoubtedly is, reporters are concerned to derive from it the best estimate possible of both the stresses and supports in the child's background as an essential component of their decisions.

The Children's Panel

At the heart of the hearings system is the work of "children's panels", or bodies of lay volunteers. These are recruited in each local government region and have at present about 1800 members in Scotland as a whole. Individual panels vary in size from 15 in Shetland to close on 900 in Strathclyde. A heavy responsibility rests with the Children's Panel Advisory Committees, who annually recruit and select new panel members for their area. In their scrutiny of applicants they attach particular importance to an ability to put people at their ease and to open up discussion. It is a great pity that there have been so few systematic descriptions of selection procedures and no attempts whatever to evaluate their effectiveness.

From the panels are made up groups of three members before whom individual children appear, accompanied normally by one or both parents and the social worker in the case. The child and parents are first asked whether they accept the grounds for referral. If these are denied by either the child or parent, or if the child is unable to understand the grounds, the hearing, if it does not proceed to discharge the case, must refer it to a sheriff for a decision on the facts. A high proportion of all grounds for referral involving abuse and neglect need to be tested in the sheriff court, either because they are denied by a parent or because the child is too young to understand them. Only if the sheriff confirms that the grounds for referral are valid can the hearing reconvene to decide what measures to take. A decision is then made as to whether a period of supervision by a social worker is desirable, whether the child should be required to enter a residential school or home, or whether the referral should be discharged.

A supervision requirement, with or without a residential condition, must be reviewed within a year, and may be reviewed sooner if requested by the child, parent or local authority. The child or parents may appeal to the sheriff against the decision of a hearing and, from the sheriff, on a point of law or irregularity, to the Court of Session, the highest court in Scotland. Since children's hearings are classified as tribunals, legal aid is not available for the hearing itself but may be available for the court proceeding whether at proof or in the event of an appeal.

If the hearing members feel that even with more substantial and more relevant information they are still not in a position to determine how the child's interests can best be served, there may be a possibility of seeking an independent opinion. That possibility was created by sections 66 and 103 of the Children Act 1975, which allow for the appointment of a child's representative or "safeguarder" in circumstances where the hearing chairman believes that there may be a conflict of interest between child and parents.

In reaching its decision the hearing is required to take into account not only the events specified in the statement of grounds for referral but also all relevant aspects of the child's circumstances. To that end the panel members have available social work and school reports, as well, on occasion, as reports from more specialized agencies; and they are expected before reaching a decision to involve the child and parents as fully as possible in discussion of the child's problems and of the most appropriate outcome. Above all, they are required to make a disposal that is in the best interests of the child. No one would seriously argue that these "best interests" can always be precisely determined within the limited range of alternative disposals available to the hearings. But the injunction is at the very least a clear reminder that their concern is not with retribution or deterrence or the protection of the community.

The Child in the Hearing

The formal court organization has therefore been replaced in Scotland by what is intended to be a less intimidating forum where understanding of the process, contributing to it and even accepting its outcome have been specified as desirable aims. It is an implicit assumption that full and open discussion at hearings is more likely to give rise to a decision appropriate to the child's needs as well as to make that decision more readily acceptable to everyone concerned. Perhaps in part because the architects of the Scottish system were concerned to achieve humane goals within a child welfare framework rather than to follow a strict judicial model, the participation of clients was intended as an essential feature of the hearings. Moreover, the hearings are supposed to be conducted within a legal framework that also requires standards of fairness and justice to be met.

Children's comprehension of most aspects of the hearing process is quite high. The majority say that they have no difficulty in understanding the proceedings although some have difficulty with the way questions are asked and are confused by the remarks made by panel members, especially their use of particular words and the complex structure of their sentences. Indeed, observers have noted that children usually take an intent interest in the proceedings, and, when interviewed afterwards, commonly recall not only the titles of those present but often the names as well (Martin et al, 1981). This suggests that the introductions at the beginning of the hearing do succeed in personalizing the proceedings. In contrast, a number of studies of young people processed through North American juvenile courts have generally revealed many shortcomings in children's comprehension of and involvement in court proceedings (Scott, 1959). A similar finding has emerged from studies of the English juvenile court (Morris & Giller, 1977).

In the Scottish context, a study by Patricia Erickson (1982) has shown that children attach considerable significance to the hearing event and their reactions to it are very much affected by the practice of panel members. Children are quite aware of the outcome of their hearings, and relate it to the decision-making role of the panel members. This may not seem to be a noteworthy achievement for hearings until it is juxtaposed with results from other studies that show children appearing before judges or magistrates to be much less aware of the disposition or who made it.

Although the comments of children and parents who have passed through the system are not free of criticism, there is a high degree of agreement on the matter of participation. They have a sense of having been listened to, a sense of having been allowed to express themselves, a belief that panel members are genuinely interested in the views expressed and are helpful in their intentions. It seems clear that the level of informality achieved is greater than the family members expect and that they respond to this appreciatively, even though detached observers might be conscious of some discrepancies between aspiration and achievement. The satisfactory level of communication obtained in the hearing may be due in substantial measure to the fact that there is a strong concentration on safe and superficial matters. The evasions and limitations in the dialogue are understandable. To confront parents with their own shortcomings is the most difficult aspect of communication in the hearing and no-one could blame panel members for shrinking from the task.

Stress in the Hearing

When the system of children's hearings was established more than 20 years ago it was not deliberately with the intention of making hearings somehow less stressful an experience than going to court. Nevertheless, the basic underlying principles of the system have a number of elements that might lead one to expect that coming before a hearing is indeed on the whole less stressful than appearing before a court, if not a completely stress-free experience.

First, the people who appear at children's hearings are not lawyers or even magistrates in the full sense of the word: they are supposed to be fairly representative members of the community, a mixed body of ordinary people who have a high degree of acceptability in the eyes of their clients. Secondly, there is not an element of a trial—that is to say, panel members have no right to try to decide guilt or innocence. If the child denies committing the alleged offence, the sheriff has to determine whether or not there is a case to answer. The children's hearing only deals with the case if the grounds for referral are accepted or proved, and then it is a matter of deciding what is the best decision to make in the interests of the child. Thus, thirdly, the criterion of a good decision should be whether it advances the interests of an individual child. Finally, hearings are expected to avoid the extreme formalities of a court situation both in the physical layout and in the way in which the business is approached. It is also important to maximize opportunities for an open and honest discussion between the family and the panel members. All of these elements within the hearing seem to point away from any kind of high stress potential.

Nevertheless, on closer scrutiny, we can see that in spite of admirable intentions there are still a number of factors present which are stress potentialities. Many families are under noticeable stress when they are introduced. Panel members have to develop considerable skill to overcome such barriers as silence, reticence, fear or aggression. The hearing is not a meeting of equals, and would not be so even if there were less dissimilarity of social background than is at present generally the case. Although the hearing is not a court of law and does not have punishment as its aim, the child is present under compulsion and both the child and his or her parents are likely to take it for granted that they are present principally because the child is in some kind of trouble. There is a sense of wrongdoing, a sense of guilt though there is not going to be a trial. If the child fails to attend, a warrant can be issued to make sure that he or she does appear next time. Finally, of course, the panel members have powers which the parents do not have and their decisions have the force of law. One of their available dispositions is that the child should be removed from home and admitted to a residential school or home. By and large most parents and children do not want a residential decision, though just occasionally all are agreed that that is the best course of action. Therefore, ideas about what is in the child's best interests may not look exactly the same from both sides of the table.

The important question to ask is not just what are the potentials for stress avoidance but what actually happens in the live situation. The findings of research have pointed to indicators of stress in children in only a minority of cases (Martin et al, 1981, pp. 142–146). For example, it has been reported that only 5% of children and indeed of mothers burst into tears at some time during a hearing. In 10–15% of children there have been observations of behaviour clearly indicative of anxious, stressed moods. On the whole, however, the majority seem to react fairly calmly and to be able to participate without any great difficulty in the proceedings. When questioned afterwards, parents and children in most cases say they did not find the hearing experience stressful. About three-quarters of the children have nothing detrimental to say about their experience and almost none of the parents found it a difficult or painful exercise. The most common reaction was that they had come along expecting the hearing to be difficult, painful, stressful; they expected to be harangued and bullied. On the whole children were surprised and pleased by the sympathy and interest, and indeed respect, shown to them by panel members; in general it is a much less stressful experience than they come prepared for.

It has been alleged that a high price is paid for the comparative smoothness and the relatively low level of stress found in the hearing situation (Martin, 1981). In order to minimize stress the panel members are inclined to move away from potentially damaging confrontations with parents and may limit the dialogue of the hearing to safe topics. Unfortunately, the child and parents may not then be given the opportunity to comment on some of the allegations, to check unsubstantiated statements in reports, to correct and disagree with the information which is generally utilized by panel members in their decision-making. Although panel members cannot be blamed for hesitating to engage in their challenging task, in the long term it is important for parents and children to be aware of their responsibilities so that they can take an active part in the supervision process. Consequently, although at one level it is an attractive finding that children in the hearings system experience a very low level of stress, it should not be so low as to jeopardize the administration of justice and what the hearing and the subsequent supervision order are intended to achieve.

The informality of children's hearings and the simplicity of the settings in which almost all of them are conducted are intended, among other things, to avoid humiliating and degrading young people and their families. Interviews with children and parents make it clear that the participants do not see the experience as confusing, remote or hurtful. The reduction of ritual, the comparative intimacy of the setting and the use of more or less plain language all seem to contribute to this. Even if in practice the actual operation of hearings, like most human activities, may sometimes fall short of the ideal, the emphasis is on creating an atmosphere in which the children and their parents can communicate freely with panel members and openly discuss their problems, on carefully adhering to legal procedures and fully explaining individual rights.

The Scottish system of juvenile justice, now in its twenty first year, has virtues equalled by very few systems for dealing with children in trouble. Children's hearings can be dignified without pomposity, informal without casualness, sensitive without sentimentality. The underlying principle, the attempt to see the child as an individual person and not simply as an offender or a victim to whom certain procedures are automatically applied, which is the essence of the system, has a profound intrinsic value.

REFERENCES

Erickson, P. (1982). The client's perspective. In F. M. Martin & K. Murray (Eds). *The Scottish Juvenile Justice System*. Edinburgh: Scottish Academic Press.

Mackay, Lord, of Clashfern PC (1988). The child: a view across the Tweed. The Child and Co. Lecture. Public lecture given in Inns of Court School of Law, London, April 27.

Martin, F. M. (1981). Taking stock. In F. M. Martin, H. Millar & A. Sinclair. *Children's Hearings: The First Decade*. Glasgow University: Panel Training Resource Centre.

Martin, F. M., Fox, S. J. & Murray, K. (1981). *Children Out of Court*. Edinburgh: Scottish Academic Press.

Morris, A. & Giller, H. (1977). The client's perspective. *Criminal Law Review*, 198–205.

Report of the Committee on Children and Young Persons, Scotland (1964). (Kilbrandon Report) Cmnd 2306. Edinburgh: HMSO.

Report on the Evidence of Children and Other Potentially Vulnerable Witnesses (1990). Scottish Law Commission, No 125. Edinburgh: HMSO.

Scott, P. D. (1959). Juvenile courts: the juvenile's point of view. *British Journal of Criminology*, **9**, 200–210.

Social Work and the Community (1966). Cmnd 3605. London: HMSO.

Social Work Services Group (1989). Referrals of children to reporters and hearings, 1988. *Statistical Bulletin*, Scottish Education Department, CH 13, 9.

Appendix: Memorandum by the Lord Justice General on Child Witnesses*

1. The following memorandum of guidance has been prepared at the suggestion of the Scottish Law Commission: see Report on the Evidence of Children and Other Potentially Vulnerable Witnesses (Scot Law Com No. 125). Its purpose is to provide assistance to judges in the exercise of their discretionary powers, where a child is to give evidence by conventional means in open court, to put the child at ease while giving evidence and to clear the court of persons not having a direct involvement in the proceedings.

2. The general objective is to ensure, so far as is reasonably practicable, that the experience of giving evidence by all children under the age of sixteen causes as little anxiety and distress to the child as possible in the circumstances.

3. The following are examples of the measures which may be taken, at the discretion of the presiding judge, with a view to achieving that objective—

   (a) The removal of wigs and gowns by the judge, counsel and solicitors;

   (b) The positioning of the child at a table in the well of the court along with the judge, counsel and solicitors, rather than requiring the child to give evidence from the witness box;

   (c) Permitting a relative or other supporting person to sit alongside the child while he or she is giving evidence;

   (d) The clearing from the court room of all persons not having a direct involvement in the proceedings.

---

* Reproduced by permission of the Lord Justice General, Scotland

4. In deciding whether or not to take these or similar measures, or any of them, the presiding judge should have regard to the following factors—

   (a) The age and maturity of the child.

   In general the younger the child the more desirable it is that steps should be taken to reduce formality and to put the child at ease while giving evidence.

   (b) The nature of the charge or charges, and the nature of the evidence which the child is likely to be called upon to give.

   Particular care should be taken in cases with a sexual element or involving allegations of child abuse especially where the child is the complainer or an eyewitness. Children directly involved in such cases are likely to be especially vulnerable to trauma when called upon to give evidence in the presence of the accused. The giving of evidence of a relatively formal nature, especially in the case of an older child, is unlikely to cause anxiety or distress and in such cases it will rarely be necessary to take special measures in the interests of the child.

   (c) The relationship, if any, between the child and the accused.

   A child who is giving evidence at the trial of a close relative may be especially exposed to apprehension or embarrassment, irrespective of the nature of the charge. The positioning of the child and the support of a person sitting alongside the child while giving evidence are likely to be of particular importance in these cases.

   (d) Whether the trial is summary or on indictment—

   While informality may be easier to achieve in summary cases, the presence of a jury in cases taken on indictment is likely to present an anxious or distressed child with an additional cause for anxiety or distress. This makes it all the more necessary under solemn procedure that steps should be taken to put the child at ease.

   (e) Any special factors placed before the court concerning the disposition, health or physique of the child.

   All children are different, and judges should take each child's particular circumstances into account before deciding what steps, if any, should be taken to minimise anxiety or distress.

   (f) The practicability of departing from normal procedure, including the size and layout of the court and the availability of amplification equipment.

Whatever steps are taken, a child witness who gives evidence by conventional means must remain visible and audible to all those who have to hear and assess the evidence, including the jury and the accused.

5. In all cases before a witness under sixteen years is led in evidence an opportunity should be given to those representing the Crown and the defence to address the judge as to what special arrangements, if any, are appropriate. Under solemn procedure such representations should be made outwith the presence of the jury and preferably before the jury is empanelled or at least before the commencement of the evidence.

6. If a relative or other supporting person is to sit alongside the child, that person should not be a witness in the case and he or she should be warned by the judge at the outset not to prompt or seek to influence the child in any way in the course of the evidence.

7. The clearing of the court while a child is giving evidence will normally be appropriate in all cases which involve an offence against, or conduct contrary to, decency or morality: see section 166 and section 362 of the Criminal Procedure (Scotland) Act 1975. In other cases this should only be done if the judge is satisfied that this is necessary in order to avoid undue anxiety or distress to the child. The statutory provisions that *bona fide* representatives of a newspaper or news agency should not be excluded should be applied in all cases.

8. When taking any of the measures described above the judge should have regard to the court's general duty to ensure that the accused receives a fair trial and is given a proper opportunity to present his defence.

CHAPTER 9

Legal Reforms on Behalf of Child Witnesses: Recent Developments in the American Courts*

Debra Whitcomb

Education Development Center, Newton, Massachusetts

The plight of child victims in the courtroom has generated considerable attention in the United States. Because of the unique attributes of child victims—their cognitive and emotional maturity and, commonly, their position as the most critical source of evidence in sexual abuse cases—the adjudication process can add to the trauma they have already experienced. Many states have adopted laws that permit alternative techniques to alleviate the perceived stress on children when they testify. In practice, however, alternatives to traditional in-court testimony have only been used as a last resort. Other reforms, aimed at reducing the burden on child victims throughout the investigation and adjudication process, can substantially reduce the need for radical departures from tradition in the courtroom.

---

*A more detailed discussion of these developments can be found in Whitcomb, D. (1992). *When the Victim is a Child*, 2nd edition. Washington: National Institute of Justice.

Children as Witnesses. Edited by H. Dent and R. Flin
© 1992 John Wiley & Sons Ltd.

A CALL FOR CHANGE

Recognition of the child's plight in the courtroom was an outgrowth of the women's movement of the 1970s. Rape crisis centers in many communities recorded increasing numbers of children among their caseloads. Victim advocates became aware that child victims, like adult rape victims, were at a decided disadvantage in the courtroom —only more so because of their age and associated limitations. Victim advocates and prosecutors across the country began experimenting with a variety of reforms intended to reduce the stress on child victims.

Media attention to this issue gave rise to increased public concern, which soon was translated into legislative activity. In the Victims of Child Abuse Act of 1990, the federal government endorsed a number of rights and protections for child victims and witnesses, including:

- Alternatives to live in-court testimony, whether by two-way closed circuit television at trial or by videotaped depositions
- Presumption of children's competency as witnesses
- Privacy protection from public identification
- Closing the courtroom during children's testimony
- Victim impact statements from children
- Use of multidisciplinary teams to provide medical and mental health services to child victims, expert testimony, case management, and training for judges and court personnel
- Appointment of guardians *ad litem* to protect the best interests of child victims
- Appointment of a child's attendant to provide emotional support for children during judicial proceedings
- Speedy trial
- Extension of the statute of limitations for commencing prosecution of child sexual or physical abuse allegations until the child reaches the age of 25
- Testimonial aids, such as dolls, puppets, or drawings

Many of these reforms had already been adopted by state legislatures; in fact, some had been informally operating in some jurisdictions long before they were statutorily authorized. Now, as we enter the 1990s, we have, collectively, a great deal of experience with these reforms, as well as some guidance for their application from the Supreme Court. For descriptive purposes, the various techniques that have been introduced on behalf of child victims can be described as courtroom reforms and system reforms.

COURTROOM REFORMS

Testimony via Videotape or Closed Circuit Television

Perhaps the most radical of the proposed reform measures are those that attempt to shield the child from direct confrontation by the accused in court: broadcasting the child's live testimony into the courtroom via closed circuit television, videotaping the child's testimony at a deposition apart from the trial itself, or erecting a screen in the courtroom. All these techniques involve physical separation of the child from the defendant, although there may be provision for the child to see the defendant over a television monitor.

By blocking direct confrontation between victim and accused, these techniques pose a serious threat to the Sixth Amendment to the US Constitution, which guarantees every defendant the right to confront his accusers "face to face". None-the-less, trial courts have experimented with improvised measures designed to protect sensitive victims from the direct gaze of the defendant during their testimony, meeting with mixed results at the appellate level.[1] And, as of December 31, 1989, 31 states had enacted legislation permitting the use of closed circuit television and 36 had provided for videotaped depositions as alternatives to in-court testimony. Twenty-two states provided for both forms of alternative testimony; only seven states provided for neither.[2]

Interestingly, the first child witness case to reach the US Supreme Court on the issue of alternatives to in-court testimony did not involve videotechnology (*Coy v. Iowa*, 487 U.S. 1012 (1988)). Rather, a screen with "one-way" glass had been erected in the courtroom between the child witnesses and the defense table during the children's testimony. After emphasizing the deep-seated belief in the value of face-to-face confrontation as the ultimate test of truthfulness, the Supreme Court acknowledged that the right of confrontation is not absolute, and may give way to "other important interests". The Court concluded that Iowa's statute, which created a generalized presumption of trauma to child witnesses, was insufficient to justify an exception to the Confrontation Clause. Instead, the Court would require "individualized findings that these particular witnesses needed special protection".

In a number of subsequent cases, state appellate courts applied this reasoning when ruling on the use of closed circuit television or videotape in lieu of live, in-court testimony by child witnesses.[3] But some state courts remained reluctant to dispense with the right of confrontation. Most notably, the Maryland Court of Appeals reversed the conviction of a day care operator charged with sexually abusing a six-year-old child on grounds that the state's showing of necessity was insufficient to permit the child to testify via one-way closed circuit television. Experts had testified that the child victim, and several other child witnesses, would suffer serious emotional distress, interfering with their ability to communicate, if required to testify in the courtroom. The Court of Appeals ruled that, in order to satisfy the "high threshold" of necessity required by *Coy*, children must be questioned first in the presence of the defendant (to assess whether they would be traumatized), and secondarily by way of two-way closed circuit television, before the more restrictive one-way procedure can be used (*Craig v. State*, 316 Md. 551, 560 A.2d 1120 (Md. Ct. App. 1989)).

The US Supreme Court disagreed. In *Maryland v. Craig*, 110 S.Ct. 3157 (1990), the Court found that "the Maryland statute, which requires a determination that the child will suffer serious emotional distress such that the child cannot reasonably communicate, clearly suffices to meet constitutional standards". Although the Court declined to articulate a minimum standard for the finding of emotional trauma, it did offer some clarification. Before an alternative to direct confrontation can be permitted, there must be a showing that the child will be traumatized, *not by the courtroom generally, but by the defendant's presence*, and further, that the child's emotional distress will be "more than *de minimus*". In its discussion, the Court delineated four elements of confrontation: physical presence of the witness, testifying under oath, cross-examination, and observation of the witness's demeanor by the trier of fact. According to the Court, closed circuit television incorporates all these elements, thereby serving as the "functional equivalent" of live, in-court testimony.

With this decision, the Supreme Court appears to have opened the door for greater use of alternatives to testimony in open court for child witnesses. None-the-less, because it was based on a 5–4 vote, it is instructive to consider the dissenting opinion. The dissenting justices took issue with the Court's holding that the needs of child witnesses can be a sufficiently compelling interest to outweigh the protections afforded by the Confrontation Clause. They asserted that the Constitution does not permit the Court to balance interests in this way. Citing research demonstrating children's heightened suggestibility to leading questions and the disastrous case in Scott County, Minnesota[6] (in which inappropriate interviewing techniques thoroughly confounded the investigation), the dissent expressed its concern that use of alternative techniques might permit innocent people to be convicted by children who had been coached by malevolent adults. The dissent repeatedly emphasized the literal meaning of confrontation to require a face-to-face meeting, concluding that the Sixth Amendment applies to *all* criminal prosecutions and that exceptions cannot be carved for child witnesses in the interests of public policy.

A review of state legislation permitting videotaped or closed circuit testimony in lieu of in-court testimony reveals that the Supreme Court is actually less restrictive in its interpretation of the Confrontation Clause than are many of the states. While some state laws actually express a preference for the alternative procedures in cases involving young children, and others require only a finding of "good cause" before these techniques may be used, still others require a finding of medical or other unavailability, and some even require a finding that the child was harmed or violently threatened by the defendant. Several statutes stipulate factors which judges must consider when contemplating the use of closed circuit television or videotape, using language that parallels that of the Scottish Law Commission in its *Report on the Evidence of Children and Other Potentially Vulnerable Witnesses* (1990):

> A court should authorise the use of a pre-trial deposition procedure, a screen, or a live closed circuit television link only on cause shown, taking into account matters such as: the age and maturity of the child; the nature of the offence; the nature of the evidence which the child is likely to be called on to give; the relationship, if any, between the child and the accused; the possible effect on the child if required to give evidence in open court; and the likelihood that the child may be better able to give evidence if not required to do so in open court. (Paragraphs 4.38–4.42; clause 4)

Referring again to the Supreme Court's decision in *Maryland v. Craig*, the pertinent issue is whether the child will be adversely affected specifically by confrontation *with the defendant*. Neither the language quoted above, nor that contained in many American statutes, addresses this issue directly. It remains to be seen how the American courts will operationalize this requirement, along with the showing that the child's stress will be more than "*de minimus*". If the courts require expert testimony from mental health professionals, prosecutors may refrain from using alternative techniques to avoid opening the door for adversarial defense experts to examine the child and report conflicting findings, thereby precipitating a "battle of the experts".

Furthermore, several commentators have argued that inherent properties of a televised (or videotaped) trial—its limited perspective, distortion of images, and similarity to television as an entertainment medium—detract seriously from the viewer's ability to grasp a complete and accurate picture of the witness's demeanor, thereby threatening the defendant's right to a fair trial (Armstrong, 1976; Brakel, 1975).

Research suggests, however, that videotape tends to improve jurors'
retention of trial-related information and to enhance witness credibility (see Miller 1976; Ross et al, 1989). Interestingly, in some cases, the
courts themselves have expressly acknowledged the superiority of
videotape technology over other methods of reproducing a witness's
testimony when the witness is unavailable for trial (such as an audio
or written recording of the preliminary hearing or having someone
relate the witness's testimony).[4] And, in fact, the new technology is
reportedly gaining popularity within the courts as an effective and
cost-efficient means of conducting certain proceedings, such as
arraignments.[5]

In sum, despite the encouraging opinion in *Maryland v. Craig*, it
appears as though alternatives to in-court testimony will remain
techniques of last resort. Research findings notwithstanding, live
testimony is believed by many prosecutors to be more persuasive to the
jury. To lessen the trauma of in-court confrontation, some prosecutors
prefer simply to instruct children to look elsewhere while they testify,
preferably at a supportive family member or victim advocate, or to tell
the judge if the defendant is "making faces". Such instructions may
not completely eradicate the child's fear of seeing the defendant in
court, but they help to impart a small sense of control.

Statutory Hearsay Exceptions

Another category of courtroom reform includes statutes that create
special exceptions to the hearsay rules for out-of-court statements
made by child sexual abuse victims. Under American jurisprudence,
out-of-court statements are considered inherently unreliable and thus
they are generally not admissible in court. It is not uncommon,
however, for young sexual abuse victims to make innocent remarks
that quite explicitly describe sexual activities that should be unknown
to a child. At least 28 states have created a special exception precisely
crafted to permit such statements into testimony. These statutes have
generally been upheld by the courts, provided they are tailored to meet
certain requirements set forth in *Ohio v. Roberts*, 448 U.S. 56 (1980):

> The court finds, in a hearing, conducted outside the presence of the jury
> that the time, content, and circumstances of the statement provide
> sufficient indicia of reliability; and the child either testifies at the
> proceedings; or is unavailable as a witness.

Some statutes have added a corroboration requirement when the
child is unavailable.

However, in a recent decision, the US Supreme Court imposed some important limitations on the admissibility of children's out-of-court statements (*Idaho v. Wright*, 110 S.Ct. 3139 (1990)). In that case, a child's statements made to a pediatrician had been admitted after a finding that the child was incapable of communicating with the jury and was therefore unavailable to testify. Instead, the doctor was permitted to testify as to statements the child had made in response to his questions.

In ruling that it was error for the trial court to admit the child's hearsay statement, the Supreme Court found that the child's statement to the doctor lacked sufficient guarantees of trustworthiness to satisfy the reliability requirement set forth in *Roberts*. Among the factors that had contributed to the lower court's decision to admit the child's statement, the Supreme Court accepted only two as relevant to the reliability of the statement: whether the child had a motive to fabricate the allegations, and whether the child's description of the alleged abuse was consistent with the cognitive abilities and sexual awareness of so young a child. Physical evidence of the abuse, corroborating statements from another witness, and opportunity for the defendant to commit the abuse—all were rejected as not pertinent to the making of the statement itself and therefore inappropriate in weighing its reliability.

The dissent in this 5–4 decision argued that excluding corroborating evidence apart from the statement itself flies in the face of common sense, legal precedent, and "the considered wisdom of virtually the entire legal community that corroborating evidence is relevant to reliability and trustworthiness". Furthermore, the dissenting justices observed, it is preferable to consider other corroborating evidence (such as medical findings of abuse) since that evidence can at least be examined by the defendant and the trial court "in an objective and critical way".

Legal commentators are divided in their opinions about the likely effect of *Idaho v. Wright* on the admissibility of out-of-court statements made by child victims who do not testify. The existence of corroborating evidence may no longer be considered in determining whether a child's statement possesses particularized guarantees of trustworthiness; rather, prosecutors must search for indicators surrounding the making of the statement itself. In fact, statutes that require corroboration, in addition to "sufficient indicia of reliability", are responding not to constitutional requirements but rather to the widespread concern that defendants might otherwise be convicted solely on the hearsay statement of a child witness who is unavailable for cross-examination (see, for example, Tuerkheimer, 1988). Interestingly, the

English Advisory Group on Video Evidence appears less concerned about the need for corroboration. In its 1989 Report (*Report of the Home Office Advisory Group on Video Evidence*, 1989), the Advisory Group recommended:

> that at trials on indictment for sexual offences any rule or practice which makes it obligatory for the court to give a direction to the jury about the danger of convicting the accused on the uncorroborated evidence of the complainant should be abolished (Paragraphs 5.30–5.31)

Videotaped Interviews or Statements

As of the end of 1989, 15 states had enacted legislation making videotaped statements or interviews with child witnesses admissible at trial under certain circumstances. Two of these statutes simply include videotaped interviews as a specific form of out-of-court statement that may be admissible under the special statutory hearsay exception described above. Other statutes, however, are less explicit in their assurances that the elements of confrontation will be met when videotaped statements are introduced. Salient features of these laws include questioning of the child by a non-attorney; availability of the interviewer for direct and cross-examination at trial; and availability of the child to testify at trial.

These statutes clearly do not contemplate videotape as an alternative to in-court testimony, since the child must be available for trial. Rather, protecting the child from the presumed trauma of trial testimony appears to be an implicit agenda. The state is not required to produce the child during its case-in-chief and, in practice, it is often left to the defense to call the child for cross-examination. However, many defense attorneys choose *not* to call the child for fear of angering a jury that may be sympathetic to the child's plight. As a result, the unchallenged videotape of a child's statement given to a law enforcement officer, social worker, or mental health professional may stand as the only evidence provided by the child.

Although the US Supreme Court did not rule directly on the issue of videotaped interviews, the recent opinion in *Idaho v. Wright* suggests that most videotaped interviews and statements will be ruled inadmissible *unless the child testifies and is cross-examined*. As Graham (1985) explains:

> It is ... extremely doubtful that a child's statement to a police officer, social worker, or someone specially trained to interview children will be found to possess equivalent circumstantial guarantees of trustworthiness, whether or not the statement was videotaped or otherwise recorded.

The normal timing of such an interview, its investigative function, the frequent use of suggestive questions by a person in authority, and the fact that the child will usually have made several earlier statements relating to the alleged sexual contact all militate against admissibility. (p. 57)

In fact, in another pertinent aspect of this opinion, the Court rejected videotaping as one of several procedural guidelines that had been recommended by the Idaho Supreme Court (the other directives were that interviewers have no prior knowledge of the child's allegations and ask no leading questions). Calling this approach a "preconceived and artificial litmus test", the Court recognized that such guidelines are not inherent indicators of the reliability of a child's statements.

The English Advisory Group on Video Evidence apparently shares the concerns of many American jurists that the accused should not be convicted solely on the basis of unchallenged statements. In its 1989 Report (*Report of the Home Office Advisory Group on Video Evidence*, 1989), the Advisory Group recommended that a special preliminary hearing be held during which the videorecording is shown and the child is subject to questioning by the prosecution and the defense. Both the original videorecording and the videorecording of the preliminary hearing would be shown at trial in place of the child's live testimony. (Paragraphs 2.29, 2.31, and 2.35)

Perhaps the most striking difference between the approaches taken in the United States, England, and Scotland lies in the American courts' strong historical reliance on *confrontation* as central to the discovery of truth and the imposition of justice. Particularly in the recommendations of the Advisory Group on Video Evidence, the intent to protect children from the perceived trauma of courtroom testimony is quite clear: "No child witness to whom our proposals apply should be required to appear in open court during a trial unless he or she wishes to do so" (*Report of the Home Office Advisory Group on Video Evidence*, 1989, paragraphs 2.25–2.26). Conversely, in the United States, child witnesses are expected to testify in court unless there is an individualized finding that a particular child will be traumatized, "more than *de minimus*", by confrontation with the defendant.

Competency Requirements

Another potentially promising courtroom reform is the elimination of special competency requirements for child witnesses. There is presently wide variation in what the states require. The majority of states

either assert that every person is competent or impose no age requirement provided certain minimum requirements are met. A few states
explicitly presume that children are competent witnesses; conversely,
some states still require children under a certain age to demonstrate
competency before testifying. Nine states specifically exempt child
sexual abuse victims from competency requirements. In practice,
however, regardless of the statutory language, most child witnesses
younger than about seven years of age are required to demonstrate
competency before they are permitted to testify.

There is likewise wide variation in the process of determining
competency. At one extreme, children demonstrate that they know
colors and know they get in trouble if they lie. At the other extreme,
children are questioned about the alleged incident in efforts to ascertain their memory and recall of specific events. In recent years, there
has been a trend among defense attorneys to request psychological or
psychiatric examinations for the purpose of assessing a child's competency as a witness. Appellate courts have usually upheld the trial
courts' denials of these motions, generally on grounds that such
assessments encroach on the jury's rightful role in evaluating the
credibility of witnesses. Such exams tend to be permitted only when
(1) existing mental illness or serious disability indicates there is reason
to question the child's competence; or (2) the prosecution has opened
the door by offering its own expert assessments of the child's competence or credibility (Bulkley, in press).

The problem appears to be that competency and credibility have
become inappropriately intertwined. In American jurisprudence, the
determination of competency belongs to the court; the assessment of
credibility belongs to the jury. Children should be allowed to testify to
the best of their ability, as adults do, and the jury should weigh the
credibility of their testimony using traditional layman's standards.

SYSTEM REFORMS

Courtroom reforms, by definition, are available only to those children
whose cases actually go to trial. System reforms benefit every child
whose abuse is disclosed to authorities. Although many system reforms
do not require statutory authorization and pose no threat to constitutional protections, they may be just as difficult to implement as court
reforms because implementation depends on cooperation and coordina-
tion among multiple agencies.

Among the most common system reforms is provision of a support
person for the child. Many communities have active victim assistance

programs whose mission it is to provide support and encouragement to child victims throughout the adjudication process. The role of the victim assistant is typically confined to explaining the adjudication system, preparing child witnesses for court testimony, and accompanying them to court proceedings. Many victim assistants also advise prosecutors as to a child's ability to withstand a courtroom appearance. Some victim assistance programs have developed educational videotapes, coloring books, dollhouse-sized courtrooms and other child-friendly techniques to complement their supportive efforts. In at least two large counties in California, "court school" programs engage small groups of child victims in structured sessions involving education, discussion, and role-play during the weeks preceding their court appearance. (See also Dezwirek-Sas, Chapter 11, and Sisterman Keeney et al, Chapter 12, this volume.)

A small number of jurisdictions assign a guardian *ad litem*, ie an independent representative, to advocate for the best interests of child victims in criminal proceedings. The reasoning is that the state's concern in prosecuting a case is gaining a conviction, which may not be consistent with the needs of the child. In practice, under most circumstances, the role of the guardian *ad litem* is quite similar to that of the victim assistant, but there is a potential for direct communication with the court.

Another cluster of system reforms is targeted at streamlining the system. Responding to research suggesting that delay adversely affects children's performance as witnesses and emotional well-being, many states have passed laws directing some form of speedy disposition for child sexual abuse cases. These laws appear to have little practical effect, however, since other categories of cases often take priority (for example cases in which the defendant is being held in custody). There may actually be greater potential in efforts to persuade individual judges to limit the number of continuances they grant in child sexual abuse cases, although some are reluctant to deny defense requests.

Perhaps the most fertile ground for system reform lies in attempts to limit the number of interviews children must undergo between the time abuse is disclosed and final disposition of the case. Parallel investigations by law enforcement and social service agencies, followed by independent inquiries conducted by the prosecutor's office, translate to repeated interviews with the victims which can compound their trauma while opening the door to inconsistencies, contradictions, and defense challenges.

Many communities have sought ways to reduce the redundancy inherent in the investigation process. For example, many larger jurisdictions have established special prosecution units for child abuse cases. These units are characterized by vertical prosecution, in which the same prosecutor handles the case from beginning to end, and smaller caseloads. Sometimes the unit has specially trained and assigned investigators, child interviewers, or victim advocates. Cross-reporting laws, enacted in a number of states, require law enforcement and social service agencies to notify each other upon receiving a report of child abuse, and further, to coordinate their response. The net effect of these efforts is a better organized, less fragmented approach to case development.

Even in the absence of legislative mandates for cooperation, police officers and social workers in some communities respond jointly to calls and interview child victims together. Multidisciplinary case review teams, in which agency representatives meet regularly to discuss new and ongoing cases, are increasingly popular ways to coordinate investigations and decision-making about the desirable course of action in any given case. Unfortunately, in some communities, efforts to build multidisciplinary teams are stymied by legal limitations on the agencies' freedom to share information about cases and difficulty in overcoming long-standing "turf" conflicts.

There is also a growing movement to designate a central location for children's interviews. At a minimum, such a location consists of a room specially furnished to accommodate children and often including a one-way mirror to enable viewing by other agency representatives. In fact, at least 40 communities have created "children's centers", following a model pioneered in Madison County (Huntsville), Alabama (see Sisterman-Keeney et al, Chapter 12, this volume). Under this model, all children's interviews occur in a single location, to which agency representatives travel rather than bouncing the child from one government building to another for repetitive interviews. Weekly team meetings are also held at the children's center to coordinate the investigation process.

Videotape technology is used in some communities to preserve the child's first statement and to reduce the number of subsequent interviews, but the technique remains controversial. Although videotapes have limited evidentiary value for the prosecution, especially in the wake of the Supreme Court's decision in *Idaho v. Wright*, they can be useful as aids to the charging decision or as leverage to encourage guilty pleas. On the other hand, videotaped interviews are sometimes used by the defense to attack questioning techniques and to support an argument that the child was coached. The issue turns on the skill of the interviewer and the policies and guidelines for conducting and videotaping the interview. The Advisory Group on Video Evidence is to be applauded for its foresight in recommending the establishment of a

Code of Practice to guide the conduct of videotaped interviews with child victims (see Spencer, Chapter 7, this volume).

CURRENT AND EMERGING ISSUES

Accompanying the movement to reform child protection and criminal justice systems on behalf of child victims in the United States is an increasingly visible "backlash" movement. For example, one outcome of the highly publicized, ill-fated multiple victims case in Jordan, Minnesota, was the formation of a group known as VOCAL, or Victims Of Child Abuse Legislation. With chapters operating nationwide, VOCAL has been moderately successful in lobbying state legislatures to be more protective of parents' rights in considering proposals that would benefit child victims.

Another disturbing trend is the growth of expert witnesses as a lucrative industry in child abuse litigation. It is an unfortunate byproduct of the adversarial justice system that the prosecution and defense seek "experts" to support their respective arguments. In sexual abuse cases, which often lack medical findings, physical evidence, or eyewitnesses, and where the victim's testimony may be weak or unconvincing, the role of mental health experts assumes greater prominence. This role may be even further augmented with the Supreme Court's clear direction requiring individualized findings of need before alternatives to confrontation may be used. With increasing reliance on mental health professionals in child sexual abuse cases, there will be greater potential for these cases to become "battles of the experts" in which contradictory psychological testimony threatens to overshadow the facts.

A third outgrowth of the intense public interest in hotly contested cases, and particularly those involving divorce, custody, or visitation disputes, is the emergence of an "underground railroad". This grass-roots network assists parents who claim that they and their children have been poorly served by the justice system by transporting them to new locations with new names and assurances of protection from the accused.

Meanwhile, researchers are attempting to address a number of unanswered questions that continue to confound the courts. For example:

- Does children's memory differ from that of adults? If so, in what ways? How can interviewers help children retrieve important facts?

- Are children more susceptible than adults to leading questions? Are there more effective techniques for interviewing children?
- Is there a "foolproof" way to determine whether a child is telling the truth about sexual abuse?
- Do anatomically detailed dolls encourage children to fabricate sexual abuse?
- How do jurors assess the credibility of child witnesses? Does this assessment differ when the child's testimony is televised?
- What is the impact of the adjudication process on child victims, and do any of the suggested reforms actually have the intended beneficial effect on the children's well-being and the outcome of prosecution?

A tremendous amount of research is underway to address these and other questions that surround the role of children as witnesses in court. The ensuing challenge will be to convey the emerging knowledge to judges, prosecutors, and other court personnel to improve current practices.

CONCLUSIONS

Although there is much we do not know, we cannot afford to wait for definitive answers before we take action to protect children who are victimized in our society. Efforts to coordinate, streamline, and otherwise strengthen the investigation process will benefit all children who become enmeshed in the "system". Furthermore, if these cases can be handled expeditiously and effectively, with minimal intrusion and maximum support for the child victims, chances are they will be disposed by guilty plea; if not, most children should possess the confidence and strength to withstand a traditional trial.

In the rare circumstance that a child has been severely traumatized by abuse, courtroom reforms are important to have available. Without them, the most needy children will be the least likely to have their day in court, and justice will not be served.

NOTES

1. See, for example, *State v. Mannion*, 57 P. 542 (Utah Sup.Ct. 1899) (seating arrangement whereby defendant could not see or hear the witness's testimony violates the right of confrontation); and *State v. Strable*, 313 N.W.2d 497 (Iowa 1981) (the fact that the witness testified behind a blackboard was, at most, harmless error).

2. Information on the number of states having enacted selected statutes was provided by the American Prosecutors Research Institute, Alexandria, Virginia.
3. See, eg, *State v. Tafoya*, 108 N.M. 1, 765 P.2d 1183 (N.M. App. 1988), finding that the necessity prong was satisfied by testimony from three experts and the children's parents that testifying in court would cause these children "unreasonable and unnecessary harm". See also *People v. Henderson*, 554 N.Y.S.2d 924 (A.D. 2 Dept. 1990), reversing a babysitter's conviction because the trial court's finding of the children's "vulnerability", necessitating the use of two-way closed circuit television to obtain their testimony, was based solely on an expert's testimony that *all* sexually abused children would benefit from this procedure, not the specific children involved in the case.
4. See, for example, *State v. Hewitt*, 545 P.2d 1201 (Wash. App. 1976), and *Hutchins v. State*, 286 S.2d 244 (D.Ct.App.Fla., 1973).
5. TV arraignment breaks new ground to streamline courts, *Government Technology*, 2 (July 1989).
6. Humphrey, H. H. (1985). Report on Scott County Investigation. Minnesota Attorney General, 111, Feb. 12.

REFERENCES

Armstrong, J. (1976). The criminal videotape trial: serious constitutional questions. *Oregon Law Review*, **55**, 567–585.

Brakel, S. (1975). Videotape in trial proceedings: technological obsession. *American Bar Association Journal*, **61**, 956–959.

Bulkley, J. (in press) Major legal issues in child abuse cases. In W. O'Donahue & J. Geer (Eds). *The Sexual Abuse of Children: Theory, Research and Therapy*. New Jersey: Lawrence Erlbaum.

Graham, M. H. (1985). Indicia of reliability and face to face confrontation: emerging issues in child sexual abuse prosecutions. *University of Miami Law Review*, **40**, 19–95.

Miller, G. R. (1976). The effects of videotaped trial materials on juror responses. In G. Bermant, C. Nemeth & N. Vidmar (Eds). *Psychology and the Law*. Mass: Lexington.

Report on the Evidence of Children and Other Potentially Vulnerable Witnesses (1990). Scottish Law Commission, No 125, HMSO.

Report of the Home Office Advisory Group on Video Evidence (1989). (Pigot Committee Report). London: Home Office.

Ross, D., Dunning, D., Toglia, M. & Ceci, S. (1989). Age stereotypes, communication modality and mock jurors' perceptions of the child witness. In S. Ceci, D. Ross & M. Toglia (Eds). *Perspectives on Children's Testimony*. New York: Springer-Verlag.

Tuerkheimer, F. M. (1988). Convictions through hearsay in child sexual abuse cases: a logical progression back to square one. *Marquette Law Review*, **72**, 47–62.

CHAPTER 10

Children in the Witness-Box

Rhona Flin

Robert Gordon Institute of Technology, Aberdeen

Ray Bull

Portsmouth Polytechnic

Julian Boon

Leicester University

and

Anne Knox

Glasgow Polytechnic

A child giving evidence from the witness-box is not an everyday occurrence in British courtrooms; however, there are indications that the number of children involved in criminal trials is not insignificant and that this figure may be increasing. There are no official records of the numbers or ages of children required to attend court as witnesses but two recent Scottish studies suggest that children observe a wide range of offences. In Aberdeen (population 200 000) a total of 226 children under the age of 16 were cited as witnesses for criminal trials in a one-year period (Flin et al, 1988) and in Glasgow (population 800 000) the comparable figure was 1440 children (Flin et al, 1990). Certainly in Scotland the majority of these witnesses are not victims of sexual

Children as Witnesses. Edited by H. Dent and R. Flin
© 1992 John Wiley & Sons Ltd.

abuse but more typically bystander witnesses to assaults or breaches of the peace (see Flin et al (1992) for a detailed breakdown of these samples). The frequency with which children are called to give evidence may be higher in Scotland than in other parts of the United Kingdom (although no English data are available) due to the Scottish legal rule that all evidence is corroborated (see Nicholson & Murray, Chapter 8, this volume) and to the practice in England and Wales of (until recently) rarely calling children under eight years to testify in criminal courts. However, in England the increase in reported sexual abuse crimes and recent legislative changes are likely to create a concomitant rise in the numbers of cases involving children being called as witnesses.

Participation in the Scottish or English criminal justice systems presents a number of problems for children who are required to give evidence as victims or bystanders in criminal trials. These include lack of legal knowledge (Flin et al, 1989), long delays before the trial (Flin et al, in press; Plotnikoff, 1990), unsuitable court facilities, and the demands of an adversarial trial (see Spencer & Flin, 1990; Flin, in press, for recent reviews). Such problems are not unique to the United Kingdom (see Dezwirek-Sas, Chapter 11, Sisterman Keeney et al, Chapter 12 and Whitcomb, Chapter 9, this volume, for a North American comparison and see Loesel, in press for a European overview.) This chapter focuses on what may be the most critical element of the process—when the child enters the witness-box to give evidence. At this stage there are potential difficulties not only for the child but also for the lawyers who have the task of presenting the child's evidence in court or testing that evidence by cross-examination. Drawing on our own courtroom observations and the research findings of other psychologists, we describe what actually happens when a child enters the witness-box and the impact these procedures appear to have on the child.

COURT OBSERVATION STUDY; GLASGOW 1988–1989

Despite mounting concern about child witnesses' ability to cope with British criminal court proceedings and recurring media reports of children being traumatized in our courtrooms, there have been no empirical studies of children's behaviour in the witness-box or of the ability of our courtroom lawyers to present or test children's evidence. This chapter presents the first data from an observational study of child witnesses in Scotland giving evidence in criminal trials. A brief outline of the methodology is presented below and the principal results are discussed with reference to (i) courtroom practices; (ii) the legal examinations; (iii) the child's demeanour during the examinations. (A more detailed description of the study can be found in Flin et al, 1992.)

Following a pilot study in which qualitative observations had been made of 22 children giving evidence in Aberdeen during 1986 and 1987 (Flin et al, 1988), it was decided to establish a second project in Glasgow to observe a larger sample of child witnesses and to record more systematic observations.

We knew that a very similar exercise was being conducted in Denver, Colorado, where psychologist Gail Goodman and her colleagues were observing children on the witness stand as part of a large-scale assessment of the effects of giving testimony on child victims (Goodman et al, 1988, in press). They were tracking a sample of 218 child sexual assault victims referred to District Attorneys' offices in Denver between 1985 and 1987. As part of this investigation they recorded interview and observational data on 40 children testifying at preliminary hearings, eight children at competence hearings and 17 children who testified at trial. The researchers watched each child testifying and recorded their observations on a set of specially designed rating scales. In order to standardize our own recording technique and in the hope of facilitating a cross-cultural comparison, we contacted Gail Goodman, who sent us copies of their observational scales which we were able to adapt for use in Scotland.

With the cooperation of the Procurators Fiscal (public prosecutors) in Glasgow, we received notification of every child under the age of 16 years cited to attend court as a prosecution witness from 1988 to 1989 (1800 witnesses in a 15-month period). An attempt was made to observe as many of these children as possible within a period of 12 months. It should be emphasized that the majority of witnesses cited to give evidence will not actually find themselves in the witness-box or even in the courtroom. Accused persons frequently change their "not guilty" pleas to "guilty" in the run-up to the trial; this may happen as late as several minutes before the trial is due to start. Not all trials listed will actually run on the first date scheduled and not all witnesses cited are required to give evidence. Given a very small project team (one and a half full-time researchers), the fact that several trials involving children could be running on the same day and the geographical dispersion of the courts in Glasgow, it was necessary to adopt a prioritizing procedure in favour of trials involving younger witnesses and more serious crimes. Of 366 children we were able to track up to their attendance at court, we were able to observe 89 of them while they were giving evidence in the courtroom.

With the permission of the presiding judge at each trial, the researcher sat in a discreet position, as near to the child as possible to permit unobtrusive recording of observations using the Court Room Observation Schedule (Scotland). This instrument was designed to record a comprehensive picture of the Court, those present, the case, the examinations and the child witness. It was subdivided into three parts as follows.

Part I recorded basic demographic details (eg the child's age, sex, victim or bystander, relationship to the accused, type of crime, date of incident, type of court, accompanying adults).

Part II was used to record court details (eg number of people present), procedures (eg adjournments), and the use of special practices (eg removing wigs and gowns, clearing the court, screening the child, seating the child outside the witness-box).

Part III consisted of four sets of scales for rating the child's demeanour during (i) the judge's competency assessment; (ii) the examination-in-chief by the prosecution; (iii) the defence cross-examination; (iv) the prosecution reexamination.

DETAILS OF CHILD WITNESSES

A total of 89 children (62 boys and 27 girls) were observed in a total of 40 trials, their ages ranged from five to 15 years with 10 children (11%) aged 5–8 years, 25 children (29%) aged 9–13 years and 54 children (60%) aged 14–15 years. The trials (figures in brackets represent number of children) took place at all four levels of Scottish criminal courts ranging from District Courts (Justice of the Peace = lay magistrate) (6); Sheriff Court—summary procedure (judge alone) (33); Sheriff Court—solemn procedure (judge plus jury) (16); through to the High Court (senior judge plus jury) (34). The principal charges libelled for each trail were assault (29); murder/attempted murder (28); sex-related (16); road traffic accident (5); theft (5); other (6).

The children had waited an average of 193 days (6.5 months) since witnessing the alleged incident (range 30–718 days). (It should be noted that there can sometimes be a delay between the alleged offence and the initial complaint, eg this can happen in sexual assault complaints.) The summary data showed that 75% of the children were bystander witnesses and 25% were victims; 34% of the sample were giving evidence against strangers, 56% against known persons, and 9% against a relative (for one case the relationship could not be ascertained).

COURTROOM PRACTICE AND PROCEDURE

Child witnesses, in common with adult witnesses, may have to wait several hours or longer at the courthouse before they are called to give evidence. In our sample we found that 64% of the children gave their evidence on the day they were told to attend court, 5% gave their evidence the following day and 31% on a later day still (max. = nine days).

In Scotland any special measures which are adopted for taking children's evidence are at the discretion of the presiding judge. There was no provision for the use of live videolinked evidence at the time of the study although this will be introduced to a number of Scottish courts in 1992. Of the children observed, 13 were permitted to give their evidence from outwith the witness-box. In most cases these children were seated in the well of the court, but one nine-year-old girl giving evidence in a serious assault case (involving her uncle) was allowed to sit up on the bench alongside the Sheriff. We observed only two children (the case involved incest and lewd and libidinous behaviour with girls aged 11 years) giving evidence while the accused was hidden from view behind a screen. One simple practice for reducing courtroom formality is for the lawyers to remove their wigs and gowns. This measure was not adopted very frequently—for six children wigs were removed, and in five of these cases gowns were also removed.

When the court is open to the public there may be a large audience present to listen to the child's evidence. For 38 children in the sample this meant being examined in front of more than 40 people. It is at the discretion of the presiding judge as to whether or not the court is closed and for 18 children the public were excluded when they gave their evidence. However, in cases which were tried before a jury, even when the public were excluded, there were still a significant number of people present: namely the 15 jurors, the judge, the lawyers, the stenographer, the clerk, the uniformed police and court officers, and the accused.

In general our experience was that the adoption of special measures for child witnesses was sporadic and appeared to be dependent more on the personal views of the presiding judge than on the basis of a coherent set of guidelines. Since this research was completed, the Lord Justice General has issued a memorandum which offers general guidance for Scottish judges and which will hopefully bring more uniformity to such decisions (see Nicholson & Murray, Chapter 8, Appendix, this volume, for a copy). A similar variety in courtroom procedures for child witnesses has also been reported in other jurisdictions. Morgan and Plotnikoff (1990) in an English study of child victims observed a number of trials and concluded, "A wide variety of procedures are now available which may ameliorate stress for the child witness and facilitate the giving of testimony, but the way in which they are used is fairly haphazard. There appears to be little shared information and experience among courts about the treatment of child witnesses" (p. 192). Likewise Goodman et al reported that in Denver, while some practices were more regularly adopted, such as permitting a victim assistant or non-offending parent to remain in the courtroom, other techniques such as live closed circuit television or screens were used relatively infrequently.

Many experts have argued that most courtrooms are by their very nature unsuitable for conducting examinations of younger children and victims. Recent moves to take children out of the courtroom and to allow them to give their evidence via a videolink would seem to be a step in the right direction. (See Davies & Westcott, Chapter 13, this volume, Myers, in press, and Cashmore, 1991a for a more detailed discussion of this technique.) The problem with the videolink is that the child still has to wait for months attempting to maintain a clear memory of the incident and will still be required to attend the court building on the day of the trial. It has also been argued (Spencer & Flin, 1990) that it would be better for some children if their statement could be recorded on videotape as soon as possible after the incident, and if the prosecution and defence examinations could be conducted and videotaped as soon as possible thereafter. While the new Criminal Justice Act (1991) will permit the admission of videotaped evidence for children in English courts, they may still be required to attend the trial for live cross-examination (see Spencer, Chapter 7, this volume).

LEGAL EXAMINATIONS

The major part of the study focused on the questioning techniques used by the prosecution and defence lawyers to examine the 89 child witnesses observed. Many of the children were questioned initially by the judge to determine if they were competent to give evidence and/or to take the oath. (The only child (aged four years) whom we were not permitted to observe was not deemed competent and therefore did not give evidence.) None of the younger children, aged 5–8 years, were asked to take the oath before they gave evidence, but the older children were normally sworn.

Given the heterogeneous nature of the sample, it was not surprising to find a wide variation in the number of examinations given and their duration. Following the initial examination-in-chief by the prosecuting lawyer, 65 of the children were cross-examined by one or more defence lawyers. (If there are multiple accused each may have a different defence lawyer who may want to conduct a cross-examination of the child.) A reexamination was required by the prosecution lawyer for 20 of the children who had been cross-examined. The average duration of the examination-in-chief was 16 minutes (range: 3–92 min). The cross-examinations lasted for an average of 10 minutes (range: 1–59 min) and the reexaminations lasted for an average of 4.5 minutes (range 1–18 min).

The number of examinations required of each child became less predictable where there were multiple accused. Although 52 (58%) of the children appeared in cases which involved a sole accused, 26 (19%) gave evidence in cases where there were five or more accused persons. In one case, involving eight accused, a child was examined 10 times —once by the examination-in-chief, eight cross-examinations, and a final reexamination by the prosecution. On occasion, the child's evidence could be interrupted by an adjournment (eg when a point of law required consideration outwith the presence of the witness, or when a witness was too upset to continue, or for a lunch break). For the cases observed, 15 children had their evidence interrupted by one adjournment, five children by two adjournments and one child by three adjournments. In some circumstances such breaks can be helpful, in other cases they were clearly distracting or even disruptive for the child. On balance, it would appear sensible to avoid interrupting the child's examination by unscheduled adjournments if possible, unless this would obviously be in the child's interest. These data are quite similar to the findings of Goodman et al (in press) from their observations in Denver, USA. They reported that in preliminary hearings, children spent 4–90 minutes (mean 27 min) on the stand, in competence examinations the time ranged from 4 to 21 minutes (mean 10 min) and in trials from 13 to 270 minutes (mean 69 min). Due to a lack of comparable adult data it is impossible to know whether lawyers generally take more or less time to conduct their examinations when it is a child in the witness-box rather than an adult.

For each separate examination, the researcher would make ratings of the verbal performance of each child. There were six scales which recorded (i) fluency; (ii) amount of detail; (iii) age-appropriateness of the lawyer's vocabulary; (iv) age-appropriateness of the grammar; (v) the child's confidence in his or her statements; (vi) the number of "don't know" or mute responses. (A more detailed breakdown of these data and their interobserver reliability is given in Flin et al, 1992.) The majority of children were found to be relatively fluent and able to provide at least some detail. However, this will not necessarily be indicative of effective communication between the lawyer and the child. Difficulties could emerge as a result of questions being put to the child by the lawyer which were age-inappropriate in terms either of vocabulary or grammar. While the majority of children (85%) were asked age-appropriate questions in terms of the grammar used, 40% of the cross-examinations contained some vocabulary that the child did not understand, compared to only 12% of the examinations-in-chief. Likewise, Goodman et al (in press) found that while most questioning they observed was reasonably age-appropriate, defence attorneys used more age-inappropriate wording of their questions than prosecutors. In neither study were records or transcripts studied of the actual language used. However, a detailed study of the linguistic difficulties which can occur when children are cross-examined was conducted using transcripts from 26 Australian cases (Brennan & Brennan, 1988). They documented 13 "strange aspects" of lawyers' courtroom language including multifaceted questions, unclear or confused expressions, negative constructions and repetitions of previous responses. Of course, cross-examining lawyers may have their own reasons for asking questions which witnesses perceive as convoluted, confusing or ambiguous. The aim of cross-examination is definitely not to have an opposing witness give a clear, complete and convincing account of the alleged incident. As one legal text on advocacy skills explains, "The purposes of cross-examination are to destroy or weaken the evidence of your opponent's witnesses, or to undermine their credibility" (Hyam, 1990, p. 84).

While the tactics of cross-examination may be a good method of testing the honesty of articulate adults, it may not be the best way of testing the evidence of a child (see Spencer & Flin, 1990). There has been a resurgence of interest in the linguistic aspects of courtroom interactions between adults (see Levi & Walker, 1990; Wilkinson 1981), and in the present climate of concern regarding the interview techniques used to take statements from child victims (Butler et al, 1991) more attention should be paid to the questioning techniques and language being used in the courtroom to test children's evidence (see Cashmore, 1991b). The Irish Law Commission has recently addressed this issue, stating in its 1989 Consultation Paper on child sexual abuse, "The lawyer needs to be able to understand the language of children and to be able to communicate with children, not in the esoteric language of the law, but in language appropriate to the particular stage of the child's development" (p. 195).

This is especially important in sexual abuse cases, where the child's terminology for body parts can be very different from that of an adult. Dezwirek-Sas (Chapter 11, this volume) quotes a 10-year-old girl who defined a subpoena as "a male's private part" and Goodman and Aman

(1991) found that preschool children pointed to their ears and arms when asked to indicate their private parts. A study by Schor and Sivan (1989) produced an interesting terminology of young children's labels for sexual body parts, and child interviewers (in or out of court) need to be familiar with the sexual language of the child's family and peer group (see also Gordon et al, 1990).

Even when the choice of vocabulary and grammar would appear to be age-appropriate, there may still be misunderstandings between the child and the examining lawyer. Children being interviewed by a stranger in a formal and highly unusual situation may be reluctant to say that they have not understood a question or to contradict the interviewer. (See Garbarino & Stott, 1989; Saywitz & Snyder, in press, for discussions of potential difficulties in interviewing child witnesses.)

In our study the children rarely said that they did not understand a question, although occasionally it would transpire during the examination that the child had not in fact understood a previous question. It was found that 40% of the children did answer "I don't know" to at least some of the questions. However, as children sometimes give this response when they do know but are not prepared to say (for example to sensitive questions), the frequency with which children in court respond "I don't know" when they genuinely do not know the answer cannot be estimated from our data. Only a few children (6%) expressed uncertainty in the content of their answers, and against a pattern of generally confident responses it is difficult to detect when a child is offering a best guess as opposed to a robust answer. Where problems in comprehension did occur they were not always with the youngest children and the lawyers appeared to be conscious of the need to keep questions very simple with this age group.

The lawyers' interviewing styles were rated on two scales, (i) degree of supportiveness and (ii) amount of questioning on peripheral details. In general the prosecution lawyers were rated as being more supportive of the child than the defence lawyers, a finding also reported by Goodman et al (in press). This is hardly surprising given that in both studies all the children were prosecution witnesses. Questions about peripheral details (which have been characterized as a means by which lawyers may cast doubt on witnesses' testimony) were relatively infrequent in our sample. The majority of questions at direct examination (93%), cross-examination (83%) and reexamination (89%) were judged to focus on information central to the incident. Goodman et al (in press) had found that at child sexual assault trials the defence attorneys compared to the prosecutors were judged to focus more on peripheral information than the assault, and perhaps this pattern of defence questioning is more typical in abuse or more serious cases.

THE DEMEANOUR OF THE CHILD WITNESSES

The third aspect of the trials we examined was the child's behaviour or demeanour during the trial. This was based on the observations recorded while the child was giving evidence. These are obviously subjective assessments and, as Goodman et al (in press) point out, they parallel the judgements made by the untrained observers who will judge the quality of a child's evidence—that is, the jury.

The majority of children gave their evidence without becoming so obviously upset that they were reduced to tears. In the examinations-in-chief and the cross-examinations, five children cried in each. It was usually the older children (8–15 years) who cried rather than younger children. While few children actually became tearful, a rather higher percentage appeared to be unhappy and tense while giving their evidence. In the examinations-in-chief and cross-examinations, 50% of the children were rated as being either unhappy or very unhappy, with 40% of the children reexamined by the prosecution appearing unhappy. Similarly, approximately half the children were rated as being tense or very tense during their examinations.

Ratings were also made as to the degree of self-confidence the children showed while delivering their evidence. These were made on the basis of the child's demeanour while giving evidence and not the degree of confidence a child expressed in his or her statements to the court. For example, we observed children who seemed very shy and timid in the delivery of their testimony but who were clear and firm as to the sequence and nature of events they were asked to describe. Conversely, we also observed children who showed high confidence and unabashed irritation at being pressed for details which they had already indicated they could not remember clearly. The ratings on this scale showed that the children varied considerably in the degree of self-confidence displayed. The majority of children were not overwhelmed by the court proceedings. In the initial examination-in-chief and in the cross-examination, 46% of the sample were able to cope to a reasonable extent and a further 40% showed some degree of confidence. The remaining 14% of children were rated as lacking in self-confidence but it is impossible to determine whether this was a feature of the child's personality or a reaction to the trial proceedings. Goodman et al (in press) found that 11 (65%) of 17 child sexual abuse victims giving testimony in trials were rated as experiencing some distress or as being very distressed.

It is interesting to note that in neither study were there any major differences in the children's demeanour between direct and cross-examinations. There are several possible explanations for this finding:

(i) there are differences but the observational method is not sufficiently sensitive to detect changes in emotional state; (ii) there are differences but they only occur in certain types of trial; (ii) there are no differences because children's anxiety relating to the trial proceedings in general outweighs any specific pressures caused by the cross-examination; (iv) there are no differences because children do not fully comprehend the trial proceedings and therefore fail to appreciate the distinction between the stages of questioning; (v) there are no differences because the prosecution and defence examinations may actually be more similar in style when the witness is a child rather than an adult.

Defence lawyers often claim (some psychiatrists say disingenuously) that it would not be in their interests to be seen to be putting a child under stress in the witness-box, since it might well lose them, and therefore their client, the sympathy of the court. This argument, coupled with the need sometimes for prosecution lawyers to exert a degree of pressure to persuade children to respond, might account for the comparability in the ratings between prosecution and defence examinations in terms of the children's reactions. Whatever the explanation, additional data will be required to explore these competing hypotheses.

CONCLUSIONS

One of the principal concerns about children as witnesses is that they are disadvantaged compared with adults in terms of their relative ability to understand court proceedings, to cope with the emotional demands of a trial and to give competent evidence. Our data are based on a very small and an extremely heterogeneous sample of cases and they should be regarded as a preliminary foray into uncharted waters. However, there is clearly a need for further detailed study of how children's evidence is elicited and tested in the courtroom in order to judge the effectiveness and fairness of our trial proceedings for child victims and witnesses.

Our findings indicated that although there were a significant number of exceptions, the majority of children appeared to be able to give their evidence reasonably well in terms of providing at least some details relatively fluently. Nevertheless, a large percentage of children did appear to be tense and unhappy while giving their evidence. In cases where children are giving detailed evidence about violent or sexual crimes they should be allowed to do so in a more informal, private context than a courtroom. In our view this could only have a beneficial effect both on the children and on the quality of their testimony. It is crucial that the rights of the accused are also safe-guarded whatever changes to legal procedure are enacted, but it is difficult to see how maximizing the accuracy and completeness of a child's testimony threatens the rights of an innocent accused.

ACKNOWLEDGEMENTS

This research was supported by the Scottish Home and Health Department, and the project was based at Glasgow Polytechnic. The views expressed in this chapter are those of the authors and do not necessarily represent the position or policy of the funding body.

REFERENCES

Brennan, M. & Brennan, R. (1988). *Strange Language*. Wagga Wagga: Riverina Literacy Centre.

Butler, J., Glasgow, D. & McEnery, A. (1991). Child testimony: the potential of forensic linguistics and computational analysis for assessing the credibility of evidence. *Family Law*, **21**, 34–37.

Cashmore, J. (1991a). The use of videotechnology for child witnesses. *Monash Law Review*, September.

Cashmore, J. (1991b). Problems and solutions in lawyer–child communication. *Criminal Law Journal*, **15**, 193–202.

Flin, R. (in press). Hearing and testing children's evidence: the British experience. In G. Goodman & B. Bottoms (Eds). *Understanding and Improving Children's Testimony: Developmental, Clinical and Legal Issues*. New York: Guildford.

Flin, R., Bull, R., Boon, J. & Knox, A. (1992). Child witnesses in Scottish trials. Manuscript submitted for publication.

Flin, R., Boon, J., Knox, A. & Bull, R. (in press). The effects of a five month delay on children's and adults' eyewitness memory. *British Journal of Psychology*.

Flin, R., Bull, R., Boon, J. & Knox, A. (1990). *Child Witnesses in Criminal Prosecutions*. Report to the Scottish Home and Health Department.

Flin, R., Davies, G. & Tarrant, A. (1988). *The Child Witness*. Report to the Scottish Home and Health Department.

Flin, R., Stevenson, Y. & Davies, G. (1989). Children's knowledge of legal proceedings. *British Journal of Psychology*, **80**, 285–297.

Garbarino, J. & Stott, F. (1989). *What Children Can Tell Us*. San Francisco: Jossey-Bass.

Goodman, G. & Aman, C. (1991). Children's use of anatomically correct dolls to recount an event. *Child Development*, **61**, 1859–1871.

Goodman, G., Taub, E., Jones, D., England, P., Port, P., Rudy, L. & Prado, L. (1988). Emotional effects of criminal court testimony on child sexual assault victims. A preliminary report. In G. Davies & J. Drinkwater (Eds). *The Child Witness: Do the Courts Abuse Children?* Leicester: British Psychological Society.

Goodman, G., Taub, E., Jones, D., England, P., Port, P., Rudy, L. & Prado, L. (in press). Emotional effects of criminal court testimony on child sexual assault victims. SRCD Monograph.

Gordon, B., Schroeder, C. & Abrams, J. (1990). Age and social-class differences in children's knowledge of sexuality. *Journal of Clinical Child Psychology*, **19**, 33–43.

Hyam, M. (1990). *Advocacy Skills*. London: Blackstone.

Irish Law Reform Commission (1990). *Report on Child Sexual Abuse*; (1989) *Consultation Paper on Child Sexual Abuse*. Dublin.

Levi, J. & Walker, A. (Eds) (1990). *Language in the Judicial Process*. New York: Plenum.

Loesel, F. (Ed.) (in press) *Proceedings of the Second European Conference on Law and Psychology*, Nurnberg.

Morgan, J. & Plotnikoff, J. (1990). Children as victims of crime: procedures at court. In J. Spencer, G. Nicholson, R. Flin & R. Bull (Eds). *Children's Evidence in Legal Proceedings*. Available from Cambridge University Law Faculty.

Myers, J. (in press). *Legal Issues in Child Abuse and Neglect Practice*. San Francisco: Sage.

Plotnikoff, J. (1990). Delay in child abuse prosecutions. *Criminal Law Review*, 645–647.

Saywitz, K. & Snyder, L. (in press). Preparation of child witnesses: closing the gap between system requirements and children's capabilities. In G. Goodman & B. Bottoms (Eds). *Understanding and Improving Children's Testimony*. New York: Guildford.

Schor, D. & Sivan, A. (1989). Interpreting children's labels for sex-related body parts of anatomically explicit dolls. *Child Abuse & Neglect*, **13**, 523–532.

Spencer, J. & Flin, R. (1990). *The Evidence of Children*. London: Blackstone.

Wilkinson, P. (1981). A case for conversational analysis of courtroom interaction. Working Paper. Centre for Socio-Legal Studies, Wolfson College, Oxford.

CHAPTER 11

Empowering Child Witnesses for Sexual Abuse Prosecution

Louise Dezwirek-Sas

London Family Court Clinic, Ontario

INTRODUCTION

Scope of the Problem

The 1980s in Canada were witness to dramatic changes in societal awareness and understanding of the phenomenon of child sexual abuse. The country was seriously shaken in 1984 when Dr Robin Badgley released the results and recommendations of his three-year Royal Commission Inquiry into the incidence of child sexual abuse, child pornography and juvenile prostitution (Badgley, 1984). The Inquiry, whose mandate was to determine the adequacy of Canadian laws to protect children from sexual abuse, documented the experiences of over 10 000 cases of child sexual abuse. It reviewed the ability of the criminal justice system to cope with the problem, as well as the ability of community agencies across the country to enforce the then existing laws. This Commission made no less than 52 recommendations ranging in scope from broad suggestions on how to increase social awareness through public education to specific amendments of Canadian criminal law.

The Commission found that the legislation was seriously lacking in its ability to prosecute the varied nature of sexual acts perpetrated

Children as Witnesses. Edited by H. Dent and R. Flin
© 1992 John Wiley & Sons Ltd.

against children. It therefore recommended revisions to the criminal offence code to better reflect the reality of what was happening to Canadian children and suggested fundamental changes to the law to allow children to be able to speak directly for themselves at legal proceedings.

Federal and provincial government bodies reviewed the Royal commission's findings, but an official response was not forthcoming until nearly two years later. In 1986, the Canadian government tabled Bill C-15 in Parliament. This was passed in 1987 and in January 1988, a full two years later—and following intense lobbying efforts, new sexual abuse legislation was proclaimed into force.

Bill C-15: Sexual Abuse Legislation

Three overall thrusts form the broad intent of Bill C-15. The first is to afford better protection of Canadian children through the provision of several new sexual abuse offences. The second thrust is to enhance the successful investigation and prosecution of cases in court, by allowing more children access to court to give their testimony. A dramatic change in the willingness to receive and give weight to children's evidence has resulted in younger children being able to testify on their own behalf in court (see Vogl & Bala, 1989). Given that the most vulnerable victims are usually younger children who are abused in secrecy with no material/physical evidence, this amendment will have far-reaching implications. More and younger children are expected to testify in court across Canada, and it appears that they will now be heard despite the lack of corroboration in some cases and, at times, an inability to understand the oath.

The third thrust is to improve the experiences of child victims in the court through the provision of modifications to court procedure. Recognition of the difficulties children experience in a courtroom setting, in particular their fears of intimidation by the accused, is evident in Bill C-15. Provisions exist for the use of a screen (Section 442[2.1]) to ensure that child witnesses are able to give a full and candid account of their victimization. The potential to employ closed circuit television in order to physically remove the child from the courtroom also exists (Section 442[2.1]). Videotaping of children's disclosure and investigative interviews is yet another avenue whereby children can be protected from having to recount the sordid details of their abuse in a full courtroom and in front of their abuser (Section 643.1). Children, however, must still adopt the contents of the tape.

Bill C-15 is now three years old and a formal legislative review is planned for 1992. Despite the legislative changes, implementation in communities across Canada is slow and the reality remains that many child victims of sexual abuse are still further traumatized by a criminal justice system insensitive to their needs and ignorant of their plight.

Effects of Sexual Abuse and Criminal Justice System Involvement on Children

The negative effects, both short and long-term, of sexual abuse on children are well documented in Browne and Finkelhor's (1986) review of the literature on the impact of child sexual abuse. More recent research continues to reveal the diverse nature of both initial and long-term symptomatology (Peters, 1988; Bagley and Ramsay, 1986; Wolfe & Wolfe, 1988). Disclosure of sexual abuse for most child witnesses brings forth a host of added pressures, at a time when their capacity to cope with more stress is already well over the limit. As a result of their disclosure, they find themselves on the threshold of involvement in the court system. This means that they have to face a complex adult-oriented and at times incomprehensible criminal justice system, despite their pronounced fears.

The last decade saw an increasing number of research articles dealing with the potential trauma of court testimony and involvement in the criminal justice system for children (Goodman et al, 1988; Jaffe et al, 1987; Runyan et al, 1988; Weiss & Berg, 1982; Wolfe et al, 1987). The finding in many of these research studies and clinical reports is that the negative emotional effects evident in child witnesses parallel those which have been documented in other research on adult female rape victims when they testify and are revictimized in court (Veronen & Kilpatrick, 1983). System stressors combined with the emotional sequelae related to the abuse itself can result in a high level of stress in children, a factor which can negatively affect their ability to provide competent and compelling evidence in a court of law.

THE LONDON CHILD WITNESS PROJECT

In 1987 the Federal Health and Welfare Department announced that funds were going to be made available to help evaluate and develop programs for child sexual abuse victims in the areas of assessment, treatment and criminal prosecution. The London Family Court Clinic (a children's mental health centre in London, Ontario) was successful in obtaining funding and set up The Child Witness Project, a three-year demonstration project, with the goal of reducing the traumatization of child witnesses in the Canadian criminal justice system.

Dealing with System Stressors

Project staff in their daily observation of the criminal justice system documented a number of stressors which contribute to the secondary victimization of child witnesses. Table 11.1 provides an outline of those areas.

Table 11.1. Criminal justice system stressors

1. Delays	Numerous unforeseen adjournments, lengthy delays which span many months, even years in a child's life
2. Public exposure	Having to recount embarrassing and frightening incidents in a public courtroom at an age where speaking publicly about oneself is difficult
3. Facing the accused	Having to face the accused person when on the stand despite intense fear for personal safety
4. Understanding complex procedures	Being exposed to court procedures that are foreign and easily misunderstood by children who do not know the legal terminology or the adversarial context
5. Change of Crown Attorneys	Having changes in Crown Attorneys on their case just prior to or on the day of court, which undermines their sense of security and self-confidence. The lack of a supportive/comfortable relationship when entering into court with their counsel because insufficient time had been spent together
6. Cross-examination	Being cross-examined by a defense lawyer, who can be very aggressive. At times withstanding cross-examination that can be downright harassing, in that it exploits the child's sensitivity and vulnerability
7. Exclusion of witnesses	Being "alone" in court because the removal of witnesses results in the child finding himself/herself in court on the stand without significant adult figures in his/her life (ie family) present as support
8. Apprehension and placement outside the home	Being removed for safety reasons from one's home while the accused is allowed to stay. Children are often the ones to leave and are then stripped of their extended family support while the accused remains home
9. Lack of preparation for the role of witness	Not being aware of the expectations of them because they are child witnesses. Most children are totally unprepared to give testimony, and do not understand the adversarial system

Overview of Court Preparation

In order to help child witnesses cope with these system stressors, a court preparation protocol was developed with the goal of: (a) demystifying the courtroom through education; and (b) reducing the fear and anxiety related to testifying through stress reduction. It was felt that empowering the child victim through education and stress reduction would readjust the imbalance that exists in court between the accused and the child complainant by providing support for and advocacy on behalf of the child witness. The underlying philosophy guiding the choice of components for the court preparation protocol was based on our belief that children, due to their inherent vulnerability caused by their tender years, limited social awareness, lack of life experiences, and naive understanding of the criminal justice system, are generally ill-prepared for the demands made of witnesses in a court of law. We felt that their lack of knowledge about the court process, along with their obvious confusion and ignorance of legal terms and concepts, would interact with their fears of facing the accused in court.

The Child Witness Project was set up to work with child witnesses on an individual basis. As a result, great effort was spent in: (a) assessing the individual needs of child witnesses *vis à vis* the court preparation; and (b) designing an intervention which would meet those needs. In order to determine the child's overall status, a number of critical factors were identified as they related to each child's ability to testify. These are described in Table 11.2.

Assessment of these factors was dependent on information obtained through several means. An in-depth intake was done with the parents or guardians. During this time the child witness was administered a battery of psychological tests and questionnaires which, together with the background information, helped the therapist determine the fac-

Table 11.2. Factors related to a child's ability to testify

The child's level of cognitive social functioning—his/her knowledge of court and his/her ability to understand court proceedings and withstand difficult questioning

The child's level of anxiety and fear related to the accused and to testifying in general

His/her feelings of ambivalence and guilt about the disclosure and the prospect of testifying (this is more of an issue in intrafamilial situations)

The availability of family support, in particular that of the mother, and agency support where appropriate for the family

The child's overall temperament and premorbid history

The child's emotional sequelae related to the sexual abuse, in particular any PTSD-related symptomatology

tors that were operating to either enhance or interfere with each child's ability to testify. The child witness court preparation protocol involved three major areas which were covered in anywhere from three to eight individual sessions. Parents were included in sessions from time to time, as the need arose, but the majority of the work was carried out with the child alone. The purpose of the educational component of the protocol was to prepare the child witness in such areas as court procedures and etiquette, legal terminology, preparation on the oath and the criminal justice system process. Innovative equipment and aids were used to teach the child about the criminal justice system in a creative and non-directive manner.

Assessment

In the first session, the therapist referred to the results of a Knowledge of Court Questionnaire, developed at the project, and the results of the Peabody Picture Vocabulary Test (Dunn & Dunn, 1981) before beginning the court preparation with the child witness. The score on the Knowledge of Court Questionnaire indicated the extent of what the child knew, or did not know, about court, while the Peabody Picture Vocabulary Test (PPVT) provided a good indicator of the level of the child's overall cognitive functioning. A vocabulary checklist, which listed 23 commonly used words and concepts in the criminal justice system, was used by the therapist to mark the dates when each item was discussed. The therapist also noted the child's level of comprehension and whether more repetition was required. Other checklists were used by the therapist to ensure that material was covered. General etiquette and court decorum, and techniques on giving one's testimony and withstanding defense tactics were all included as part of the protocol.

Material and Procedures

Courtroom model and dolls A wooden courtroom model (36 × 36 in) and dolls, designed and made by the Family Court Clinic staff members, were used to assist in the teaching. Soft dolls (non-anatomically correct) represented court personnel, the child witness and his/her family, support people and the accused. In addition, the court model was used to give the child an awareness of where he/she and others would sit during the court proceedings. The therapist encouraged the child witness to take himself/herself through an imaginary court hearing and to rehearse the sequence of events that would transpire. Children of all ages enjoyed this educative aid.

Booklets such as *So You Have To Go To Court* (Harvey & Watson-Russell, 1988) and an excellent colouring book, *What's My Job in Court?* (Gaitskell, 1989), were also used for court preparation. This latter booklet contains "pop out" people in a courtroom as well as descriptions of court procedures, and it was given to the child witness as an adjunct to the educative sessions.

Judge's gown and role-playing A judge's gown worn during the role-playing of courtroom scenarios was used as another preparation technique. The focus of the role play was to familiarize the child with the roles of the judge, crown attorney, and defense lawyer. The child witness was encouraged to wear the gown and questions were rehearsed around the oath in creative play. The technique was also used to reinforce other aspects of the court preparation such as proper voice projection, articulation of "yes" or "no" answers, attentive listening and appropriately assertive behavior.

Homework Most child witnesses were given homework assignments on understanding the importance of telling the truth and their appreciation of the seriousness of the allegations. Children were also asked to draw pictures of themselves in court, showing all the key courtroom personnel.

Court tour The Victim Witness Assistance Program staff arranged a court tour for the child witness and a crown appointment approximately 7–10 days before the court date. A Provincial Division court tour (before preliminary hearings) and a General Division (previously known as district court) court tour (before trial) were conducted. In each case the child was brought into an empty courtroom so that he/she could become familiar with the setting.

Stress Reduction

Assessment The decision to include a stress reduction component in the preparation was based on our clinical findings that the majority of child victims expressed much fear and anxiety over their court dates and in particular over their participation in the hearings and trials as key witnesses. The five most salient fears documented in a pilot study of child witnesses were: (a) facing the accused person; (b) being hurt by the accused in the courtroom or outside; (c) being on the stand or crying on the stand; (d) being sent to jail; and (e) not understanding the questions.

Techniques The stress reduction component involved a combination of techniques : (1) deep breathing exercises: (2) deep muscle relaxation: (3) development of a fear hierarchy; (4) cognitive restructuring and empowerment; (5) emotional support; and (6) systematic desensitization, when needed. Two alternate forms of muscle relaxation therapy were available as part of the stress reduction. An imagery-based relaxation script (Koeppen, 1974) was employed with younger child witnesses (under age 10) to teach them to identify the somatic counterpart to their stress and to gain control over it. With older children, non-imagery based deep muscle relaxation exercises (Bernstein & Berkovec, 1973) were employed.

All child witnesses were taught to employ deep breathing relaxation exercises as a strategy for managing their anxiety and nervousness in court. Frequent practice of this technique was encouraged. The aids and equipment used for this component of the preparation protocol involved a tape-recorder and microphone, muscle relaxation scripts, audiotapes and inexpensive portable tape players, and a recliner chair. Depending on the level of fear and anxiety related to testifying in court, children were offered a range of stress reduction techniques. For some of the child witnesses who endorsed many fears, and who were manifesting post traumatic stress disorder (PTSD) related symptomatology, individual relaxation tapes were made. The tapes were always made *in vivo* with the child, in the therapist's office. The tapes were highly individualized and the child's name was used by the therapist throughout the instructions. In conjunction with the therapist, child witnesses were asked to generate a hierarchy of their five most salient fears related to testifying in court.

For a small number of child witnesses, systematic desensitization was employed to induce relaxation and reduce fears. This involved having the children imagine their fears on their hierarchy and master each fear through deep muscle relaxation. The fears were dealt with in gradual succession from least to most anxiety-provoking.

Empowerment and Support

Empowerment of the child witnesses was a difficult task, given their history of victimization. As part of the stress reduction, a cognitive restructuring intervention was carried out with the child witnesses. Kendall et al (1988) have expounded on the benefits of cognitive behavioural treatments for anxious children. In our sessions, positive self-statements of mastery and strength were used to assist children in reversing their feelings of helplessness, giving them inner strength and self-confidence. Child witnesses were encouraged to generate some positive reasons for attending court, to review their support base, and to develop strategies for dealing with different court scenarios. Role-playing of courtroom vignettes helped prepare the child witnesses to answer simple questions competently even though the actual facts of the case were never discussed. The concept of a team attending court with the child victim was a successful way of reducing the stress the child witnesses felt at "carrying the case alone". Children were encouraged to think about their inner strength and external supports. The children were reminded that *they* were not on trial, but that their complaint was being taken seriously by a court of law. Child witnesses were encouraged to bring a "lucky charm" to court, something small but meaningful which would strengthen their resolve and bring them good luck.

In addition, the Child Witness Project therapist continually provided emotional support and encouragement to the child during the educative and stress reduction sessions and, when needed, this support was extended to the family. In cases of incest where family support was of a dubious nature, the Project therapist's support was probably the most important service offered.

EVALUATION DESIGN

Given that the overall purpose of the Child Witness Project was to develop a successful model of intervention for child sexual abuse victims testifying in court, such that their potential for secondary trauma was lessened, it was decided that a client-focused outcome evaluation was required. The outcome evaluation addressed the treatment efficacy of the court preparation in reference to the psychological adjustment and court performance of the child witness. Given that the Child Witness Project worked cooperatively with other agencies in the community to advocate for child witnesses by planning the nature of their involvement and exposure to the criminal justice system, it was determined that results of the impact of the Child Witness Project on the community's handling of sexual abuse cases were also required.

In addition to the general evaluation design described, an experimental design was incorporated within the Project to determine the significance of the preparation component relative to a control group. Thus, all child witnesses in the Project were randomly assigned to either the "treatment condition" (involving preparation sessions in the Child Witness Project) or a control condition (involving the standard procedure provided to all child witnesses). The control condition involved a tour of the courtroom and one individual discussion with the child of court procedures by the Victim Witness Assistance Program, but no individual preparation by the Child Witness Project.

The evaluation design, coupled with the experimental design contained within the evaluation, was thus able to address three major issues of pertinence to the topic of preparing children for court testimony. First of all, this evaluation clarified the process necessary for children to learn the basic information and skills for testifying in court. Secondly, the evaluation was able to address the question of whether or not preparation for court testimony made a difference in their adjustment and performance, in comparison to children who were only given a tour of the court. Finally, the complicated and multifaceted issue of how children's victimization experiences may influence their psychological adjustment and subsequent court performance was addressed in this study. A prediction model was developed to assist in understanding what factors were most influential in determining children's outcome in court and subsequent psychological adjustment. These factors included demographic characteristics (eg the child's age, sex, etc) related to the abuse itself (eg the duration of the abuse, the child's relationship to the offender, etc), and factors related to their criminal justice system involvement (length of time in the system, whether they testified, and if they received court preparation).

Measuring the Effects of Court Preparation

In order to evaluate the effectiveness of the Child Witness Project in reference to the child's general psychological adjustment, the child's specific court fears, the child's understanding of the criminal justice system, the child's actual courtroom performance, and his/her and his/her family's perception of the services, a series of instruments were incorporated into the evaluation procedures at several different points in time during the child's trajectory through the criminal justice system. Table 11.3 provides the schedule for obtaining the outcome measures.

Child's General Psychological/Social Adjustment

There were two data sources for measuring the child's general psychological and social adjustment: the child, through self-report, and the parent or parent surrogate, through a checklist and intake interview. Because some concerns have been expressed in the literature regarding

Table 11.3. Child witness outcome measures

Pre-intervention testing & intake	Post-intervention before court	At preliminary hearing	Post-preliminary hearing	At trial	Post-trial	Follow-up	Completed by
CDI	—	—	CDI	—	CDI	CDI	Child
CMAS	—	—	CMAS	—	CMAS	CMAS	Child
FSSR–SAFE	—	—	FSSR–SAFE	—	FSSR–SAFE	FSSR–SAFE	Child
PPVT	—	—	—	—	—	—	Child
Court fears	Court fears	—	—	—	—	—	Child
Court knowledge	Court knowledge	—	—	—	—	—	Child
CBCL	—	—	CBCL	—	CBCL	CBCL	Parent
—	—	Court perf. rating if child testifies	—	Court perf. rating if child testifies	—	—	Research assistant
—	—	—	Feedbacks	—	Feedbacks	—	Crown/police
—	—	—	Feedbacks	—	Feedbacks	—	Crown/police

the extent to which children and adolescents are able to accurately report their feelings (Kazdin, 1981), it was felt that a multimethod evaluation of the child witnesses was necessary. The child's abuse-related fears and anxieties were measured by the administration of the Fear Survey Schedule for Children-Revised (Ollendick, 1983), the SAFE (Wolfe & Wolfe, 1988), and the Children's Manifest Anxiety Scale (Reynolds & Richmond, 1978). The child's level of depression was measured by the Children's Depression Inventory (Kovacs, 1983).

Child's Specific Court Fears and Knowledge of Court

A Fears of Court measure was designed to measure the child's personal fears related to testifying. A Knowledge of Court Questionnaire was designed to measure the child's understanding and knowledge of court personnel and procedures as well as of his or her "witness" role. The nature of the fears canvassed in the first questionnaire covered five basic aspects of a child witness's potential court experience. Eight items dealt with the accused, facing the accused, having feelings of fear regarding personal safety because of the accused, and dreading the outcome in court as it pertained to the accused. Five items tapped the child's fears of personal inadequacy as a witness, not understanding questions, forgetting events, losing emotional control on the stand, and/or becoming ill on the stand. Other items attempted to measure the child's fear of public exposure, humiliation, and embarrassment at being identified or labelled as a victim of sexual abuse. Several items focused on the impact of the child's decision to testify on his or her family system. The Knowledge of Court Questionnaire was designed to assess a child's basic knowledge and understanding of courtroom procedures and process. It consisted of 21 open-ended questions which require verbal or written responses. The pool of items was developed from a list of key terms and procedures that were felt by Child Witness Project staff to be integral to testifying in a courtroom. The answers to the questions were written down but could be given verbally by the child.

Child Witness Performance in the Courtroom

Court performance rating scale The court performance rating scale was developed by the Child Witness Project for use by the research assistant in the courtroom. It examined how children performed on the stand (ie their ability to swear an oath, respond to questions, resist defense strategies, and consistently respond to questions regarding the past abusive events). It also examined other areas of difficulty for child witnesses. The research assistant observed and rated all preliminary hearing and trial testimonies of child witnesses on the court performance rating scale. In addition, police and crown attorneys were asked to rate the child witnesses with respect to their understanding of court procedures and etiquette, legal terminology, and general orientation.

Parent/Child Perception of Project Service

Parent/child questionnaires Lastly, the families of the child witnesses and the children themselves who received the court preparation were asked to complete feedback questionnaires at two points in time (preliminary hearing and trial). The questions in the parent feedbacks required that the parents rate the general helpfulness of the Child Witness Project, the value of the preparation in educating and reducing the child's stress, and the amount of emotional support they and their child received.

Results

Description of the Child Witnesses in the Study

Demographics The Child Witness Project accepted 144 consenting child witness referrals into the evaluation study between January 1, 1988 and January 1, 1990. In all of these cases charges had been laid by police under Bill C-15 on behalf of children who were either victims of or witnesses to sexual abuse. The study sample consisted of 114 girls and 30 boys (male 21%: female 79%, a ratio consistent with previous findings in the literature on sexual abuse victimization (Russell, 1984). The ages of the children referred ranged from five to 17, with the majority of the children falling between the ages of 10 and 15. The mean age overall was 11.5. Of interest was the finding that over 20% of the sample were in special classes within the school system and were described by their parents as low functioning with respect to their academic achievements.

Although the Child Witness Project was primarily geared towards victims who were required to testify, it became apparent to us that a sizeable number of children were being called as witnesses to sexual crimes perpetrated on other children. Of the 144 referrals to the Child Witness Project there were 128 victims and 16 witnesses. Eight children were both victims of sexual abuse and witnesses to the abuse of others. In the majority of the cases (83%) the victimization was by someone the child knew, and in many instances a family member was the abuser. All manner of methods of coercion were used on these children to obtain their compliance in the abuse, and it was painful to hear how children's emotions and loyalties were manipulated and their fears aroused by intimidation and force. Nearly half of the children were threatened or were physically restrained. The actual sexual acts perpetrated against the children varied a great deal as well, but over one-third were victims of some form of sexual intercourse and many had been involved in repeated acts of abuse over long periods of time.

Abusive incidents The abusive incidents described in the police charge sheets and by the parents to the intake worker varied a great deal in their severity. The most frequently alleged abuse was one in which the abuser touched the victim on the victim's private parts: 74% of the children complained of this. The next two most frequently alleged abuses were: (a) exposure of the abuser (29%), and then of the victim (28%), and then touching the abuser (21%). This was followed by oral–genital contact (17%), mutual masturbation (10%), and anal intercourse (8%). Simulated intercourse (8%) and vaginal intercourse (7%) also occurred. Several children described having their clothes partially torn off or being restrained but nothing more taking place.

Coercive inducements by abusers The means by which the abuser obtained the children's compliance was another area examined in great detail. Physical force was used in one-third of the abusive situations and threatened in another 23% of the situations. Presenting oneself as an authority figure was a manipulation used in nearly 40% of the abusive situations. Children often reported that the abuser's parental, teaching, counselling, or supervisory role was implied as a reason why they should acquiesce to the sexual demands. In another 20% of the cases, children reported being threatened with dire consequences which were sufficiently alarming to them that they chose not to disclose. For some children, legitimization of the behaviour encouraged them to be involved. Bribery through money, gifts, and special privileges was a much less frequently used method of coercion, as were "trickery" and "pretences".

A review of all the methods suggested that the use of authority, threat, and some physical force by the abuser most often resulted in children's compliance.

Child witness fears The child witnesses expressed many fears about going to court but the most prominent fear was facing the accused. The fears were manifested in the children having difficulty relaxing, falling asleep, or concentrating at school. Many children felt powerless to control their fears. Nearly half of the child witnesses evidenced PTSD related symtomatology (80% reexperiencing, 64% avoidance, 67% arousal, 49% PTSD).

Goodman et al (1988) noted significant adjustment problems on the part of child victims. She reported that the children who were frightened of the accused while testifying were less able to answer questions and more likely to say that testifying had affected them adversely. Out of our sample of 144 child witnesses, 63 testified at the preliminary hearing, 71 at trial, and 50 at both. In our examination of child witnesses' fears of going to court, we found that the older children expressed more fears than the younger children and that girls expressed more fears than boys, in particular about their personal safety.

As well, the children who had suffered intrafamilial abuse experienced more fears related to familial pressure and the potential negative impact on the family due to their testimony (see also Kreiger & Robbins, 1985). The complicated nature of the stressors brought to bear on intrafamilial child witnesses—concern for family, excessive guilt, lack of emotional support and even familial abandonment in favour of the accused—were not unusual and made court preparation all the more challenging. We found that court preparation which took into consideration the special issues that were present for incest victims maximized the therapeutic benefits of testifying.

Child witness ignorance In addition to their anxieties and fears about court, child witnesses did not know very much about the court process, a finding consistent with the results of Flin et al (1989) in a study on the knowledge of court of Scottish children (non-witnesses). In our study, older children knew and understood more legal terms but were still fairly ignorant about the workings of the criminal justice system and court procedures. Many child witnesses had gross misconceptions about how hearings were held, and as a result were clearly at a disadvantage compared to the knowledge available to the adult abusers. One of the more comical responses to our Knowledge of Court questionnaire was the definition for a subpoena given by a 10-year-old girl as "a male's private part". All humour aside, the child witnesses were certainly in need of education on *all* aspects of court proceedings.

Outcome Results

Results of the final evaluation indicate that the court preparation offered by the Child Witness Project benefited the child witnesses in four distinct ways:

1. By educating them about court procedures
2. By helping them deal with their stress and anxieties related to the abuse and to testifying
3. By helping them tell their story competently on the stand in court
4. By providing an advocacy role on their behalf with the other mandated agencies in the criminal justice system.

The difficulty inherent in assessing the benefits of court preparation for child witnesses is due to the multifaceted nature of the factors affecting all the outcome measures. In an attempt to address this reality, several multiple regression analyses were conducted in which groups of important variables (child's background and criminal justice system factors) were entered into a regression equation model to determine their relative impact on the post-court outcome. The most significant finding from these analyses was that the Child Witness Project's court preparation served to mitigate the negative effects of a documented major stressor, "length of time in the criminal justice system", and resulted in better adjustment in some of the psychological measures of fear, increased knowledge of court, and better performance (ie testimony) by child witnesses as rated by crown attorneys (see Dezwirek-Sas et al, 1991 for full details).

CONCLUSION: THE CRIMINAL JUSTICE SYSTEM'S EXPERIENCE FOR CHILD WITNESSES

It is often the case that we find our attempts to help the sexually abused child result in significant and unintended negative consequences. In our observations of the criminal justice system we saw first hand the negative side: how sometimes laying charges and going to court resulted in the child being thrown into a system which was extremely slow moving, required frequent recall of the abuse, led to stigmatization through public exposure, and exacerbated feelings of self-blame, guilt and fear during cross-examination. On the positive side, however, we also saw cases where it empowered children, reversing their feelings of helplessness and providing a public affirmation that the child was *not* responsible for what happened and that the abuse was wrong and unacceptable to society. For some child witnesses it was even a cathartic experience which then signalled the beginning of their emotional recovery. The problem is that upon entering the courtroom it is hard to predict with any certainty how the events will play themselves out—there are too many factors that cannot be controlled. Our observations from tracking the criminal justice system for the child witnesses in our study lead us to believe that the negatives still loom large. The delays and length of time in the system were very difficult for the vulnerable children, especially the younger ones who tired out and often gave up the fight. An excellent research study by Runyan et al (1988) has concluded that awaiting criminal court proceedings can impede the resolution of depression, and Tedesco and Schnell (1987) found that children who testified were *still* upset two and a half years later. As well, although testifying does not necessarily cause more emotional disturbance in all child victims, it does appear to prevent children from healing. Our experiences confirm other research findings in that the majority of our child witnesses frequently verbalized their inability to get on with their lives until court was over. Unfortunately, this "in limbo" state often stretched up to two years.

Having completed a three-year evaluation study on the benefits of court preparation for child witnesses, a strong recommendation is made for more legislative amendments to court procedures. As much as possible, children should be provided with alternatives to facing the accused when giving their evidence, either through a screen or closed circuit television provision. In addition, the child witnesses should be accompanied by a known person whom they trust when they go up on the stand. The Child Witness Project played a major advocacy role on behalf of child witnesses with respect to modifying the courtroom/ proceedings. It also demonstrated that preparing child witnesses using education, stress reduction and empowerment is effective. Much can be done to help child witnesses cope within the criminal justice system, but further research and lobbying efforts are needed.

REFERENCES

Badgley, R. (1984). *Sexual Offences Against Children*. Report of the Committee on Sexual Offences Against Children and Youths. Canada.

Bagley, C. & Ramsay, R. (1986). Disrupted childhood and vulnerability to sexual assault: long-term sequels with implications for counselling. *Social Work & Human Sexuality*, 4, 33–48.

Bernstein, D. A. & Borkovec, T. D. (1973). *Progressive Relaxation Training: A Manual for the Helping Professionals*. Campaign: Research Press.

Bill C-15 (1987). *An Act to Amend the Criminal Code and the Canada Evidence Act*, R.S.C. 1985, c. 19 (3rd suppl.) Ottawa: Canadian Government Publishing Centre.

Browne, A. & Finkelhor, D. (1986). Impact of child sexual abuse: a review of the research. *Psychological Bulletin*, **99**, 66–77.

Criminal Code, Revised Statutes of Canada, 1985 c. C-46.

Dezwirek-Sas, L., Hurley, P., Austin, G. & Wolfe, D. (1991). *Reducing the System-Induced Trauma for Child Sexual Abuse Victims Through Court Preparation, Assessment and Follow-Up.* Ontario: London Family Court Clinic.

Dunn, L. M. & Dunn, L. M. (1981). *Peabody Picture Vocabulary Test—Revised: Manual for Forms L and M.* Circle Pines: American Guidance Service.

Flin, R. H., Stevenson, Y. & Davies, G. M. (1989). Children's knowledge of court proceedings. *British Journal of Psychology*, 80, 285–297.

Gaitskell, S. (Ed.) (1989). *What's My Job in Court?* Ontario Ministry of the Attorney General.

Goodman, G. S., Jones, D. P. H., Pyle, E., Prado, L., Port, L. P., England, T., Mason, R. & Rudy, L. (1988). The child in court: a preliminary report on the emotional effects of criminal court testimony on child sexual abuse victims. In G. Davies & J. Drinkwater (eds), *Proceedings from the Oxford Conference on Children in Courts: Do the Courts Abuse Children?* pp. 46–54. Oxford: British Psychological Association.

Harvey, W. & Watson-Russell, A. (1988). *So You Have to Go to Court* (2nd edn). Toronto: Butterworths.

Jaffe, P., Wilson, S. K. & Sas, L. (1987). Court testimony of child sexual abuse victims: emerging issues in clinical assessments. *Canadian Psychology*, 28, 291–295.

Kazdin, A. E. (1981). Assessment techniques for childhood depression. *Journal of the American Academy of Child Psychiatry*, 20, 358–375.

Kendall, P. C., Howard, B. & Epps, J. (1988). The anxious child: cognitive-behavioral treatment strategies. *Behaviour Modification*, 12, 281–310.

Koeppen, A. J. (1974). Relaxation training for children. *Elementary School Guidance and Counselling*, October, 14–21.

Kovacs, M. (1983). A self-rated depression scale for school-aged youngsters. Unpublished manuscript, University of Pittsburgh School of Medicine.

Kreiger, M. J. & Robbins, J. (1985). The adolescent incest victim and the judicial system. *American Journal of Orthopsychiatry*, 55, 419–425.

Ollendick, T. H. (1983). Reliability and validity of the Revised Fear Survey Schedule for Children (FSSC-R). *Behaviour Research Therapy*, 21, 685–692.

Peters, S. D. (1988). Child sexual abuse and later psychological problems. In G. Wyatt & G. J. Powell (Eds), *Lasting Effects of Child Sexual Abuse*, pp. 101–117. Newbury, CA: Sage.

Reynolds, C. R. & Richmond, B. O. (1978). What I think and feel: a revised measure of children's manifest anxiety. *Journal of Abnormal Child Psychology*, 6, 271–282.

Runyan, D. K., Everson, M. D., Edelsohn, G. A., Hunter, W. M. & Coulter, M. L. (1988). Impact of legal intervention on sexually abused children. *Journal of Pediatrics*, 113, 647–653.

Russell, D. H. (1984). *Sexual Exploitation.* Beverly Hills, CA: Sage.

Tedesco, J. F. & Schnell, S. V. (1987). Children's reactions to sex abuse investigation and litigation. *Child Abuse and Neglect*, 11, 267–272.

Veronen, L. J. & Kilpatrick, D. G. (1983). Stress management for rape victims. In D. Meichenbaum & M. E. Jaremko (Eds). *Stress Reduction and Prevention.* New York: Plenum.

Vogl, R. & Bala, N. (1989). *Testifying on Behalf of Children. A Handbook for Professionals.* The Institute for the Prevention of Child Abuse. Toronto: Canada.

Weiss, E. H. & Berg, R. F. (1982). Child victims of sexual assault: impact of court procedures. *Journal of the American Academy of Child Psychiatry*, **21**, 513–518.

Wolfe, V. V. & Wolfe, D. A. (1988). Sexually Abused Fear Evaluation (SAFE). Unpublished measure.

Wolfe, V. V., Sas, L. & Wilson, S. K. (1987). Some issues in preparing sexually abused children for courtroom testimony. *The Behavior Therapist*, **10**, 107–113.

CHAPTER 12

The Court Prep Group: A Vital Part of the Court Process

Kathryn Sisterman Keeney, Ethel Amacher
and
Julie A. Kastanakis

National Children's Advocacy Center, Huntsville, Alabama

INTRODUCTION

As reports of child sexual abuse increase and the number of cases set for prosecution grows, children are being required to testify in courts with increasing frequency. In many cases, due to the lack of physical evidence or corroborating witnesses, the prosecutor's case rests in large part on the testimony of the child victim.

Testifying before a court can be frightening and confusing for anyone of any age; for a child already bearing the stress and psychological repercussions of child sexual abuse, a court appearance can be traumatizing.

Goodman compares a child's position in a courtroom as a key witness—regardless of the type of case—to the position of a rape victim. The child's credibility is disbelieved and attacked, opening the child to further emotional trauma (Goodman, 1984). In the case of child sexual abuse, a situation in which a child is already questioning his or her own self-worth, this type of legal maneuver can be particularly damaging. Therefore, one of the primary concerns of many professionals in the field of child sexual abuse is the effect of the trial experience

Children as Witnesses. Edited by H. Dent and R. Flin
© 1992 John Wiley & Sons Ltd.

on the child victim. There is an on-going debate as to whether the experience of giving testimony will result in a therapeutic gain of empowerment and control or in damaging feelings of stigmatization, powerlessness, self-blame, and guilt (Goodman, 1984; Runyan et al, 1988; Schwartz-Kenney et al, 1990; Whitcomb, 1990).

Numerous citations in the literature of anecdotal research describe the responses of children in the courtroom. Many of these were found to be highly detrimental to the prosecution's case as well as damaging to the child's own emotional well-being (Whitcomb et al, 1985). Goodman (1984) presents the case of a young boy charged with arson in which the boy denies completely his presence as a bystander at the fire, and even the existence of the fire itself, because he thought that if he could make the judge believe that there had been no fire he would not be found guilty. Others have given examples of children who became very frightened in the courtroom or completely misunderstood the court process (Berliner & Barbieri, 1984; Pynoos & Eth, 1984).

The possibility of further traumatizing a child through a courtroom experience is a valid concern. In order to reduce the potential damage, those facets of the judicial process that could become stressors on the child and his or her family, such as unfamiliar language or unclear procedures, should be minimized as much as possible (Berliner & Barbieri, 1984; Burgess & Holmstrom, 1978; Whitcomb et al, 1985). Saywitz (1989) proposes a very convincing argument for this minimization using a medical model. She states that when children face unfamiliar and frightening medical procedures, an attempt is made to reduce their anxiety through techniques based on a firm knowledge of what will happen to them, including desensitization and anticipatory coping strategies. It seems clear that the same techniques could be used for the unfamiliar and frightening judicial procedures that confront a child giving evidence in court (Dezwirek-Sas, Chapter 11, this volume).

As Goodman (1984) points out, children testify in the context of their own understanding of the court process. In order to make a child's appearance in court as beneficial as possible to him/herself and to his or her case, it is clear that professionals in the field need to work to improve the child's level of understanding of the court process.

THE COURT PREP GROUP

The National Children's Advocacy Center has a program which attempts to minimize the stress inherent in the judicial process, using a children's court preparation group. The Court Prep Group evolved from a program originally developed by the multidisciplinary team of Nashville, Tennessee. Mary Hausman, counsellor, observed that traditional procedures used to familiarize children with the courtroom did not prepare them for the impact of the actual experience. Children who had seen the courtroom, and who knew the roles and positions of the court personnel, still froze when they had to testify at trial. To address this problem, the first Court Prep Group was created.

THE DEVELOPMENT OF THE PROGRAM

The team learned that the anxiety associated with a court appearance could be reduced by providing sessions over a four- to six-week period, thus allowing time for desensitization and learning to occur. As the program became more structured, the team designed each session to address one or more of the fears most frequently expressed by children and others involved in the criminal justice system: facing the defendant; testifying on direct and cross-examination; expectation of retaliation by the defendant; fears of judge and jury; and the unfamiliarity of the courtroom itself (Goodman et al, 1988; Whitcomb et al, 1985). The court*house* was found to be as intimidating to some children as the court*room*, so a tour of the building was incorporated as a part of the Court Prep program. Art and Gestalt techniques are used to help the children with their fears and feelings, and role-playing is employed to educate them about court personnel and their functions. These activities are aimed at demystifying the courtroom and diminishing the anxiety it evokes.

Throughout the group sessions, the central message underlined for the children is "tell the truth". Courtroom etiquette and protocol are also explored, discussing the rules of the court and the roles of its personnel. The next section gives a brief outline of the group sessions. This outline can be modified to better fit various needs and timeframes.

OUTLINE OF GROUP SESSIONS

Session 1—held in a neutral setting

A. Introductions and information
    1. Artwork: Decorating and personalizing name tags, personal folders
    2. Goal of group: Facts and feelings about court

B. Parents leave for their own information and support group
C. Beginning group exercise: An icebreaker with focus on group purpose. Assemble large table-size puzzle depicting court personnel and functions (can be made with cardboard)
D. Personal experiences since disclosure: A move toward individual participation. On a chalkboard, list people encountered in the system
E. Artwork: "Feeling faces" are used to open the discussion of feelings about going to court. Each child is asked to draw a face that shows how he or she feels about going to court
F. Closure: Cool-down time and preview of next session

Session 2—held in a neutral setting

A. Artwork as children arrive provides a baseline for assessment
    1. Free drawing and/or
    2. Draw or write about one or more:
        (a) What I learned last time
        (b) What I need to know
        (c) How I feel about going to court
        (d) How I feel about_____
B. Begin concrete information about court
    1. Reassemble puzzle
    2. Handouts: "Fill-in" drawings of the courtroom. Each child writes or draws the "court characters" in their appropriate places
C. First role-play
    Materials: Judge's robe, gavel, role-play cards, scenario cards
    1. Role-play cards describe courtroom personnel and one or two simple questions/statements to ask/say
    2. Scenario cards describe:
        (a) Robbery when perpetrator is a friend (used for first role-play)
        (b) Robbery when perpetrator is someone you are angry with
        (c) Robbery when perpetrator makes threats, witness initially lies to police
    3. Leaders verbally assist role definitions and review court terms: continuances, objections, pleas, overruled, sustained, etc.

Session 3—held in the courthouse
A. Tour of courthouse: Victim assistance office(s), bathrooms, jury room, courtroom
B. Game: Numbers are hidden on the positions (seats/tables) of

12 "court characters". The children are given a list of the characters and must find the number and match them to the people. In playing this game, the children crawl in, out and over the entire courtroom, bringing them a familiarity that greatly reduces anxiety for both children and adolescents

C. Review of roles: Role-play scenario cards

Sessions 4 and 5—held in the courthouse

A. Mock court role-play: Scenario (a), (b) or (c), depending on group age, comprehension, and ability level. Children choose roles and take turns. One way of assessing a child's attitude and readiness to testify is by how soon the child chooses to play the witness role
B. Focus on appropriate witness behavior
C. Discuss feelings that emerge during role-play
D. With younger children, use videos that show the court process

Session 6—held in a neutral setting—assessment/closure

A. Focus on individual case planning/coordination
B. Artwork, poetry, writing for next group: What I learned, how I feel, etc
C. Review of group experience
D. Graduation certificates. The graduation exercise is a positive way to end the group. It emphasizes that, regardless of the outcome of the trial, each child has successfully accomplished the primary goal: willingness to participate in, and thereby assist, the criminal justice system in becoming more equitable for child victims

Note: Depending on the size and needs of the group, only one session may be spent in the courtroom. However, experience indicates that greater confidence and less anxiety results from several role-playing sessions in the courtroom itself.

TIMING THE COURT PREP GROUP IN RELATION TO COURT APPEARANCE

Every effort is made to schedule children for the Court Prep Group closest to their actual court date. In Huntsville, Alabama, the grand jury indictment list is used to prioritize participants. The court docket is scheduled after the grand jury hands down its indictments. Even after the docket is set, it may be some time before a case is actually tried; the knowledge of the victim advocates is relied on to more realistically estimate the court schedule. In addition to these regularly scheduled cases, direct referrals for the Court Prep Group are taken from support persons. Occasionally a support person, such as a child's therapist, becomes aware of a child's need to experience Court Prep Group at an earlier date in an effort to gain a sense of empowerment and control over his or her victimization. If there is enough time and it is believed to be beneficial, the child can later repeat those segments of the program designed to familiarize him or her with the courtroom and the court process. Also, the group leaders review the status of each child at the end of a Court Prep Group program to evaluate the need for repeat attendance, either individually or in another group.

GROUP LEADERS OR FACILITATORS

In Tennessee, the original group leader was a Department of Human Services social worker. Subsequent groups were assisted by a victim advocate from the district attorney's office and the child sexual abuse community coordinator (Amacher, 1989). In Huntsville, the Court Prep Groups are facilitated by National Children's Advocacy Center staff therapists and by two victim advocates. A prosecutor from the Child Sexual Assault Prosecution Unit and a member of the clinical staff at the National Children's Advocacy Center lead the information/support group for parents and caretakers. Leaders of a Court Prep Group can, however, come from a range of sources. The necessary characteristics of a leader are a therapeutic manner and an ability to work at the level of the children involved.

GROUPING THE PARTICIPANTS

Though court schedules make it difficult to limit a group by age, it seems to work best to break the groups into age ranges of 6–12 years and 13–17 years. Often, all ages are included in the first and last sessions of a Court Prep Group and the age groups are split for the middle sections. This allows the leaders to refine the sessions of a particular age group's level of understanding. Children under six and older adolescents can be grouped separately and/or worked with individually, drawing from the same preparation outline. Usually, siblings are grouped together unless the circumstances of a specific case dictate otherwise. Emergency cases are added as they arise.

Age and developmental levels are very important factors to consider in planning groups. In a recent study of children's knowledge of the courtroom, Saywitz (1989) found that age and level of experience were the primary factors affecting the expectations the children brought to the courtroom, and that the children's expectations were consistent with their age-related developmental abilities. Saywitz (1989) also noted that prior experience with the legal system did not lead to enhanced knowledge or understanding of the process. Other studies have found that children may think they understand a legal term but, when asked to define it, provide a very different, non-legal definition concurrent with their age and level of development (for example interpreting jury to mean jewelry) (Saywitz & Jaenicke, 1987; Warren-Leubecker et al, 1989). The ramifications of this type of misunderstanding are alarming. Emphasis must be placed on the clarity of definitions of court processes and personnel, with special attention paid to the children's perceptions of those definitions. Court Prep Group leaders make a particular effort to check and review the children's understanding of terms such as continuance, object, judge, jury, and overruled. The leaders often ask the children to define these terms and then reflect clear definitions back to the children using their own terminology. It is important to note that specific case issues are not addressed, and prosecutors are not involved in the children's group sessions.

The support the children gain from being with other victims is one of the most immediately apparent benefits of the Court Prep Group. The group process underscores the child's realization that his or her victimization is not unique or rare, that he or she is not the only child to have been abused or to testify. This helps to reduce the child's sense of aloneness. Separate group sessions for parents and caretakers have now been incorporated as part of the program in order to provide them with much needed information and support.

SUMMARY

Because fear of the unknown can cause stress, it is very important that the child and family know what to expect when their case is set for prosecution. Court Prep Group benefits the child and family in a number of ways. The group provides materials and a defined program for re-enforcing reality while reducing anxiety, teaches improved coping skills and provides a safe setting to work through the effects of post-traumatic stress disorder, and allows for the support of peers as additional "team-mates" when court delays and continuances occur (Amacher et al, 1987).

Court Prep Group was designed to be part of a therapeutic intervention system. This involves a continuum of supportive, therapeutic contacts from initial investigative interviews through assessment, treatment, and resolution in the legal system. Given the complexity of this system and the need for a therapeutic approach, the ability to be adaptable and creative is very important in developing a court preparation program.

REFERENCES

Amacher, E. (1989). Group preparation of children for court: an idea whose time has come. *Roundtable Magazine*, 1(2), 14–17.

Amacher, E., Dozier, S., Greene, B., Shearon, T., Hausman, M. & Thurman, T. (1987). Court preparation for the sexually abused child. Presentation at the Third National Symposium on Child Sexual Abuse, Huntsville, Alabama.

Berliner, L. & Barbieri, M. K. (1984). The testimony of the child victim of sexual assault. *Journal of Social Issues*, 40(2), 125–137.

Burgess, A. W. & Holmstrom, L. L. (1978). The child and family during the court process. In A. W. Burgess, A. N. Groth, L. L. Holmstrom & S. Sgroi (Eds). *Sexual Assault of Children and Adolescents*. Lexington, MA: Lexington Books, pp. 205–229.

Goodman, G. (1984). The child witness: an introduction. *Journal of Social Issues*, 40(2), 1–7.

Goodman, G., Jones, D. P. H., Pyle, E. et al (1988). The child in court: a preliminary report on the emotional effects of criminal court testimony on child sexual assault victims. In G. Davies & J. Drinkwater (Eds), *Do the Courts Abuse Children?* Leicester: British Psychological Society.

Pynoos, R. S. & Eth, S. (1984). The child as witness to homicide. *Journal of Social Issues*, 40(2), 87–108.

Runyan, D., Everson, M., Edelshohn, G., Hunter, W. & Coulter, M. (1988). Impact of legal intervention on sexually abused children. *The Journal of Pediatrics*, 113(4), 647–653.

Saywitz, K. (1989). Children's conceptions of the legal system: court is a place to play basketball. In S. J. Ceci, D. F. Ross & M. P. Toglia (Eds). *Perspectives on Children's Testimony*. New York: Springer-Verlag, pp. 131–157.

Saywitz, K. & Jaenicke, C. (1987). Children's understanding of legal terms: a preliminary report of grade-related trends. Paper presented at the biennial meeting of the Society for Research on Child Development, Baltimore, MD.

Schwartz-Kenney, B. M., Wilson, M. E. & Goodman, G. S. (1990). An examination of child witness accuracy and the emotional effects on children on testifying in court. In K. Oates (Ed.). *Understanding and Managing Child Sexual Abuse*. Sydney: Harcourt, Brace, Jovanovich.

Warren-Leubecker, A., Tate, C. S., Hinton, I. D. & Ozbek, I. N. (1989). What do children know about the legal system and when do they know it? First steps down a less travelled path in child witness research. In S. J. Ceci, D. F. Ross & M. P. Toglia (Eds). *Perspectives on Children's Testimony*. New York: Springer-Verlag, pp. 158–183.

Whitcomb, D. (1985). Prosecution of child sexual abuse: innovations in practice. *Research in Brief.* Washington, DC: National Institute of Justice, US Department of Justice.

Whitcomb, D. (1990). When the victim is a child: past hope, current reality and future promise of legal reform in the United States. In J. R. Spencer, G. Nicholson, R. Flin & R. Bull (Eds), *Children's Evidence in Legal Proceedings: An International Perspective.* Cambridge: University of Cambridge, Faculty of Law.

Whitcomb, D., Shapiro, E. & Stellwagen, L. D. (1985). *When The Victim is a Child: Issues for Judges and Prosecutors.* Washington, DC: US Department of Justice, National Institute of Justice.

CHAPTER 13

Videotechnology and the Child Witness

Graham Davies

University of Leicester

and

Helen Westcott

National Society for the Prevention of Cruelty to Children, London

One of the most controversial issues to emerge from recent concern over the plight of child witnesses has been the use of videotechnology in the courtroom. Professionals campaigning on behalf of child witnesses were quick to see the potential of videotechnology as a facilitator for children required to testify in court (eg Libai, 1969; Bernstein & Claman, 1986; Bulkley, 1985; Colby & Colby, 1987; Spencer, 1987). The role of video is twofold. First, it can be used at the trial itself, to allow the child to testify via closed circuit television outside the intimidating arena of the courtroom. Secondly, it may be employed to prerecord interviews with the child which can be used to complement or substitute for the child's actual appearance in court. The first use of video for in-court facilitation will be referred to as the video or live link, while the second use of prerecorded material will be referred to as videotapes or videorecordings.

Set against the particular difficulties children experience in testifying effectively in court, video evidence appears to offer major advantages. As regards the live link, its use can obviate confrontation with

Children as Witnesses. Edited by H. Dent and R. Flin
© 1992 John Wiley & Sons Ltd.

the defendant, one of the major fears expressed by child witnesses who are called to court (Flin et al, 1988; Goodman et al, 1988). Moreover, by testifying from a small room with social support (see Moston, Chapter 3, this volume), anxiety about speaking out in court, with its alien, adult and often intimidating setting, may be reduced (Davies, 1991).

As regard the use of videotapes, these too can offer significant advantages for the child witness. In recent years there has been a gradual reassessment of children's cognitive capacities (eg Ceci et al, 1987; Cole & Loftus, 1987), with the result that researchers are now generally more optimistic about the quality of memory of children as young as three or four years and their potential as witnesses (Davies et al, 1986). However, recent research suggests that children may be even more susceptible than adults to long delays between the storage and recall of information, so that their capacity to remember accurately details (especially peripheral details) diminishes over time (Brainerd & Ornstein, 1991; Flin et al, 1990). According to its advocates, videotape offers the opportunity to capture the child's first-hand account of events as soon as an allegation is made. Moreover, this record can be preserved and produced as evidence at trial, obviating the frequently long delays which occur between an initial report and the case coming to court (Davies, 1988; Spencer & Flin, 1990).

These apparently powerful arguments have not gone unchallenged. Many lawyers remain unconvinced that these theoretical advantages can be achieved in practice, and question the empirical basis of the assertions for the value of videotechnology for empowering child witnesses (eg Grant, 1987; King, 1988; Wilson, 1990). In this chapter we examine first the existing evidence for the effectiveness of the live link, paying particular attention to its use in the United Kingdom. We then go on to consider critically the practical advantages and difficulties associated with the use of videorecordings as evidence in cases involving child witnesses, in the light of the proposals embodied in the 1990 Criminal Justice Bill.

THE LIVE LINK

The use of closed circuit television to separate the child physically from the accused during testimony has been pioneered in the United States. State legislatures began to introduce provision for the use of links for children in criminal trials in 1983 (Spencer & Flin, 1990) and now some 29 states have such legislation on their statute books (Cashmore, 1990). Subsequently, Canada, Australia, New Zealand and the United Kingdom have all moved to permit testimony to be given in this way. However, the form of the link and the range of cases for which its use is permitted vary widely.

The form of the link usually involves the child testifying from an adjacent room with the television picture being relayed to the main courtroom. One exception to this was the pilot study in Western Australia where the accused was placed in the adjacent room and watched on television as the child gave evidence in open court (Cashmore, 1990). However, such an arrangement appears to lose one of the major perceived advantages of the live link: that the child be able to give evidence away from the alien setting of the conventional courtroom.

Another perceived benefit of the system is that the child need never have sight of the accused throughout his or her testimony. If necessary a television link can be one-way so that the child never sees the courtroom and only the image of the child is broadcast to the main court. In the United States the child is closeted with counsel and the questions and answers are relayed to the court. This has led to successful legal challenges on the grounds that the defendant's right to brief counsel was violated (Grant, 1987). In the United Kingdom, this problem is overcome by the use of a two-way link where the child is on-screen continuously for viewing by the defendant. Careful selection of camera angles combined, if necessary, with some minor modifications to the architecture of the courtroom can ensure that the child never sees the accused on camera. Once again, there are some exceptions to this general rule: Cashmore (1990) states that in Alabama and Georgia the defendant is actually in the same room as the witness, an arrangement which would appear more stressful for the child than an in-court confrontation!

There are also large variations in the circumstances under which a link is invoked and in the age group to which the provision applies. Most court systems employ the technique for victims of sexual offences, while others allow its use for both physical and sexual assaults. Still others (Australian Capital Territory, Alabama and Iowa) encourage its use in all cases where children may be called upon to testify. Again, there are large variations in the age limit for which the scheme is employed. According to Cashmore (1990), these vary from an upper age limit of 10 in California and Indiana to 18 in Australian Capital Territory. Likewise, the circumstances under which the link may be employed show a similar variation. In many legislatures, including some in the United States, it is necessary to show that the child will suffer severe emotional damage by testifying in open court. The establishment of this, as Spencer & Flin (1990) note, may be more traumatic than an actual court appearance. In England and Wales, however, an application to the judge is sufficient to trigger the necessary arrangements.

THE ENGLISH EXPERIENCE

In England and Wales provision for the live link was included in the 1988 Criminal Justice Act which came into force in January 1989. The legislation was restricted to Crown Courts. This meant that children could still be cross-examined in the conventional way at committal proceedings; this anomaly awaits abolition as part of the 1991 Criminal Justice Act. The use of the link was initially confined to cases involving violence or sexual assault and to witnesses under the age of 14, but the 1991 Act extends this to 17 in sex cases.

Closed circuit television equipment was installed initially in some 14 Crown Court centres throughout England and Wales and was later extended to 30 further courts to provide a comprehensive geographical coverage. After some initial reservations detailed in the Scottish Law Commission Report (1988), parallel legislation was introduced in 1990 in Scotland.

The systems installed in the courts all involve a two-way, closed circuit link where the child testifies from an adjacent room. Some systems are voice-activated, displaying an image to the receiver of whoever is talking, while others allow the judge to override and control what appears on screen. In addition to a combined camera and monitor available to the child, equipment is available to the judge, defence and prosecution barristers. Additional monitors for relaying the proceedings are placed around the court for the benefit of the defendant, the jury and the general public. While the defendant can observe the child, the defendant should never be in shot for the child. In giving evidence, the child is normally accompanied by an usher and sometimes an adult such as a relative or social worker at the discretion of the judge (Davies, 1991).

As in the United States and Australia the actual use of the equipment has been less frequent than was originally anticipated. During the first eight months of employment, some 115 applications to use the link had been heard by judges of which all but nine had been approved. These figures concealed quite widespread variation between courts: at one extreme, Liverpool and Nottingham had each heard 17 cases while Southwark and Manchester had heard just two. Of the 106 successful applications, only 61 went to trial, the remaining 45 all resulting in late guilty pleas (Davies, 1991). It is tempting to see in these figures evidence of the perceived potency of the link in concentrating the mind of the accused, a view publicly endorsed by the Lord Chancellor (Mackay, 1990). Other explanations are possible, however, and a final verdict must await the outcome of a formal comparison of committal rates for courts with and without the link being conducted for the Home Office by the first author.

A survey by the Lord Chancellor's Department in 1989 established that the experiment was a technical success despite early hitches such as the tendency of voice-activated cameras to respond to rustling papers or scraping chairs as well as legal exchanges. It is evident from public comment, however, that reservations about the effectiveness of the link survive among judges and other court officials. When the scheme was first initiated, it was envisaged that all relevant cases involving children should be channelled through the link-equipped courts; this has not happened.

Judge Pigot at the Old Bailey was involved in an early link case where a 13-year-old child witness broke down under cross-examination and the trial had to be discontinued (*The Times*, 23.2.89). Subsequently, he opted to allow children to testify in open court, but to protect them from a view of the accused by an arrangement of screens. In 1989 some 100 cases involving juveniles were heard using screens at the Central Criminal Court (Morgan & Plotnikoff, 1990).

It is also evident from newspaper reports that many individual court officers have taken a decision that it is less traumatic for a child to testify in the conventional way in a non-link court than to travel long distances to a strange town in order to give evidence using the link.

The readiness of individual judges and other court officials to accept or reject the link reflects a number of implicit assumptions about the impact of the link on the child's ability to give evidence and upon the likely reaction of juries to live, as opposed to televised testimony. Such views, though strongly held, are frequently based on single experiences and anecdote rather than objective research. The following section examines what research is available on the impact of video testimony on child and jury.

COMMUNICATION AND CREDIBILITY

Little research has yet been published on the impact of the link on the child witness. As Cashmore (1990) notes, one of the major claims for the technique is that the child who is isolated from the courtroom will be more relaxed in giving testimony and will be able to provide a more confident and comprehensive account of events. Only two experimental studies, however, have examined the view that closed circuit television will empower young witnesses, with equivocal results.

Hill and Hill (1987) compared the quality of testimony given by child volunteers who were questioned about an argument seen on television. Questioning was either in a small room similar to that typically employed in videolink cases or in an orthodox courtroom in the presence of the "defendant" (the actor in the film), judge and counsel. Children reportedly gave more complete and accurate information in the small room and were less nervous and anxious during the experience, though the data fell short of conventional statistical significance.

A study conducted by the authors (Westcott et al, 1991a) compared the quality of evidence concerning a staged event produced by children aged 7–8 years or 10–11 years. Questioning was conducted either face-to-face or via the link. Older children reported more information and were more accurate than younger children under both media of communication, but there was no difference in the amount of information elicited under either direct or indirect questioning.

In the Westcott et al study the method of questioning was open-ended and friendly, rather than leading or adversarial, and the content of both incidents was innocuous rather than quasi-criminal. Thus, such results need to be treated as suggestive rather than indicative. Nevertheless, there is no evidence available to support the view that the use of the link, as such, is a bar to effective communication between witness and questioner. But what of the impact of video testimony on jurors?

Once again studies of witness credibility are few but there is no shortage of opinion. Attitudes towards the link are sharply differentiated between those who place significance on the importance of confrontation and those who give primacy to oral evidence. For the former, the absence of the witness from the stand and the limited view afforded by the television camera seriously reduce the information available to a jury (King, 1988). For the latter, the very absence of the child will force the jury to concentrate upon what the child has to say, a position consistent with the oral evidence tradition of English common law (Spencer & Flin, 1990).

The authors' own research tends to support the "oral evidence" viewpoint. In one study (Westcott et al, in 1991b), children aged 7–8 years or 10–11 years were videotaped answering questions about a visit the class had paid to a museum. In fact only half the children had been on this trip, the remainder having seen a short video film of the visit and then being asked to respond as though they had been present. Adult jurors faced with this material were only 59% accurate in their detection of children who were telling the truth or lying, a figure modestly, but significantly, above chance. Adults' decisions were more accurate on younger children, particularly boys telling the truth, but overall their performance was not very impressive. Such data are entirely consistent with other more orthodox laboratory studies which suggest that untrained adults are poor at detecting cues to deception (DePaulo et al, 1985).

When asked, however, what cues they relied upon in making decisions, 86% of judgements were based on the child's verbal behaviour, of which the factual content formed the major component. This finding, that the videolink channels jurors' attention towards the oral evidence, is also consistent with earlier work with adult witnesses appearing in videotaped trials conducted by Miller and Fontes (1979).

These latter authors also demonstrated that type of shot (full face, close up or medium) influenced juror perceptions of credibility. English legislation does not specify such production details but all equipment gives a head-and-shoulders view of the witness to the jury. These shots are preferred in that they make it evident to those in court that the child's supporters are not prompting answers in any way. A third study by the authors (Westcott et al, 1991a) suggests that this preferred view has no adverse impact upon sample jurors compared to close-up, though close-up might have significant advantages in eliminating differences in perceived credibility due to age (see also MacFarlane & Krebs, 1986).

Such experiments, however, leave unaddressed a number of legal concerns. One such is the impact of the withdrawal of the witness from the court on the perceived guilt of the accused: is the accused too dangerous to be allowed near the child? A judge will often instruct a jury that they should draw no pejorative implication from the child's use of the link in these circumstances. However, it is unclear whether this is sufficient to eliminate prejudice in the eyes of the jury (Myers, 1987).

There is also the question of the impact of the medium itself: does television enhance the status of the evidence in that it is seen as more authoritative than conventional oral testimony? Or as MacFarlane (1985) has argued, does television flatten the emotional impact of a child's evidence relative to a live court appearance? One observer has described a jury filing out for a teabreak when a child broke down giving particularly harrowing testimony as acting as though they were experiencing a "commercial break" in a television programme (Sharp, 1989).

There is as yet no research with children which addresses these issues directly. Research with adults suggests there is no generalized advantage for live over televised presentation, but rather, large differences between individual witnesses (Miller & Fontes, 1979). One study at least suggests that video testimony, by its very unusualness, does lead to juries giving it special attention. Thomson (1989) compared evidence from an adult witness given via television with the same evidence presented in court in the conventional way. Jurors spent much longer debating the video extract than they did when the same information was presented in an orthodox manner.

The introduction of the videolink in Britain and other countries arose from a genuine concern to ease the ordeal of the child witness giving evidence in court. However, this innovation was launched without any systematic research on closed circuit television's effect either on the quality of the child's evidence or on the perceptions of the jury. Such work is now being undertaken and none has yet questioned the principle of the televised link. Currently, there is a wide variation in the deployment and application of the basic conception of the link. Research both in and outside the courtroom can be expected to produce an optimal configuration for the system with a consequent increase in its acceptance in legal systems which share the adversarial tradition. However, such links do little to help very young children who cannot or will not tell their story in court. For them, prerecorded videotape evidence offers one prospect of justice.

PRERECORDED INTERVIEWS WITH CHILD WITNESSES

The potential of prerecording videotape interviews with witnesses was recognized by many North American judges and researchers as far back as the late nineteen sixties (eg Libai, 1969; McCrystal, 1972). At this time, videotechnology was a relatively new commodity, but its potential for speeding up the judicial process was quickly recognized (Armstrong, 1976; Kornblum, 1972). Professionals were attracted to the possibility of recording witness statements out-of-court and at a convenient time, and then inserting the videotape into the trial process (McCrystal, 1972). Indeed, the possibility of recording the whole trial to show to the jury was considered as a means of clearing the backlog of cases awaiting trial (Miller & Fontes, 1979).

Professionals working with child witnesses have turned to video-technology for different reasons. The existence of a videorecording of the interview with the child removes the need for repeated interviews with other professionals. Further, the child is then able to participate in therapy and work through the psychological consequences of the abuse. It is also alleged that the existence of the videorecording relieves the pressure on children from other family members who wish them to retract their statement (Bernstein & Claman, 1986; MacFarlane, 1986; Whitcomb et al, 1985).

Recent years have seen attempts in Britain to permit these video-taped interviews to be entered as evidence in cases involving alleged child sexual abuse. This has been particularly so in the civil courts, where the burden of proof is less stringent than that in the criminal courts (Spencer & Flin, 1990). The evidentiary value of videotapes has been widely debated (eg Bulkley, 1985; Clark-Weintraub, 1985; Colby & Colby, 1987; MacFarlane, 1986), with the key issue being whether they can be admitted as evidence in exception to the hearsay rule, and without sacrificing the rights of the defendant (Spencer, 1987, 1989; Spencer & Flin, 1990).

Until the 1991 Criminal Justice Act comes into effect, these tapes remain essentially inadmissible in English and Scottish criminal courts, except for a few (mostly inapplicable) situations where they fall under an exception to the hearsay rule (Spencer, 1989; Spencer & Flin, 1990).

The advantages of such videotaped interviews have been highlighted by clinicians and researchers who see the evidential potential of the videorecording (Davies, 1988; Vizard, 1990). The interview can take place in a non-threatening environment, in a room equipped with child-sized furniture and toys. Recording early interviews with child victims/witnesses preserves an accurate record of their account while the event witnessed is still fresh in the mind. It enables the viewer to hear the story in the child's own words, accompanied by the child's non-verbal behaviour.

It is argued that the videotape can act as an additional source of support for the child's testimony if the child must still testify. Alternatively, videotape could replace the child's testimony, thus removing the need for the child to appear in court. If children's live evidence is replaced with a videorecording, they will not have to testify in an unfamiliar and public place about a frightening and possibly embarrassing experience, and are less likely to be intimidated by their surroundings or the presence of the alleged perpetrator (MacFarlane, 1986). Multiple interviews are avoided, removing a source of stress and confabulation (Benedek & Schetky, 1986; Burgess & Holmstrom, 1978; Butler-Sloss, 1988: Whitcomb et al, 1985). This view is endorsed by the terms of the 1991 Criminal Justice Act. A further, possibly unantici- pated, consequence of videorecording the child's interview is that it may encourage guilty pleas from defendants who have viewed the tape (Spencer & Flin, 1990; Mackay, 1990; Whitcomb et al, 1985). However, several potential problems arise when the child's interview is recorded in this way. The first of these is the contention that the use of videorecorded interviews deprives the defendant of the right to con- front the witness (Bulkley, 1985; Colby & Colby, 1987). This "right" of physical confrontation is strongly entrenched in American law (Grant, 1987), though less so in the United Kingdom (Spencer, 1987). Defen- dants, however, must be able to cross-examine witnesses for the prosecution, in order to argue their case. When children are inter- viewed, the interviewer will strive to question them alone (Vizard et al, 1987). If such a tape were used as the sole evidence, and in the absence of the child, there would be no opportunity for the defendant to put any questions to the child. Further, it has been argued that use of videorecordings will implicitly suggest the guilt of the alleged abuser, and thus impair the defendant's right to a fair trial (King, 1988).

The quality of the video equipment used is obviously of great importance, and a high-quality recording of the interview is required in order for those involved in the trial to accurately assess the credibility of the child (MacFarlane, 1986). Armstrong (1976) and Grant (1987) raise concerns that the video presentation will affect jurors' abilities to assess the witness's credibility, by failing to show subtle changes in pallor, or through the influence of different camera shots and other recording techniques. It has also been queried whether the use of a videorecording will interfere with jurors' attention to the testimony (Bermant et al, 1975; Miller & Fontes, 1979), although the work of Bermant et al (1975) provides no support for this contention. Jurors in this study were positively disposed towards receiving prere- corded testimony.

Finally, there is a concern that by questioning the child in a more comfortable and less inhibiting environment, this may give the testi- mony a more relaxed "tone", which in turn may suggest that the child was not emotionally affected by the alleged abuse, or that the testi- mony was "learned" (MacFarlane, 1985). All these issues require serious evaluation when the potential of videotechnology is consid- ered; however, most can be overcome when careful implementation and usage is maintained.

FORMAL ASPECTS OF TAPING

Professionals conducting the child's initial interview have generally been those from child welfare agencies, for example social workers, clinical psychologists, psychiatrists, or police (Boat & Everson, 1988; MacFarlane, 1986; Vizard et al, 1987). The increasing awareness of child sexual abuse has also resulted in educational psychologists and schoolteachers preparing for such interviews with children (Schwartz & Schwanenflugel, 1989). However, videotaping is likely to be performed mainly within institutions which can afford not only the equipment, but also appropriate facilities for recording, such as a bright, relatively quiet room. These financial and physical considerations can exert considerable limitations on the possibility of videotaping interviews, even when the professionals involved are eager to facilitate the recording.

The training and experience these professionals have in interviewing children seems to vary widely (Benedek & Schetky, 1987; Boat & Everson, 1988; Walker, 1990), although it would seem most important that interviewers have received some guidance in interviewing skills and developmental considerations (see Dent, Chapter 1, this volume; MacFarlane & Krebs, 1986). This issue has been particularly highlighted by the recent legal reviews (Butler-Sloss, 1988; Pigot, 1989; Scottish Law Commission, 1990), and projects set up in England to develop interagency cooperation in dealing with child sexual abuse have served to stress the need for facilities for training in child interviewing skills (see Aldridge, Chapter 14, this volume; Metropolitan Police and the London Borough of Bexley, 1987). The 1991 Criminal Justice Act envisages a code of conduct being drawn up for such interviews following consultation with interested parties.

When the interview is being video recorded, the interviewer needs to be aware of factors arising from the position and operation of the camera equipment, as MacFarlane (1986) has commented. Not only must interviewers be able to interview the child in front of the camera, but also they are responsible for gauging the child's reactions to it.

The oft cited interview by Jones (Jones & Krugman, 1986) illustrates the key role of the interviewer in questioning a child about an alleged assault, and the benefits of proper training in child psychology. Here, the psychiatrist was able to question a three-year-old girl about her abduction and assault, eliciting such accurate testimony that her abductor was subsequently identified, arrested and admitted the offence.

The amount of prior information held by the interviewer about the alleged abuse or facts of the case has also been subject to debate. Some authors argue that knowledge of all available information prior to conducting the interview empowers interviewers, and enables them to guide their questioning appropriately (eg Boat & Everson, 1986; MacFarlane & Krebs, 1986). Others, however, argue that the interviewer should have no previous knowledge of the case to prevent biased questioning or unnecessary focusing on certain aspects of the testimony (White et al, 1987). In the final analysis, this matter would seem best left to the judgement of the interviewer, who will decide which mode of operation is preferable.

Most interviewers see the child alone, so that the accompanying adult is unable to influence the child's testimony in any way (eg Vizard et al, 1987; White et al, 1987), but recent research by Moston (see Moston, Chapter 3, this volume) has suggested that the presence of informed peers may facilitate the child's recall. For very young children, it may be necessary to allow a non-involved supportive adult to be present throughout, although this person may not contribute to the actual interview (Boat & Everson, 1988). Where the interview is videotaped, all personnel present in the room should be identified (Pigot, 1989).

THE NATURE OF THE INTERVIEW

The most notable difficulty that arises when children who are suspected of being sexually abused are videorecorded is to clarify the exact function of the interview. As noted earlier, the primary purpose of the videorecordings, at least initially, was to facilitate the interviewer's assessment of the case. However, with increasing numbers of children being reported victims of sexual assault, the possibility of using these videotapes as evidence in custody hearings has become a very real one (Family Law Reports, 1987; Spencer & Flin, 1990). The conflict that exists between the evidentiary and therapeutic needs of such an interview has been well documented (Douglas & Willmore, 1987; Family Law Reports, 1987; MacFarlane, 1986; Vizard et al, 1987; Walker, 1990).

In conducting a therapeutic interview with the suspected victim of sexual abuse, the primary aims are to establish the risk to the child and to assess the child's therapeutic needs (Vizard & Tranter, 1988). It has been noted that, in most cases, the child victim has been subjected to much emotional pressure and blackmail by the abuser, who attempts to keep abuse of the child a secret (Burgess & Holmstrom, 1978; Conte et al, 1989). In order for the clinician to assess the situation, therefore, much coaxing is often required to break the child's frightened silence, and indicate that she/he is allowed to talk about the abuse. The techniques clinicians use to enable children to reveal the details of their abuse in this way frequently involve the employment of "leading" and hypothetical questions (Vizard, 1987).

Leading questions, by their very nature, suggest the answer that is expected. However, while employing leading questions fulfils the therapeutic role of the interview, it immediately causes problems for the interviewer should the taped interview be put forward as evidence (MacFarlane & Krebs, 1986; Vizard, 1987). The forensic needs of the interview require that only objective questions are used to elicit the details of the suspected abuse; the use of leading questions significantly weakens the evidentiary value of the videorecording (Waite, J. in *Family Law Reports*, 1987). Further, the forensic value of the videotape depends also on the precise details being elicited from the child of the date, time and place of the abuse, and the unequivocal identification of the suspect as the abuser. Frequently, children are insufficiently aware of such details to be able to provide them, and, anyway, this information may not be crucial to the therapeutic assessment (Walker, 1990).

While the desirability of developing interviewing techniques which fulfil both therapeutic and evidentiary needs is recognized by most professionals (Dent, Chapter 1, this volume; Spencer, Chapter 7, this volume; Vizard & Tranter, 1988), the enormity of the task is daunting (Latey, J. in *Family Law Reports*, 1987). In sum, it seems that excessive use of suggestive questioning will continue to prevent interviews being admissible in court (Pigot, 1989), and that clinicians must reserve use of such questions till the final stages of the interview. By delaying leading questions in this way, it is hoped that the child will have volunteered details of the abuse either spontaneously or in response to objective, non-leading questions (the "stepwise interview" technique—Yuille, 1988).

INTERVIEW AS EVIDENCE

The needs of the child frequently dictate that one interview is not sufficient to both establish a rapport and elicit details of the alleged abuse (Bannister & Print, 1989). The problem then arises as to which of the interviews should be videotaped, and which videorecording should be submitted as evidence (MacFarlane, 1986). This possibility does not appear to have been given wide attention in the published literature, although it could pose serious practical problems. For example, the presentation of numerous videorecordings at a trial could lead to lengthy delays, and could possibly affect the response of those personnel involved in the case; Walker (1990) mentions cases where the judge has appeared to have fallen asleep! If only one of the interviews is recorded, the clinician will be questioned in detail as to why this is so (MacFarlane, 1986). This problem could be overcome if the child was only interviewed once, but with members of both the child welfare agencies and police force present, so that each could ask the questions relevant to their enquiries (Bannister & Print, 1986; Metropolitan Police and the London Borough of Bexley, 1987; Butler-Sloss, 1988).

A serious cause for concern has been the question of ownership of the videorecording, and the associated issue of confidentiality (MacFarlane, 1986; Smith, 1988; Vizard, 1990). If the videotape is to be used as evidence, then the defendant and his/her counsel must be permitted to view the tape. However, many professionals feel this is a breach of the child's confidentiality, and is not what the tape was originally intended for (Smith, 1988). Further, should the clinician destroy the recording in order to protect the child, then there is the possibility that he/she will be charged with destruction of, or tampering with, evidence and/or perverting the course of justice (*Family Law Reports*, 1987; MacFarlane, 1986; Smith, 1988); the courts have the power to subpoena the tape as evidence, regardless of the wishes of the child or the professional involved (Vizard, 1987).

The question of ownership and storage is also a practical problem (Pigot, 1989). Large numbers of videorecordings will have to be stored for up to 20 years, and their usage regulated to prevent abuse or misappropriation. The question then arises as to which agency will be responsible for their storage, and who will be able to prevent the videotapes being misused (Vizard, 1987). The Pigot Committee (Pigot, 1989) has recommended that ownership of videorecorded interviews should be vested in the responsible police force, who will also regulate viewing of the tape by the defendant and his counsel and loaning of the tape to social services or prosecution counsel. How the 1991 Criminal Justice Act will handle this delicate matter is, as yet, unclear.

All these issues have led to serious misgivings on the part of professionals called to interview children, and even to some abandoning their use of video equipment to record interviews (MacFarlane, 1986; Vizard, 1987). At best, clinicians are encouraged not to promise the child that no-one will see the tape (Butler-Sloss, 1988), while the issue of guidelines or a Code of Practice for the ownership and viewing of the videotapes is urged (MacFarlane, 1986; Pigot, 1989; Smith, 1988).

Many professionals are also unhappy at the prospect of unqualified, often inexperienced judges and counsel using the interviewer's style as a means of undermining the child's evidence (Smith, 1988; Vizard et al, 1987). The willingness of certain psychiatrists to act as expert witnesses for the defence has been noted (MacFarlane, 1986; Vizard et al, 1987) who criticize the interviewing methods employed, frequently in the absence of any personal training or experience in child psychology. Additionally, the videotape is assessed in isolation, without the benefit of the interviewer's written notes or assessment of the interview (Smith, 1988). As with the use of anatomical dolls as aids in interviews (Westcott et al, 1989), this situation would seem best resolved by the continuing efforts of professionals to share their experiences and knowledge with each other. Butler-Sloss (1988) and Pigot (1989) have urged that appropriate training in legal and developmental matters be made available to all professionals involved in dealing with child sexual abuse.

The issue of editing is important when videotaped interviews are considered. As noted above, there may have been several interviews with the child which may produce large amounts of irrelevant material. At times, this could lead to the child's credibility being questioned. Whitcomb et al (1985) cite a case where a young girl hesitated when asked if she had a pet dog; the child's apparent uncertainty was then used to discredit her whole testimony.

It might be tempting to see editing as a possible solution (Spencer, 1987), with only the essential statements by the child being submitted as evidence. Most professionals, however, work on the premise that editing will be unacceptable to the courts, and that some method of timing the interview should be incorporated into the recording, either using an in-built mechanism in the camera itself or by showing a clock at the beginning and end of the tape (MacFarlane, 1986). Pigot (1989) recommends that the interviewer should state the names of the people present and the time and location at the beginning of the interview. Although editing is not explicitly mentioned or forbidden in the report, it is stated that "explanations should also be given for any interruptions in the proceedings" (p. 41). From this position, it would seem best that interviewers proceed as before, with the assumption that any editing will be conducted by the judge prior to trial in consultation with counsel. The 1991 Criminal Justice Act proposes to deal with these issues through a written Code of Conduct.

CONCLUSIONS

Videotechnology in the form of both the videolink and the videotaped interview has opened up new prospects as well as problems for all professionals who must deal with child witnesses. At a legal level, the debate persists as to how such technology can be reconciled with traditional legal notions such as confrontation and hearsay. At a psychological level, research continues on optimal methods for interviewing children which can combine the maximum elicitation of knowledge with the minimum of leading or suggestive questioning. At the ethical level, the question of the ownership of tapes and the notion of informed consent continue to concern psychiatrists and social workers. The law cannot turn its back on technological change and the potential it brings for extending the protection of the judicial system to young children, but it must not underestimate the difficulties.

However, it seems unlikely that technology alone will remove the genuine fears and anxieties of children testifying under the adversarial system. Under the 1990 Criminal Justice Bill, young witnesses using the videolink will still face cross-examination, with all its potential for humiliation and confusion for the child. Even if the enlightened proposals of the Bill are accepted, such examination will continue with even younger children, albeit in an arena less intimidating than the courtroom. Only when these primitive and wayward processes of truth-divining are replaced by a truly scientific method of establishing witness-credibility will the traumas of witnessing be fully banished for children.

REFERENCES

Armstrong, J. J. (1976). The criminal and videotape trial: serious constitutional questions. *Oregon Law Review*, **55**, 567–585.

Bannister, A. & Print, B. (1989). *A Model for Assessment Interviews in Suspected Cases of Child Sexual Abuse*. London: NSPCC.

Benedek, E. P. & Schetky, D. H. (1986). The child as witness. *Hospital & Community Psychiatry*, **37**, 1225–1229.

Benedek, E. P. & Schetky, D. H. (1987). Problems in validating allegations of sexual abuse. *Journal of American Academy of Child and Adolescent Psychiatry*, **26**, 912–921.

Bermant, G., Chappell, D., Crockett, G. T., Jacoubovitch, M. D. & McGuire, M. (1975). Juror responses to pre-recorded videotape trial presentations in California and Ohio. *Hastings Law Journal*, **26**, 975–995.

Bernstein, B. E. & Claman, L. (1986). Modern technology and the child witness. *Child Welfare*, **65**, 155–163.

Boat, B. W. & Everson, M. D. (1986). *Using Anatomical Dolls: Guidelines for Interviewing Young Children in Sexual Abuse Investigations*. Chapel Hill, NC: University of North Carolina.

Boat, B. & Everson, M. (1988). Interviewing young children with anatomical dolls. *Child Welfare*, **67**, 337–352.

Brainerd, C. & Ornstein, P. (1991). Children's suggestibility: the developmental backdrop. In J. Doris (Ed.). *The Suggestibility of Children's Recollections.* Washington: American Psychological Association.

Bulkley, J. A. (1985). Evidentiary and procedural trends in States Legislation and other emerging legal issues in child sexual abuse cases. *Dickinson Law Review*, **89**, 645–668.

Burgess, A. & Holmstrom, L. (1978). The child family during the court process. In A. Burgess, A. Groth, L. Holmstrom & S. Sgroi (Eds). *Sexual Assault of Children and Adults.* Lexington, MA: Lexington Books.

Butler-Sloss, E. (1988). *Report of the Inquiry into Child Abuse in Cleveland in 1987.* London: HMSO.

Cashmore, J. (1990). The use of video technology for child witnesses. *Monash University Law Review*, **16**, 228–250.

Ceci, S. J., Toglia, M. P. & Ross, D. (1987). *Children's Eye-witness Memory.* New York: Springer-Verlag.

Clark-Weintraub, D. (1985). The use of videotaped testimony of victims in cases involving child sexual abuse: a constitutional dilemma. *Hofstra Law Review*, **14**, 261–296.

Colby, I. C. & Colby, D. N. (1987). Videotaped interviews in child sexual abuse cases: the Texas example. *Child Welfare*, **66**, 25–34.

Cole, C. B. & Loftus, E. F. (1987). The memory of children. In S. J. Ceci, M. P. Toglia & D. F. Ross (Eds). *Children's Eyewitness Memory.* New York: Springer-Verlag.

Conte, J., Wolf, S. & Smith, T. (1989). What sexual offenders tell us about prevention strategies. *Child Abuse & Neglect*, **13**, 293–301.

Davies, G. M. (1988). Use of video in child abuse trials. *The Psychologist*, **1**, 20–22.

Davies, G. M. (1991). Children on trial? Psychology, video-technology and the law. *The Howard Journal of Criminal Justice*, **30**, 177–191.

Davies, G. M., Flin, R. & Baxter, J. (1986). The child witness. *The Howard Journal*, **25**, 81–99.

DePaulo, B., Stone, J. & Lassiter, G. (1985). Deceiving and detecting deceit. In B. Schlenker (Ed.). *The Self and Social Life.* New York: McGraw-Hill.

Douglas, G. & Willmore, C. (1987). Diagnostic interviews as evidence in cases of child sexual abuse. *Family Law*, **17**, 151–154.

Family Law Reports (1987). Sexual abuse of children. Special issue, **1**, 269–346.

Flin, R. H., Bull, R., Boon, J. & Knox, A. (1990). *Child Witnesses in Scottish Criminal Prosecutions.* Report to the Scottish Home and Health Department.

Flin, R. H., Davies, G. & Tarrant, A. (1988). *The Child Witness.* Final Report to the Scottish Home and Health Department under Grant 85/9290.

Goodman, G. S., Jones, D. P. H., Pyle, E. A., Prado-Estrada, L., Port, L. K., England, P., Mason, R. & Rudy, L. (1988). The emotional effects of criminal court testimony on child sexual assault victims: a preliminary report. In G. M. Davies & J. Drinkwater (Eds). *The Child Witness: Do the Courts Abuse Children?* Issues in Criminological and Legal Psychology, No. 13. Leicester: British Psychological Society.

Grant, J. P. (1987). "Face—to television screen—to face": testimony by closed-circuit television in cases of alleged child abuse and the confrontation right. *Kentucky Law Review*, **76**, 273–299.

Hedderman, C. (1987). *Children's Evidence: The Need for Corroboration.* London: Home Office.

Hill, P. E. & Hill, S. M. (1987). Videotaping children's testimony: an empirical view. *Michigan Law Review*, **85**, 809–833.

Home Office (1987). *The Use of Video Technology at Trials of Alleged Child Abusers*. London: Home Office.

Jones, D. P. H. & Krugman, R. (1986). Can a three-year-old child bear witness to her sexual assault and attempted murder? *Child Abuse & Neglect*, **10**, 253–258.

King, M. (1988). Use of video in child abuse trials: a reply to the Professional Affairs Board of the Society. *The Psychologist*, **1**, 167–169.

Kornblum, G. D. (1972). Videotape in civil cases. *Hastings Law Journal*, **24**, 9–26.

Libai, D. (1969). The protection of the child victim of a sexual offence in the criminal justice system. *Wayne Law Review*, **15**, 977–1032.

McCrystal, J. L. (1972). Ohio's first videotape trial. *The Ohio Bar*, **45**, 1–4.

MacFarlane, K. (1985). Diagnostic evaluations and the use of videotapes in child sexual abuse cases. *University of Miami Law Review*, **40**, 135–165.

MacFarlane, K. (1986). Videotaping of interviews and court testimony. In K. MacFarlane, J. Waterman, S. Conerly, L. Damon, M. Dunfee & S. Long. *Sexual Abuse of Young Children: Evaluation and Treatment*. London: Guildford Press.

MacFarlane, K. & Krebs, S. (1986). Techniques for interviewing and evidence gathering. In K. MacFarlane, J. Waterman, S. Conerly, L. Damon, M. Dunfee & S. Long. *Sexual Abuse of Young Children: Evaluation and Treatment*. London: Guildford Press.

MacKay, J. (1990). Opening address to the International Conference on Children's Evidence. In J. R. Spencer, C. G. B. Nicholson, R. H. Flin & R. Bull (Eds). *Children's Evidence in Legal Proceedings: An International Perspective*. Cambridge: Cambridge University Faculty of Law.

Metropolitan Police and the London Borough of Bexley (1987). *Child Sexual Abuse: Joint Investigative Programme. Final Report*. London: HMSO.

Miller, G. R. & Fontes, N. E. (1979). *Videotape on Trial: A View from the Jury Box*. California: Sage.

Morgan, J. & Plotnikoff, J. (1990). Children as victims of crime: procedure at court. In J. R. Spencer, C. G. B. Nicholson, R. H. Flin & R. Bull (Eds). *Children's Evidence in Legal Proceedings: An International Perspective*. Cambridge: Cambridge University Faculty of Law.

Myers, J. E. B. (1987). *Child Witness Law and Practice*. New York: Wiley.

Pigot, T. (1989). *Report of the Advisory Group on Video Evidence*. London: Home Office.

Schwartz, A. R. & Schwanenflugel, P. J. (1989). Eyewitness testimony of children and the School Psychologist. *School Psychology Review*, **18**, 235–246.

Scottish Law Commission (1988). *The Evidence of Children and Other Potentially Vulnerable Witnesses*. Edinburgh: Scottish Law Commission.

Scottish Law Commission (1990). *Report on the Evidence of Children and Other Potentially Vulnerable Witnesses*. Edinburgh: Scottish Law Commission.

Sharp, F. (1989). Video evidence—a doubtful benefit for children. *Journal of Child Law*, April/June, 95–97.

Smith, G. (1988). Use of video recordings in legal proceedings. *The Psychologist*, **1**, 405.

Spencer, J. R. (1987). Child witnesses, video-technology and the law of evidence. *Criminal Law Review*, 76–83.

Spencer, J. R. (1989). When is the videotape of an interview with a child admissable in criminal proceeding? *Journal of Child Law*, **1**, 38–41.

Spencer, J. R. & Flin, R. H. (1990). *The Evidence of Children: The Law and The Psychology*. London: Blackstone Press.

Thomson, D. M. (1989). Video recorded evidence: psychological and legal issues. Paper presented at the Police Powers Conference of the Society for the Reform of the Criminal Law, Sydney, Australia.

Vizard, E. (1987). Interviewing young, sexually abused children—assessment techniques. *Family Law*, 28–33.

Vizard, E. (1990). Interviewing children suspected of being sexually abused: principles and practice. In C. Hollin & K. Howells (Eds). *Clinical Approaches to Sex Offenders and their Victims*. Chichester: Wiley.

Vizard, E., Bentovim, A. & Tranter, M. (1987). Interviewing sexually abused children. *Adoption and Fostering*, **11**, 20–27.

Vizard, E. & Tranter, M. (1988). Helping children describe experiences of child sexual abuse—a guide to practice. In A. Bentovim, A. Elton, J. Hildebrand, M. Tranter & E. Vizard (Eds). *Child Sexual Abuse Within the Family: Assessment and Treatment*. Bristol: John Wright.

Walker, L. E. A. (1990). Psychological assessment of sexually abused children for legal evaluation and expert witness testimony. *Professional Psychology: Research and Practice*, **21**, 344–353.

Warren-Leubecker, A., Tate, C., Hinton, I. & Ozbek, N. (1989). What do children know about the legal system and when do they know it? In S. J. Ceci, D. F. Ross & M. P. Toglia (Eds). *Perspectives on Children's Testimony*. New York: Springer-Verlag.

Westcott, H., Davies, G. & Clifford, B. (1989). The use of anatomical dolls in child witness interviews. *Adoption and Fostering*, **13**, 6–14.

Westcott, H., Davies, G. & Clifford, B. (1991a). The credibility of child witnesses seen on closed-circuit television. *Adoption and Fostering*, **15**, 14–19.

Westcott, H., Davies, G. & Clifford, B. (1991b). Adults' perceptions of children's videotaped truthful and deceptive statements. *Children and Society*, **5**, 123–135.

Whitcomb, D., Shapiro, E. R., Stellwagen, L. D. (1985). *When the Victim is a Child: Issues for Judges and Prosecutors*. Washington, DC: National Institute of Justice.

White, S., Strom, G., Santilli, G. & Quinn, K. M. (1987). Guidelines for interviewing pre-schoolers with sexually anatomically detailed dolls. Unpublished manuscript.

Wilson, J. (1990). A perspective on the Canadian position. In J. R. Spencer, C. G. B. Nicholson, R. H. Flin & R. Bull (Eds). *Children's Evidence in Legal Proceedings: An International Perspective*. Cambridge: Cambridge University Faculty of Law.

Yuille, J. C. (1988). The systematic assessment of children's testimony. *Canadian Psychology*, **29**, 247–262.

CHAPTER 14

The Further Training of Professionals Dealing with Child Witnesses

Jan Aldridge

University of Leeds

WHERE DO WE GO FROM HERE?

Awareness of the potential evidential contribution of children is growing apace. Despite a historical neglect of and bias against the child witness (Goodman, 1984), in the last decade an increasing body of informed research on children as witnesses has been rapidly accumulating (see Spencer & Flin, 1990; Doris, 1991 for recent reviews). Whether or not this research-based knowledge will be applied within the legal system depends at least in part on a commitment by a range of agencies, organizations and individuals to increased education and broader based training.

There is general agreement that good training is necessary to reduce the systemic abuse endured by many children once they have entered the legal process (Butler-Sloss, 1988). Further, it is widely acknowledged that a degree of specialist input should form part of the training of the legal profession, child protection workers and law enforcement officers (MacFarlane et al, 1986). Few police officers and lawyers, for example, have any specialized training on how to communicate with young, potentially traumatized children, just as few mental health

Children as Witnesses. Edited by H. Dent and R. Flin
© 1992 John Wiley & Sons Ltd.

professionals have been trained about the legal aspects of these cases. Despite these agreements, training in relation to children and the law (with exceptions, Mapstone, 1990) has rarely formed a significant part of professional education. For the most part, practitioners have gained their training in a more or less hit-or-miss fashion on the job. Similarly, most experts have not gained their expertise through traditional avenues of formal education. In other countries the position is similar. In America, for example, there are virtually no graduate or professional schools in any discipline that offer specific programmes leading to a qualification in this area, and even specialized courses are rare (MacFarlane et al, 1986).

As well as a more general appreciation of the growing research base relevant to children in relation to the legal system, awareness of and lack of tolerance for the historical biases and constraints of our legal systems is also increasing. When Sir William Blackstone opinioned in the eighteenth century that it is better that 10 guilty persons should escape than one innocent suffer, it was in a climate where death was the penalty for relatively minor offences. In such a context the emphasis upon the rights of the defendant is understandable. However, in 1989 Judge Pigot ventured:

> In our search for justice it is often forgotten that when a guilty person is not charged, or if charged the court case does not reach its proper conclusion but is terminated abruptly because of the failure of a key witness to give evidence or come up to proof, that can be as much a failure or miscarriage of justice as if an innocent person had been convicted. ... I have never been able to understand as a matter of logic why it is better to have ten miscarriages of justice rather than one. (Pigot, 1990, p. 210)

Current thinking on reform is more flexible then in the past. Searching questions are being asked and contemporaneous discussions are raising the rights of the victim as well as the rights of the defendant (Home Office, 1990). There is an increasing awareness and consideration of the rights of victims to be spared revictimization.

Law-makers and practitioners in a number of different western countries are attempting to decide upon and implement more effective policies for child victims (see Spencer et al, 1990). Jones (1988, p. 269) suggested that these changes might be grouped into two categories:

1. Those items which could be put into practice now with little or no fundamental legal or procedural reform required.
2. Those issues which would require a much more essential change in traditional practice.

The second category sits largely within the political arena and change is slow, but within the first category new ideas are already being discussed, and research as well as evaluation is ongoing. Innovations include modifications to courtroom formalities (Nicholson & Murray, Chapter 8, this volume), child witnesses being linked by video to the main courtroom (Davies & Westcott, Chapter 13, this volume) and the preparation of children for testimony (Dezwirek-Sas, Chapter 11, this volume; Sisterman Keeney et al, Chapter 12, this volume).

One particular modification which has been the subject of considerable debate is the use and admissibility in legal proceedings of earlier interviews or statements made by a child and recorded on videotape (see Spencer, Chapter 7, this volume). Clearly such a modification has important implications for training in evidential interviewing methods.

TRAINING IN EVIDENTIAL INTERVIEWING

As videotapes are now accepted in criminal proceedings involving child witnesses (Criminal Justice Act, 1991), it is extremely important that interviews are conducted in a form acceptable to the court. Two interviewer-related factors are likely to influence the court's decision to accept or reject a videotaped interview. First, interviewers will clearly have to take note of the rules of evidence (Spencer & Flin, 1990) if such videotapes are to have any kind of legal credibility. Secondly, actual interviewer technique will also play a major part in determining the evidential strength of videotaped interviews, hence the Home Office guidelines, see Spencer, Chapter 7, this volume. At present the increase in the number of evidential interviews with potential child witnesses and the effect of limited specialist training in such interviewing has resulted in many interviews being inadequate from an investigative point of view (Yuille, 1988). There is growing understanding from the child witness literature of key issues to incorporate in training in evidential interviewing methods (Steller & Boychuk, Chapter 4, this volume). Despite many methodological differences across studies, consistent results have emerged. In general, the younger the child, the less information and the less detail are supplied in their free reports of witnessed events (Chi, 1983). Although younger children provide less information in their free reports than older children and adults, their reports are equally as accurate (Cole & Loftus, 1987) and errors in recall tend to be about peripheral aspects of events for both children and adults (King & Yuille, 1987).

It would appear that the actual questioning style used may lead to lower levels of accuracy in witnesses' reports. Research findings consistently implicate the questioning techniques used with children as greater sources of distortion to their testimony than any underlying deficits in their cognitive ability. Poor questioning strategies (such as over-reliance on leading questions and lack of attention to the child's developmental level in question structure) may result in incomplete responses which lack clarity and are contaminated by suggestion. We have reached the stage where what we know about the effects of different strategies is beginning to be incorporated into training. So far there are few training programmes which explicitly do this, although there are notable exceptions. A good general approach to helpful interview strategies with children who may have been abused is described by Jones and McQuiston (1988).

A clinically and experimentally based systematized approach which has received increasing attention over the last few years is Statement Validity Analysis. This is a development of a procedure called Statement Reality Analysis which was first developed in Germany and Scandinavia in the early 1950s (Undeutsch, 1989). It was developed within an inquisitorial legal system, and in cases in which children were involved the court could appoint an expert in Statement Reality Analysis. The task of the expert is to interview the child, interview any other relevant witnesses, review all the forensic evidence in the case and then submit to the court a report on the validity or falsity of the child's testimony. Over the last four decades a set of specific procedures to evaluate the child's testimony have been developed and in recent years these procedures have been further systematized and formalized (see Steller et al, 1987; Steller & Boychuk, Chapter 4, this volume).

Statement Validity Analysis includes an interview protocol designed for use with children. It is intended to maximize the information the child provides while minimizing the contamination of that information. Thus an explicit aim of Statement Validity Analysis is first to make every attempt to obtain information from the child which is uncontaminated by the interview. The interview proceeds to more intrusive techniques only when earlier phases have not been successful and an issue of child protection remains. The second purpose of Statement Validity Analysis is to provide a framework for the evaluation of the validity of the child's account.

As such systematized approaches to interviewing develop we need to ask the following questions:

1. Do professionals working in the area need this training, or are they informally already using the relevant knowledge and skills?

2. If it is found that professionals might benefit from training in interviewing, how should that training be delivered and how should it be evaluated?

The investigation of how interviewers actually perform on a day-to-day basis is the subject of much discussion at the present time (ESRC/Police Foundation, 1990). However, despite the importance of the area little work has yet been reported. This is understandable given the considerable practical difficulties and the feelings and concerns of the potential interviewers.

THE WEST YORKSHIRE PROJECT

Between 1986 and 1988 a joint collaborative study between the University of Leeds and the West Yorkshire Police investigated the initial interviewing of police and social workers involved in preparing the evidence of children for criminal and civil court proceedings. (For full details see Aldridge & Cameron, 1988.) The group of experienced, but not specifically trained, police officers and social workers performed poorly in terms of establishing effective rapport, overall questioning behaviour and structuring verbal communcation at appropriate developmental levels. In addition, in terms of the structure of individual questions, mainly specific-leading questions were used. It was clear from this study that there was a need for training in evidential interviewing methods.

The second aim of the study was to evaluate the efficacy of a short statement validity based training programme with police officers and social workers. The aims of the course focused specifically on two areas:

1. A framework for joint working and inter-agency cooperation between the police and social services.
2. The development of specific evidential interviewing skills for work with children. The police officers and social workers involved with the training course were all experienced workers in the field of child abuse and the course was aimed specifically at skills to be applied in investigative interviews.

In terms of instructional design, the three-day course on evidential interviewing with children drew specifically on the work of the educationalists Gagné and Briggs (1974). Appropriate capabilities to be learned were divided into intellectual skills (information about which could be presented via instructions) and cognitive strategies (internally organized strategies that govern the learner's behaviour (Bruner et al, 1956). Information on the rules of evidence and evidential interviewing was presented via a series of lectures, seminars and handouts. In terms of the development of new cognitive strategies, the important aspect is the provision of opportunities for the application of these strategies to various problem situations. Consequently, instruction was arranged in terms of experiential techniques, including videoed role plays and recorded interviews with schoolchildren about stage-managed, non-emotive incidents which had occurred previously at school. Follow-up days were arranged at three-monthly intervals.

The analysis focused on three inter-related, yet different aspects of interviewer performance: the proportion of interview time spent in different activities; the number and structure of individual questions defined in terms of openness and leadingness; and the quality of rapport behaviour and overall questioning strategies. When the interview behaviour of course participants was evaluated over the 12 months following training, they performed poorly in terms of establishing rapport, overall questioning behaviour, structuring verbalizations appropriately and asking specific-leading questions. It was apparent that the training over this duration of time was not successful in developing and maintaining the practical skills necessary to facilitate accurate and complete reporting. Three days was sufficient to inform but not to train. Perhaps there is an analogy here with other learned skills. For example, a person might theoretically learn how a car works and how to drive it in three days, but to be a reasonable driver a considerable amount of practice is needed. It is clear that if people are to be trained in the complex skills of interviewing children then they must be well trained. This means as a society we must value the skills of interviewing children and train people properly.

One explanation for the ineffectiveness of short courses of this type might lie in the discrepancy between the complexity of the task of interviewing children and the necessarily narrow aims of such a course. In the present case the course was directed specifically at evidential interviewing. The broad development of skills for interviewing children was not the aim. Interviewing children is a complex task and needs to draw upon complex cognitive strategies. Acquiring a cognitive strategy is not achieved on a single occasion, rather this kind of capability develops over fairly long periods of time (Gagné & Briggs, 1974). Instruction in this area would attempt to influence thought processes and behaviour across a range of situations and facilitate the acquisition of strategies which are broadly generalizable. In order that the strategies improve and become dependably useful there must be a number of experiences of interviewing with different children in different types of situations. Such learning experience is not possible in a three-day course.

Even if some learning does take place in a short course, such a time-limited programme raises a further recurrent problem in the area of training, namely the generalization and maintenance of behaviour change. Long-term follow-up is too often omitted, but it is obviously of considerable importance in the area of training. It is not sufficient to develop new skills: these skills must be maintained. Follow-up was for one year in the present study and the results were consistent with those from a range of studies of behavioural change (Bandura, 1977). When studies have included a follow-up the results have been found to be disappointing, the effects not outlasting the programme by more than a few months. When attempting to increase positive long-term effects, it is relevant to take note of the distinctions that social learning theory makes among the three basic sub-processes of change —induction, generalization and maintenance of behaviour. The analysis of training programmes in terms of these sub-processes can provide a more informative basis for evaluation and improvement than undifferentiated assessments of outcome. From this perspective the general issue of programme efficacy is divided into the more specific questions of whether a programme initiates changes in behaviour, whether the changes generalize across situations and response systems (behavioural, affective and attitudinal) and whether the changes are maintained over time. In the area of training it is apparent that some methods are effective for creating changes but that this alone is not enough. The specific incorporation of generalization and maintenance programmes is also required, rather than just leaving generalization and maintenance to fortuitous circumstances.

Prior to participation in the course, assumptions had been made about the overall child interviewing skills of the participants. However, when interview behaviour was assessed in the naturalistic setting it was clear that although the participants had many skills and much experience, they did not possess sufficient developmental knowledge and interviewing skills to adequately respond to children's behaviour, verbalizations and needs. These findings are supported by informal observations from police forces and child protection workers both in this country and abroad. For police officers, interviewing victims draws on vastly different skills from interviewing suspects; similarly for social workers, evidential interviewing has different aims and constraints from a therapeutically oriented interview. One of the challenges facing trainers is to bring a realization to experienced professionals that in the matter of evidential interviewing there are skills to learn. There is a need to relinquish certain patterns and develop certain skills afresh.

The numbers taking part in the present training were small, but nevertheless the study does raise the importance of the issue of evaluation. As pressure increases for training (Butler-Sloss, 1988; Home Office, 1990) and courses are established to meet this need, it is clear that evaluation should be built into them. Not only should agencies be concerned about being seen to be doing something about training, they should also be concerned that training is effective.

THE IMPORTANCE OF THEORY-BASED FOUNDATIONS

An established and comprehensive body of knowledge of child development exists. Developmental psychology has much to offer to our understanding of children and much that can be of practical help when working with them. It is essential that training courses in evidential interviewing of children are built on a firm foundation of knowledge of child development. Participants in these courses, experienced as they are, must not underestimate this need and those entrusted with training should be well versed in the processes of child development. Knowledge of cognitive development and memory functioning, an understanding of expressive language ability and normal sexual development in children of different ages are just some of the areas which have practical relevance.

Cognitive development, and in particular what children remember and why, is an area which has been well studied in and out of the laboratory. Since the mid 1970s the study of remembering, the study of early memory development for events, as well as memory for scripts and routines, has undergone a period of vigorous creative growth (Fivush & Hudson, 1990; Ornstein et al, 1991). Clearly, a working knowledge of memory development has practical implications for interviewing. With developmental psychology as an underpin, knowledge from other fields also enriches training for interviewing children. An obvious example, in which both research and practical instruction abound, is the study of communication skills (Egan, 1988; Kanfer & Goldstein, 1980; Nelson-Jones, 1983). Given that with children the quality of the information obtained depends more on the skills of the interviewer than is the case with adults, then the more skills that are available to the interviewer the better.

Once again, however, it is not just an understanding of techniques (such as pacing, listening, clarification and summarizing) that is needed, but the incorporation of these into skilful practice. In the West

Yorkshire study described above, one of the hardest skills for the interviewers to learn and to incorporate into their practice was the apparently straightforward one of pacing. They all understood the value of going at the child's pace, but the temptation to fill short pauses with further questions was overwhelming. Common difficulties were either going too fast for the child, bombarding the child with loosely related questions, or going too slowly. In the latter case interviewers would often rationalize their difficulty in moving on with the interview by arguing they were still building rapport, when the child was more than ready to get on with the purpose of the interview. Much is known about children, their cognitions, their behaviour, their memory, and how to work with them to maximize the value of their testimony. If this body of knowledge is used effectively, then the gains are potentially enormous.

DIVERSITY IN TRAINING

Training in evidential interviewing has been considered in some depth as it raises and illustrates a number of issues pertinent to the whole area of training. As our knowledge increases in a range of areas relevant to child witnesses it becomes important to explore effective ways to share and implement this knowledge with a wide group of professionals and interested parties from diverse backgrounds with varying degrees of expertise. In doing this it is essential to address the training needs of different groups, at different points in their careers, with varying types of experience. These might be considered in relation to training for four overlapping categories of need:

1. Courses to be incorporated into an overall training strategy for those newly entering their particular profession or field of work (for example pupil barristers, newly selected magistrates, social workers and police officers in training, victim support volunteers).
2. Training as a positive, ongoing opportunity for development and review incorporated into the professional role of those already working in the field (for example the judiciary).
3. Training considered in terms of the particular needs and professional development of each profession or grouping.
4. Interdisciplinary training across traditional boundaries.

In addition, the issue of training for different levels of expertise has to be considered. Training takes place at different levels, and the purpose of training needs to be explicitly addressed. For example, many more people need to be informed than to have expertise in an area. If the purpose is to inform, a very different level of training over a much shorter time-span will need to be developed than if a real level of expertise is the aim. There is an obvious danger in the confusion of levels on the part either of the trainers or of the trainees.

An example of an area where the sharing of information from recent research and practice might be considered in terms of the implications for training within these different groups and at different levels is the recent work on the preparation of child witnesses. Appearing in court is known to be stressful and intimidating not only for child witnesses but also for professionals routinely required to testify (Spencer & Flin, 1990). As more and younger children are called as witnesses, the issues of support and preparation become increasingly important. Appropriate pretrial preparation of the child witness can make a crucial difference to the child's ability to testify (Dezwirek-Sas, Chapter 11, this volume; Sisterman Keeney et al, Chapter 12, this volume), whatever method is used to obtain the child's testimony.

However, decisions about which groups of professionals might take responsibility for, or be involved in, this area of preparation have not yet been made. The outcome is that there is considerable variety between juristictions and in some a total lack of clarity. In Scotland the function of pre-trial preparation is generally undertaken by the prosecution. Its value was emphasized by the 1990 Scottish Law Commission *Report on the Evidence of Children and other Potentially Vulnerable Witnesses*. In England and Wales there is no systematic approach and the question of responsibility for the pre-trial preparation of the child witness has not been addressed. The Home Office (1990) *Victim's Charter* makes no mention of the specific orientation and support needs of child witnesses. At present, where pre-trial support and orientation is provided at all, it is usually carried out informally by police officers and social workers, although they may have little experience in the area. An added consideration is the argument advanced in some sectors that the person handling the preparation of the child should not be involved in the investigation because of the possibility of a challenge of undue influence. A similar argument has been made against the prosecutor in Scotland being the person to be involved in pre-trial preparation because of the risk of the accusation of coaching. The Scottish Law Commission (1990) doubted whether this is a real problem. Nevertheless, calls are being made for a more coordinated strategy and a general set of procedures to be developed which would be less susceptible to challenge and within which preparation strategies would be tailored to the needs of the individual child

(Plotnikoff, 1990). In doing this the range of functions upon which appropriate preparation might draw would need to be delineated (for example court-related information, psychological preparation, emotional support during the giving of testimony). These functions may, but need not, be carried out by one individual, raising the issue of who should be trained in what. In addition, some professionals, such as the Crown Prosecution Service, might need to be aware of developments and direct policy without being directly involved themselves in the preparation of the children.

The implications for training are that very different programmes would need to be provided for the varied groups. For example, for the judiciary in general, information-giving about recent relevant research findings on the preparation of child witnesses might be useful; training in managing emotional content and effective support with children might be helpful to victim support volunteers if they are available to children and their families during the lengthy time prior to a court appearance; training in the detailed assessment of children's court-related fears and coping strategies and the management of stress-related behaviour might be relevant to clinical psychologists working with selected children with considerable anxieties about the court process. There is much emphasis on interdisciplinary training and the sharing of broad-based skills. However, if the needs of the children are to be well served the value also of specialist training, geared to the needs of the different professional groups, should not be neglected.

CONCLUSIONS

It is apparent that there are a number of recurring themes in training. In particular, it is clear that experience alone is not always sufficient. Indeed, there is some agreement that direct experience is not necessarily the best teacher (Spence, 1968). If the aim of training is the development of real skill rather than awareness of a limited range of techniques, then an integrated training programme must be a careful blend of skills and experience, together with opportunities for feedback, active experimentation and ongoing learning possibilities. Considering these requirements in terms of the four stages in Kolb's learning cycle (concrete experience; reflective observation; abstract conceptualization; active experimentation (Kolb et al, 1984)), it is apparent that whatever area of expertise is being developed, the value of repeated opportunities with all four stages needs to be recognized and explicitly addressed.

Of course, exactly how these stages, their order and the overall cyclic process are incorporated into specific programmes demands a measure of flexibility. To be effective a programme needs to be tailored to meet the needs of a particular target group. Behavioural objectives, corresponding content, specific learning curriculum and choice of methods must be developed in response to the needs of the target population. The experiential model has been extensively used in the further training of professionals. Indeed, it might be argued that it is particularly appropriate to this area, given the combination of both traditional and non-traditional experience-oriented learning strategies with strong, direct supervision in attitude and behavioural awareness (Famighetti, 1981). However, this model is by no means the only one and those responsible for training must continue to explore the use of a variety of methods and creative solutions, including distance teaching and open learning (Hodgson et al, 1987). If training is to continue to develop and make a useful contribution as well as experimenting with new approaches it also needs to harness existing resources, including the resources of institutions of higher learning. Institutions must also address the part they can play in the continuing development of the abilities of professionals in this issue-orientated arena of the service world.

A further recurring theme is the quality of training and, given that effective evaluation improves the quality of training, the need for evaluation. If training is to be done, it needs to be well done. The danger is that if people are not able effectively to perform the tasks they need to do, then potentially progressive moves will be sabotaged. An example is the permitted admission in legal proceedings of child witnesses' prerecorded evidential interviews in The Criminal Justice Act (1991). If these are not skilfully done, serving the needs of the child witness, the defendant and the court, then they will not be accepted as evidence. A possible solution may be training for two levels of expertise (Butler-Sloss, 1988). One level of training would be targeted at informing and educating a broad range of people. A second, more intensive level of training would be aimed at the development of a specialist resource. After all, specialist cardiac surgery would not be performed by surgeons who had not been steeped in general surgical approaches. In the vital area of child witnesses, training should be implemented in an analogous manner. Perhaps ultimately the needs of all will be best served by well-researched and evaluated professional training programmes having their foundations properly rooted in established bodies of knowledge which can provide the theoretical base for the way forward.

REFERENCES

Aldridge, J. & Cameron, S. (1988). The evaluation of training in evidential interviewing. In J. Aldridge, K. Lawrence & S. Cameron. *Research into the Use of Video in the Investigation of Child Abuse*. London: Home Office.

Bandura, A. (1977). *Social Learning Theory*. Englewood Cliffs, NJ: Prentice Hall.

Bruner, J. S., Goodnes, J. J. & Austin, G. A. (1956). *A Study of Thinking*. New York: Wiley.

Butler-Sloss, E. (1988). Department of Health and Social Security. *Report of the Enquiry into Child Abuse in Cleveland, 1987* (CM412). London: HMSO.

Chi, M. (1983). *Trends in Memory Development*. Basel: Karger.

Cole, C. B. & Loftus, E. F. (1987). The memory of children. In S. J. Ceci, M. P. Toglia & D. F. Ross (Eds). *Children's Eyewitness Memory*. New York: Springer-Verlag.

Doris, J. (1991) (Ed.). *The Suggestibility of Children's Recollections*. Washington: American Psychological Association.

Egan, G. (1988). *You and Me: The Skills of Communicating and Relating to Others*. Belmont: Brooks/Cole.

ESRC/Police Foundation (1990). Jointly Funded Conference on the Investigation of Child Sexual Abuse, London, UK.

Famighetti, R. A. (1981). Experiential learning: the close encounters of the institutional kind experience. *Gerontology and Geriatrics Education*, **2**, 129–132.

Fivush, R. & Hudson, J. (Eds) (1990). *Knowing and Remembering in Young Children*. New York: Cambridge University Press.

Gagné, R. M. & Briggs, L. J. (1974). *Principles of Instructional Design*. New York: Holt, Rinehart and Winston.

Goodman, G. S. (1984). Children's testimony in historical perspective. *Journal of Social Issues*, **40**, 9–31.

Hodgson, V. E., Mann, S. J. & Snell, R. (1987). *Beyond Distance Teaching—Towards Open Learning*. London: Open University Press.

Home Office (1990). *Victims Charter—A Statement of the Rights of Victims of Crime*. London: Home Office.

Johnson, M. K. & Foley, M. A. (1984). Differentiating fact from fantasy: the reliability of children's memory. *Journal of Social Issues*, **40**, 33–50.

Jones, D. P. H. (1986). Case report: can a three-year-old child bear witness to her sexual assault and attempted murder? *Child Abuse and Neglect*, **10**, 253–258.

Jones, D. P. H. (1988). The child witness in court: implications for clinical and legal practice. In G. Davies & J. Drinklater (Eds). *The Child Witness—Do the Courts Abuse Children?* Leicester: British Psychological Society.

Jones, D. P. H. & McQuiston, M. (1988). *Interviewing the Sexually Abused Child*, 3rd edition. London: Gaskell.

Kanfer, F. H. & Goldstein, A. P. (1980). *Helping People Change: A Textbook of Methods*. London: Pergamon.

King, M. A. & Yuille, J. C. (1987). Suggestibility and the child witness. In S. J. Ceci, M. P. Toglia & D. F. Ross (Eds). *Children's Eyewitness Memory*. New York: Springer-Verlag.

Kolb, D. A., Rubin, I. M. & McIntyre, J. M. (Eds) (1984). *Organisational*

Psychology. Englewood Cliffs, NJ: Prentice-Hall.

MacFarlane, K., Waterman, J., Coneley, S., Damon, L., Durfee, M. & Lang, S. (1986). *Sexual Abuse of Young Children*. New York: Guildford Press.

Mapstone, E. (1990). Centre for Child Care and Protection Studies Courses 1990–91. University of Dundee.

Nelson-Jones, R. (1983). *Practical Counselling Skills*. London: Holt, Rinehart and Winston.

Ornstein, P., Larus, D. & Chubb, P. (1991). Understanding children's testimony: implications of research on the development of memory. In R. Vasta (Ed.). *Annals of Child Development*, Vol. 8. London: Jessica Kingsley.

Pigot, T. (1990). Women and children first. In J. Spencer, G. Nicholson, R. Flin & R. Bull (Eds). *Children's Evidence in Legal Proceedings: An International Perspective*. Cambridge University Law Faculty.

Plotnikoff, J. (1990). Support and preparation of the child witness: whose responsibility? *Law and Practice*, 1, 21–30.

Report of the Advisory Group on Video Evidence (1989). (Pigot committee) London: Home Office.

Scottish Law Commission (1990). *Report on the Evidence of Children and Other Potentially Vulnerable Witnesses*. Edinburgh: HMSO.

Spence, D. L. (1968). Medical student attitudes toward the geriatric patient. *Journal of the American Geriatrics Society*, **16**, 976–983.

Spencer, J. R. (1987). Child witnesses, video technology and the law of evidence. *Criminal Law Review*, Feb., 76–83.

Spencer, J. R. (1988). How not to reform the law. *New Law Journal*, **138**, 497.

Spencer, J. R. & Flin, R. (1990). *The Evidence of Children*. London: Blackstone Press.

Spencer, J., Nicholson, G., Flin, R. & Bull, R. (Eds) (1990). *Children's Evidence in Legal Proceedings: An International Perspective*. Cambridge Law Faculty.

Steller, M., Raskin, D. C. & Yuille, J. C. (1987). *Sexually Abused Children: Interview and Assessment Techniques*. New York: Springer.

Undeutsch, U. (1989). The development of statement reality analysis. In J. C. Yuille (Ed.). *Credibility Assessment*. Dordrecht: Kluwer.

Yuille, J. C. (1988). The systematic assessment of children's testimony. *Canadian Psychology*, **29**, 3, 247–262.

Index

Page numbers in *italics* refer to figures and tables.

Index compiled by Jill C. Halliday

LIBRARY
HANDSWORTH COLLEGE
SOHO ROAD
BIRMINGHAM
B21 9DP